The Theology of George MacDonald

The Theology of George MacDonald

The Child Against the Vampire of Fundamentalism

John R. de Jong

PICKWICK *Publications* · Eugene, Oregon

THE THEOLOGY OF GEORGE MACDONALD
The Child Against the Vampire of Fundamentalism

Copyright © 2019 John R. de Jong. All rights reserved. Except for brief quotations in critical publications or reviews, no part of this book may be reproduced in any manner without prior written permission from the publisher. Write: Permissions, Wipf and Stock Publishers, 199 W. 8th Ave., Suite 3, Eugene, OR 97401.

Pickwick Publications
An Imprint of Wipf and Stock Publishers
199 W. 8th Ave., Suite 3
Eugene, OR 97401

www.wipfandstock.com

PAPERBACK ISBN: 978-1-5326-7874-5
HARDCOVER ISBN: 978-1-5326-7875-2
EBOOK ISBN: 978-1-5326-7876-9

Cataloguing-in-Publication data:

Names: de Jong, John R., author.

Title: The theology of George MacDonald : the child against the vampire of fundamentalism / John R. de Jong.

Description: Eugene, OR: Pickwick Publications, 2019 | Includes bibliographical references.

Identifiers: ISBN 978-1-5326-7874-5 (paperback) | ISBN 978-1-5326-7875-2 (hardcover) | ISBN 978-1-5326-7876-9 (ebook)

Subjects: LCSH: MacDonald, George,—1824–1905. | Fantasy fiction, English—History and criticism. | Christian fiction—History and criticism. | Children's literature—History and criticism. | Religion and literature. | Criticism, interpretation, etc.

Classification: PR4969 D45 2019 (print) | PR4969 (ebook)

Manufactured in the U.S.A. SEPTEMBER 27, 2019

Scripture taken from the New King James Version. Copyright © 1982 by Thomas Nelson. Used by permission. All rights reserved.

Cover image: George MacDonald
by Elliott & Fry, published by Maclure, Macdonald & Co (photogravure, 1892).
© National Portrait Gallery, London.

"If we are not little ones of a perfect love,
I can see no sense in things."

GEORGE MACDONALD, LETTER TO LADY MOUNT TEMPLE, 1893.

Contents

Preface ix
Abbreviations xi

Introduction 1
Chapter 1: The Context of George MacDonald's Work 11
    Theology and Literature 12
    The Reluctant Congregationalist 15
    George MacDonald's Theology—Key Ideas and Influences 18
    The Influence of Romanticism 22
    The Victorian Backdrop—A Divided Evangelical World 27
Chapter 2: The Victorian Child—Social and Theological Attitudes 41
    Sin and Innocence 41
    Early- and Mid-Nineteenth-Century Attitudes to Childhood 43
    Post-Darwin and *Fin de Siècle* Attitudes to Childhood 54
    The Nineteenth-Century Child 59
Chapter 3: George MacDonald's Contribution to Childhood 60
    Childhood Sins, Adult Sinners—A Tractarian Perspective 61
    A Reading of *At the Back of the North Wind* 65
Chapter 4: The Child in MacDonald's Realist Fiction 97
    Approaching MacDonald's Realist Fiction 97
    The Innocent Child 100
    The Abused and Disturbed Child 109
    A Realist Fairyland 123
Chapter 5: An Overview of George MacDonald's Theology 125
    MacDonald's Approach to Cognition and Epistemology 125
    Doctrine of God 132
    Cosmology 146
    Anthropology 152
    The Problem of Evil 158
    Soteriology 165
Chapter 6: The View of Evangelicalism from Fairyland 174

George MacDonald's *Via Media* 174
Evangelical Views of Evil 175
"A Little World of His Own"—The View from Fairyland 181
Learning to See Again—Fairy Vision 187

Chapter 7: The Child Against the Vampire—A Reading of *Lilith* 192
Lilith—Making Strange Theology 192
Lilith—Anti-Child and Antichrist 198
The Landscape and Action in *Lilith* 200
The Tactic of Defamiliarization 205
The Battle in (and for) the Mind 206
Satan—The Great Shadow 209

Chapter 8: *Lilith*—A Summary of George MacDonald's Theology 217
A Realist Fantasy 217
An Alternative Epistemology—Shape-Shifting Truth 219
The Child Against the Vampire 223
Key Theological Proposals that Emerge from *Lilith* 229

Chapter 9: The Implications of George MacDonald's Theology 236
"Death Has Come Through Our Windows" 236
"A Problematic Attitude to the World" 238
"If We Are Not Little Ones of a Perfect Love, I Can See No Sense in Things" 251
"His Quarrel Is with All Churches at Home and Abroad" 255
"The Idea of the Universe" 265

Bibliography 271

Preface

GEORGE MACDONALD'S PROSE IS somewhat wearing on the modern reader; a tendency towards prolixity, detours into prolonged "preachments" (to use C. S. Lewis's term), and Scottish vernacular—combined with liberal helpings of Victorian sentimentality—all make for a challenging reading experience. Despite the packaging, there is, nevertheless, a pertinence and an urgency to MacDonald's work which, I believe, is relevant to every generation for he is pondering the deep, perennial theological questions at the heart of faith—of life. For although quintessentially Victorian, MacDonald is also quintessentially human and I admire him for his transparency and dogged determination not to be satisfied with conventional answers. His work is essentially a theodicy. He asks that most difficult of theological questions: If God is love, why does evil exist? Trite answers about human free will simply do not wash. He may not have the "right" answers about the *mysterium iniquitatis* (no one does), but he is asking the right questions.

On re-reading *Lilith* many years after receiving it as a gift, I realized that George MacDonald's work directly addresses many of the issues that we struggle with in the twenty-first century, particularly in relation to religious fundamentalism. For MacDonald, fundamentalism was synonymous with idolatry; a tendency within contemporary Christianity to worship concepts, soteriological schemes, dogmas—even Scripture—rather than Christ. Through "making the familiar strange" he challenges the idols that have brazenly taken up residence in Christianity and fearlessly demands exorcism or, if you prefer, gene therapy. His is a message desperately needed, not only for our age, but every age. I hope that you, as I was, will be richly rewarded by journeying with me into MacDonald's thought.

This volume is the fruit of doctoral research at King's College London under the supervision of Professor Ben Quash and Dr. Michael Ledger-Lomas to whom I am indebted for their invaluable guidance and support. I am grateful for the financial and moral support of family and friends, particularly my wife, Jeltje. Extended research is always trying for family members and I thank her for her patience in accompanying me on this long journey. I am also indebted to my elderly parents. Their support was unwavering, but they, sadly, left this earth as this manuscript was being prepared. I am also thankful for the support of Yvonne and Matt Carson, Andrew and Rebecca Whettam, and Dr. Lisa Firth. This project could not have been completed without financial support from the King's College London Theological Trust, the Mylne Trust, the Catherine Mackichan Bursary Trust, the Sir Richard Stapley Educational Trust, and the Alexis Trust, for which I am grateful.

As George MacDonald once remarked, "No man could sing as he has sung, had not others sung before him," and, as a musician, I am conscious of the many "songs" that have influenced my writing. I hesitate to name anyone for fear of missing others who should rightfully be identified as part of the choir, but, looking back over my shoulder, I feel a particular indebtedness to the writings of Stephen Prickett, John Pridmore, U. C. Knoepflmacher, Sally Shuttleworth, David Bentley Hart, and Rowan Williams (and, of course, others, many of whom are credited in the body of this work) for their scholarly ability to provide wide contextual insight—a view of the symphony that has helped me to put my own modest themes into perspective.

It is also helpful to have gifted children. Thanks are due to Benjamin Daigle and Amy de Jong for proof-reading (even picking up on wrongly-italicized commas), Jesse de Jong for correcting and advising on points of grammar, and Esther de Jong Paterson, herself a gifted theologian, for inspiring conversations and encouraging me to keep going.

John de Jong, Prague, 2019.

List of Abbreviations

The works of George MacDonald

AF	*Alec Forbes of Howglen*
AQN	*Annals of a Quiet Neighbourhood*
CW	*Castle Warlock*
DE	*David Elginbrod*
DG	*Donal Grant*
DOP	*The Disciple and Other Poems*
EA	*England's Antiphon*
Fairy Tales	*The Complete Fairy Tales*
HG	*The Hope of the Gospel*
HL	*A Hidden Life and Other Poems*
Lilith	*Lilith*
MA	*Malcolm*
ML	*The Miracles of Our Lord*
MM	*Mary Marston*
NW	*At the Back of the North Wind*
Orts	*A Dish of Orts*
PC	*The Princess and Curdie*
PG	*The Princess and the Goblin*
PH	*Phantastes*

Poems	The Poetical Works of George MacDonald
POS	The Portent and Other Stories
Rampolli	Rampolli: Growths from a Long-planted Root
RF	Robert Falconer
RS	A Rough Shaking
SF	Salted with Fire
SG	Sir Gibbie
TWC	Thomas Wingfold, Curate
US1	Unspoken Sermons: First Series
US2	Unspoken Sermons: Second Series
US3	Unspoken Sermons: Third Series
WC	Wilfrid Cumbermede
WMM	What's Mine's Mine
God's Words	God's Words to His Children: Sermons Spoken and Unspoken

Other abbreviations used

GMAW	Greville MacDonald, *George MacDonald and His Wife*.
GMWR	William Raeper, *George MacDonald*.

Note

Emphasis in quotations is in the original unless stated otherwise. New King James Version italics are omitted.

Introduction

G. K. CHESTERTON FELT that George MacDonald represented "a turning point in the history of Christendom."[1] This claim appears to be little more than Chestertonian hyperbole; nice words written by him for a devoted son's biography. History, certainly, does not seem to concur: MacDonald is generally absent these days from theological conversations and from the indices of textbooks exploring the nineteenth century—even those specializing in religion. Apart from some devoted disciples or specialists, he is all but forgotten. There is a strong case that *The Lord of the Rings* and Narnia might not exist without his inspiration, but apart from that, he seems to have made little impact on our world.

There are, perhaps, two fundamental reasons. First, that he is *so* Victorian, with a worldview and a writing style (sometimes in Scottish Doric) that, within decades of his death (perhaps even earlier), went spectacularly out of fashion. Certainly his optimism that "all will be well" was dealt a severe blow by the Great War and few modern readers have the patience to wade through what is, frankly, often tortuous, prolix, sentimental, and didactic prose. Second, he was, on principle, against any kind of systematizing of thought—"theologic chicanery," as he called it, that left religion a desiccated husk—the discarded carcass of a spider's catch. But he takes this analogy further: there is no spider at the center of religion, rather, a vampire.

Such views were no doubt fueled by exposure in youth to the fruits of the Westminster Confession in his native Scotland—a somewhat frigid and legalistic document giving birth, especially north of the border, to an equally frigid and legalistic version of Calvinism. In contrast, there is much humor in MacDonald's writing, especially when he lapses into his Doric vernacular—the language of his rustic saints—to tease the

1. *GMAW* 13.

religious establishment. There is, nevertheless, a certain Scottish stubbornness—perhaps even dourness—in his demeanor, expressed mainly in a tendency to be somewhat opinionated and in the stubborn refusal to construct anything approaching a "system" (perhaps his *Unspoken Sermons* come closest). For this reason, it is very clear what he *doesn't* believe, but hard to work out what he does believe, or what he is proposing.

There is, however, a nagging doubt when reading MacDonald that Chesterton was onto something. C. S. Lewis certainly thought so, describing the aura surrounding his prose as "holiness," and famously referring to him as his "master." This volume explores what that might be.

George MacDonald was writing at a time of Evangelical anxiety. As the nineteenth century progressed, a maelstrom of ideas challenged accepted orthodoxy in so many areas. For Evangelicals, the received wisdom of forebears was increasingly perceived to be inadequate to account for, or defend, the faith. On the moral front, God was perceived as not being so much the solution to the problem of evil as responsible for it; on the scientific front, discoveries and theories from all quarters challenged the foundations of traditional faith. The Bible, for so long considered the interpreter of history, found itself under historical-critical scrutiny. As the critical *Westminster Review* put it in 1875 (with characteristic exaggeration), "the whole theological world is at issue on points involving the very existence of many dogmas hitherto held as being beyond dispute."[2]

Social, ideological, and theological pressures resulted in a fundamental split in Evangelical lines: conservatives retreated behind the walls of received orthodoxy; others became more "liberal" in a quest to allow faith to bend with the times. But this bifurcation of Evangelicalism was, to the minds of many—including George MacDonald—unsatisfactory: neither "liberal" nor "conservative" truth-claims appeared to offer an adequate account of lived reality. The press was awash with polemical diatribes claiming to expose the hollowness of religion. Humanity, it was claimed (by those such as Herbert Spencer), had moved on. "God," proclaimed Nietzsche, "is dead." Many simply turned their back on Christianity.

For MacDonald, however, the problem was not that religion was hollow as such; the problem was the vampire in residence at its heart; a usurper, an imposter. Unlike Christ who shed his blood on behalf of the

---

2. "Religious Education of Children."

children, the idol at the center of nineteenth-century religion was, like the harlot in Revelation, sucking their blood—drunk on the blood of the saints. The church was responsible for killing her children, a prognosis which did not, naturally, appeal to those faithfully serving at the altar. As one contemporary Presbyterian rightly observed, "His quarrel is with all the Evangelical churches at home and abroad." Here, I go further and argue that his "quarrel" is with much of Western Christianity.

MacDonald's response to this state of affairs is, like Jesus, to place a child "in our midst" for our consideration. As one critic lamented, childlikeness is something he "constantly harps about," and it is true: at every page-turn we encounter a "child." At first sight, this child appears to be the incarnation of the Romantic ideal, but appearances can be deceptive. It is, rather, a radical, sacramental icon undermining false doctrines of God and challenging the human response. It is not merely a reminder that Christ called us to be children; MacDonald argues that childlikeness, being the antithesis of all that is evil, is the fundamental attribute of the deity. *God* is the child "in our midst" and it is time the vampire was put in her place. This simple theological claim pervades MacDonald's disparate opus and is, I suggest, the golden key that unlocks all his work, for however far MacDonald has strayed from the orthodox Evangelical fold, his work can only be understood as that of someone who not only remains a theologian, but an "evangelical" theologian at that; someone anxious, in other words, to reclaim and proclaim faith.

Again, though, appearances can be deceptive. At first sight of merely historical interest, on closer examination it is clear that the theological claims being made have wide-reaching implications. This volume explores those implications; in particular, the claim that there is something askew at the heart of Western Christianity which is so pervasive and corrupt that it can no longer lay claim to the title "Christian." Christianity as we know it, MacDonald is saying, equates to—or at minimum has a tendency towards—vampirism. It represents a fundamental and far-reaching challenge to the foundations of faith, particularly one based of the Reformation tendency to place more value on words than the Word with the resulting tendency towards religious fundamentalism and the violence that ensues.

In many respects, this volume is a journey into George MacDonald's mind. While this is a truism in respect to any "biography," for a writer with Romantic, mystical, and idealist leanings such as MacDonald, it is a stronger claim: mind is the stuff of the universe. In his cosmos, God is the great Mind thinking reality into being. He saw himself as having been flung into orbit at an "epistemic distance" from God (a term we will explore later), the radiating, thinking sun-God at the center of reality, but nevertheless intrinsically connected to that deity through the umbilical cord of *imagination* tethering mind to Mind. As for Coleridge before him, human imagination was "a repetition in the finite mind of the great I AM"; a force, a human–divine partnership, forging and fusing reality.

However, MacDonald's philosophical idealism never remains merely theoretical. Always the champion of action above words, just as he insists that true faith is obedient faith, so he himself is obedient to his own vision—that of a divinely-inspired ("God-breathed") imaginative mind partnering with God's in the creative process; a mind informed by God's book of nature, replete with numinous images pregnant with meaning. All his writings, therefore, are shot through with imaginative thought. This, you might observe, is true for any author, but this thinker is, above all else, imaginative rather than "logical," and therefore—through his fantasy works in particular—we find ourselves invited (sometimes explicitly) to explore the mind of this innovative thinker. At his best, he shows rather than tells, drawing the reader herself to imaginatively engage with his art, an art which, he claims, *is* divinely inspired.

Our journey begins, therefore, by exploring the world into which this mind was born. Claims that MacDonald is somehow fundamentally unique are refuted as we consider his Scottish Calvinist upbringing, his historical heroes, his Victorian interlocutors, and the social and philosophical pressures that shaped him. Although in many respects a liminal figure on the edge of the Christian establishment, he was, nevertheless, deeply aware of contemporary conversations, and—as we will explore—a significant contributor to them. Although on the edge of Christian orthodoxy (particularly as understood by Evangelicals), his connection with those such as F. D. Maurice, Charles Kingsley, A. J. Scott, John Ruskin, the Pre-Raphaelites, and others, place him near the center of at least one "school" of Victorian intellectuals, though these can hardly be described as establishment people. In short, he is a man of his times, but one that not only challenged, as Schleiermacher had phrased it, the "cultured despisers of religion," but those enamored with religion who claimed allegiance.

MacDonald, though, was by no means unique in placing a child at the center of his thought. As we explore in chapter 2, the figure of the child was central to many contemporary conversations. On the one hand, the Victorians had inherited from the Romantics a view of the child mind as a *tableau rasa* on which Nature wrote the text of life, a narrative untainted by the affectations of culture and the false mores of "adult" society. The child represented a state of innocence, of detachment from societal corruption, and of connection with divinity. Others, on the other hand, had a less benign view. The Puritans had bequeathed to the Victorians a view of the child as an accident waiting to happen. Shot through with original sin, rather than celebrating the state of childhood, it was seen as a phase in life to be left behind as quickly as possible: the child, as Calvin had insisted, did not, as a birthright, carry the *imago Dei*, rather, it was fundamentally corrupted by evil. Hell needed to be beaten out of the child. The ascendency of evolutionary thought did little to free the child from ancestral burdens; rather, origin sin was simply replaced with notions of savage simian ancestry or, at minimum, the idea that the child was somehow burdened with the legacy of antiquity. In this period at the dawn of the new science of psychology, the child was also placed "in the midst" and became the focus of anthropological musings.

MacDonald, then, places before us an apparently Romantic child as somehow exemplary of both the nature of God and the disposition of the faithful. But, as noted, there is more in this "Romantic" child than meets the eye. In chapter 3, we consider how this child represents a challenge to such contemporary views. Rather than a state to be left behind as quickly as possible, MacDonald makes a radical suggestion: that it is adulthood that should be rejected. Underpinning this claim, following F. D. Maurice, is an emphasis on "original love," that hell is not the deepest place in the universe from which some fundamental negative life-energy emerges to entrap the children of men; below that is an even deeper "abyss"—the love of God. The child does, in some sense, as Wordsworth had put it, come into the world trailing clouds of glory. There is something about the child that is inherently divine; it carries "original blessing."

Representing the case for the prosecution, we consider Archdeacon (later Cardinal) Henry Manning's severe view of "the sins that follow us" into eternity to indict us before the throne of God and how MacDonald responded theologically. (It was not only Evangelicals that were obsessed with sin.) Illustrating the case for the defense, we then meet one of MacDonald's children, Diamond from *At the Back of the North Wind*. This narrative, like all MacDonald's output, is fundamentally theological and reveals six central claims about the child and how, as an image-bearer, it reflects certain aspects of the divine nature. However, we are left with a sense that Diamond is not quite "all there"—that he represents a vision of childhood that is not quite true to life, and perhaps, as the text itself suggests, that he has learning difficulties: he cannot truly relate to the real world. Diamond, however, is making a fundamental claim: that true holiness is perceived as insanity by the ungodly. Diamond *does* have learning difficulties: he is too innocent to learn the ways of "adult" human corruption. MacDonald is, rather disparagingly, suggesting that we, as readers, in our judgement of this Christ-child, are the insane ones.

The view that something is not "quite right" with Diamond raises a fundamental question which this book seeks to answer. Is something not "quite right" with MacDonald's theology? Is the sense of inadequacy and unreality which we regularly struggle with as readers when we meet MacDonald's fictive children simply the result of second-rate dramatization—perhaps overly-sentimental Victorian prose? (C. S. Lewis, while describing MacDonald as his "master," nevertheless did not consider him to be in the first rank of authors, and "probably not in its second.")[3] Or is it because MacDonald's inadequate pictures of children reflect an inadequate theology, perhaps a Romantic naivety? Or is it a deliberate authorial strategy—for example, to challenge notions of normality? What fundamental theological claims are being made?

Before, in chapter 5, constructing an overview of MacDonald's theology as a base camp from which to explore some of his more enigmatic and opaque fantasy works, chapter 4 brings these questions into greater focus as we meet some of the children from his "realist" fiction, many of whom, like Diamond, raise questions. I cast doubt on the word "realist" because it soon becomes apparent that MacDonald's realist characters (and settings) are far from real. On closer inspection, we realize they are imports from fairyland that sometimes misread the quotidian world of humans. His children appear to float incongruously above the grime of Victorian Britain, curiously immune to its toxicity. The grime, on closer inspection, seems more of a stage prop than the detritus of humanity; or is it that the children have magical powers? So we meet children such as Gibbie, an Aberdeen stray, finding a lost earring in a gutter and sucking it clean without contracting cholera. The temptation is to simply dismiss this as "bad fiction," but, as critics, we must take into account that MacDonald's fiction does not illustrate some underlying, deeper theology; his novels do not illustrate what he thinks, they *are* what he thinks— here, the view that evil has no purchase on the childlike. There are, of

---

3. Lewis, *George MacDonald*, 14.

course, period distractions and technical issues, but the quest is to dig for theological gems which, Chesterton remarked, are "hidden in a somewhat uneven setting." That said, one must resist the temptation (perhaps Lewis's error in his *Anthology*) of ignoring those fictive settings. Literary context is as important to the critic as content.

As noted, MacDonald particularly despised "theologic" systems. In his view, they quickly became idolatrous scaffolding that hid the true nature of God. He therefore stubbornly refused to explain his work: "If my dog can't bark," he remarked, "I'm not going to sit up and bark for him." Constructing a systematic overview of MacDonald's thought is, therefore, challenging. Not only is his theology dispersed in some fifty volumes of varying genres, his cognitive and epistemological prioritizing of imagination above "logic" necessarily results in often enigmatic prose. That said, he often does "sit up and bark" from within his narratives and it is possible, from both direct thoughts from sermons, letters, and such authorial interjections, as well as from imaginative, "illustrative" prose, to construct a clear picture of what he believes. This is presented in this mid-chapter where, in particular, we explore a little-read short story, *The Broken Swords*, which summarizes MacDonald's *exitus–reditus* view of the trajectory of human life. Against the backdrop of a more nuanced understanding of the influence of those such as Jacob Boehme, a summary of his wider theology is offered under heads such as the doctrine of God, cosmology, anthropology, the problem of evil, and soteriology.

Until this point, for the most part, I purposely avoid MacDonald's two main fantasy works *Phantastes* and *Lilith* that bookended his career. The former, published in 1858, represents his youthful manifesto; the latter, his most mysterious work written when he was around seventy, is arguably a summative retrospective of his life's work. These works have been endlessly dissected from various perspectives (all, of course, richly rewarding and valid), but my motive in summarizing MacDonald's theology prior to reading these more opaque works is based on the premise that *theology* is the key that unlocks their secrets, and in using this key, more detailed theological claims are revealed or clarified.

The second half of the journey into MacDonald's mind begins (in chapter 6) by considering the Evangelical backdrop to his work in more detail and by looking more closely at his methodology. Regarding the former, we observe how "the problem of evil" was the main bone of contention between liberal and conservative Evangelicals (impacting, of course, those who claimed other faith-affiliations or none). We explore in more detail the more extreme views of both camps. (In our criticism, it is important to remind ourselves that in the nineteenth century, Evangelicalism was having its time in the sun, and, generally, considered a positive force for renewal in British and American society.)

Regarding methodology, we consider MacDonald's placement of a fairy child above the unseemly religious skirmishes of the period; a child that offers a *via media* which involves two core proposals. The first, that fighting for the truth is a waste of time. Perhaps at this point MacDonald's Romantic pedigree comes most clearly into view as a counter-Enlightenment position challenging the hegemony of logic. Enlightenment epistemology, claims the fairy child, is fundamentally flawed; truth, although it may be logically evaluated, is not *in se* "logical." Rather, truth is perceived imaginatively through an aesthetic encounter with it and its source. Furthermore, truth is not simply a matter of perception but of construction as the human mind engages with God's truth which, for the Christian, is a person, not a theory. As Augustine had put it: "Christ is the art of the omnipotent God."[4]

With this in mind, the fairy child stands aloof from the futile religious battles, and using three strategies of defamiliarization forces those at its feet to reconsider their violent, destructive, and ultimately futile fundamentalist conflicts. First, it makes the familiar strange: by forcing a fresh look at the idols that have taken residence in the religious landscape we are forced to ask the question: What right have they to be there? Second, it makes strange the familiar. This has less to do with exposing falsehood as forcing a reconsideration of the truth: has familiarity bred contempt when it comes to the content of religion? The child—in a childlike manner—describes the world through its innocent eyes; we see our world truly, perhaps for the first time, or at least with fresh vision. And lastly, the fairy child, being from fairyland, either cannot, or refuses to, name what it sees. After Carlyle, and Coleridge before him, MacDonald was suspicious of words that had become so interred in the grave of convention that not only had their true meaning been lost, they had become gravestones hiding the true nature of reality. By refusing to name what it sees, the fairy child forces *us* to give reality a "name," and in the process, evaluate its true, that is, aesthetic, identity.

These three strategies of defamiliarization are evident in *Lilith*, a book which names the vampire at the heart of what we would now call

---

4. Dods, *Works of Augustine*, 7:177 (*De Trinitate* 6.10).

fundamentalist religion. As we consider her pedigree and nineteenth-century incarnation, it becomes clear why MacDonald has chosen this vampiric *femme fatale* as his antagonist. At numerous levels she embodies all that (in his view) was wrong with contemporary religion and society: she feeds on the blood of children, claims worship, but is, in reality, the queen of Hell; she personifies the male fear that Victorian females were not as submissive as supposed; she has sold her soul to the devil, the "great Shadow," complicit in seeking out those whom *she* may devour; she is the princess of a materialistic and exploitative city that despises its poor; she is the ultimate anti-child, and therefore the antichrist. Shockingly, however, she is worshipped by those who claim faith. Since two core themes in *Lilith* are childhood and evil, a close reading of this text is necessary (chapter 7). It reveals that these are not two themes, but one: the perfection of childhood is the opposite pole of being from the depravity of vampirism. True humanity inheres in renouncing vampirism—the blood of a counterfeit Eucharist—and accepting the true Eucharist, the bread and wine of Christ.

Our reading of *Lilith* is very much a journey into MacDonald's mind. Numerous allusions to mental states, as well as the genre of fictional autobiography, allow no other reading. We are drawn into a complex web of intrigue as MacDonald bares his soul. We discover that while the narrative does feature archetypal children, such as the Little Ones, the main hero-child is MacDonald himself in the guise of Mr. Vane: a far from ideal child, full of fears, doubt, pride, sexual fantasy, and foolishness—in short, a far more "real" child that many of his other fictional characters; if not a perfect child, certainly a child in the making—a child on the *reditus* leg of its journey being inexorably drawn back to the source of its being.

In chapter 8 we pull together the theological threads from *Lilith* in a quest to weave together as coherent as possible a picture of MacDonald's "theology of childhood." His methodology—the implementation of defamiliarization strategies—is a lesson in what might be called imaginative fiduciary hermeneutics, that is, "decoding" the world imaginatively as a child through the eyes of faith. The theological proposals that emerge clarify MacDonald's view of reality as a Keatsean "system of soul-making," but what is striking is his view of life *and* the afterlife as purgatorial processes preparing the soul for the final post-mortem embrace of God. Perhaps more contentious is his expression of the universalist "larger hope" which, by implication, will result in the salvation of Lilith, the vampiric antichrist.

Rather than simply a Romantic symbol of interiority or innocence, it is clear, then, that MacDonald's child is making rather shocking theological claims—at least to those raised in the shadow of Calvin. Not only is he suggesting that a vampire has taken up residence at the heart of Christianity, he is implying that this vampire, along with its human hosts, will be "saved." Furthermore, in his theodical quest to exonerate God from charges of evil, he has, it could be argued, made God the author of evil. Since his starting point is "God is light, and in him there is no darkness," the solution he offers therefore has to be, at some level, to redefine evil as good.

These theological questions and concerns are the focus of our final chapter where we critically examine the implications of MacDonald's "theology of the child." It will be argued that his theodicy is flawed but that this does not detract from some profound theological insights which, in particular, shed light on the nature of Christian fundamentalism, an idolatry which, according to Pope Francis, is found in all religions. We discover that his views on hell and damnation, for example, chime with those such as Gregory of Nyssa and are not far removed from certain strands of Western thought.

It is easy, as some have done, to dismiss George MacDonald as a nineteenth-century oddity (some, as we shall note, even conclude that he is "not a Christian"); a "hopelessly Romantic" optimist wearing Wordsworthian rose-tinted glasses, ignoring—as one contemporary put it—"the awful controversy caused by sin." But, I argue here, this would be a mistake. Rather, his is the story of a mind walking the familiar theological tightrope across the abyss where, on the one hand, we have a good God, and on the other, apparently dysteleological, destructive evil. How can the two coexist? This, the *mysterium iniquitatis*, has exercised theological minds since Job. I suggest that MacDonald's conclusions, far from being of merely historical interest, have much to contribute to today's theological conversations, and, in particular, are a stark warning against blindly sliding into the destructive hell of fundamentalism.

1

The Context of George MacDonald's Work

LIKE MANY VICTORIANS, GEORGE MacDonald's (1824–1905) journey was one of emancipation from "childhood" ways. His was a journey away from Calvinism in favor of a more benign vision of Christianity at the center of which is the image of "the child," an axiomatic image symbolizing both the nature of God and the disposition of the faithful. One Presbyterian critic, George McCrie, lamented that "the childlike" was something that he "constantly harps about" resulting in "religious opinions, which are most unsound and dangerous."[1] The central question we explore here is: What are the theological implications of MacDonald's understanding and use of this motif?

In answering this question, it becomes apparent that "the child" (MacDonald's shorthand for all of a childlike disposition, henceforth not in quotes), far from being a submissive, acquiescent juvenile content to submit to the whims of elders—notably worldly religious elders—is, rather, a force that challenges the latter's rule and wisdom. The child represents a theology that *is* "unsound and dangerous" to those such as McCrie, for in MacDonald's mind he and those like him represented a church that had turned its back on childhood, that is, had forsaken worship of the Christ child and instead allowed a vampire to take up residence at its heart—one that drank the blood of the saints rather than offering Eucharistic life. This is the essential message of one of MacDonald's last and most enigmatic fantasy novels, *Lilith*. Before reading this narrative, however, we lay thoughts of vampires to one side as we meet various

1. McCrie, *Religion of Our Literature*, 295.

incarnations of MacDonald's child and, through these encounters, build up a picture of his theology and the world in which it was forged.

Theology and Literature

Before we begin this task, however, some comments are necessary regarding the validity of reading MacDonald's work—especially his novels—as theology. What is the relationship between theology and literature?

George McCrie's decisive rejection of MacDonald's theology highlights a deeper issue—a profound suspicion, among conservative Evangelicals in particular, of narrative writing as a medium to express or explore theology. McCrie articulates the prevailing view: being imaginative, rather than concerned with the "true facts" of Evangelical religion, it results in "our poets and novelists . . . teaching an erroneous theology with all the earnestness of missionaries"; those with aesthetic gifts have sold their souls to the devil and become "patrons of heresy." Such should stick to their role of providing entertainment, not "theologizing." "Their peculiar office is to delight and entertain the world rather than to preach or to prophecy."[2] The implication is that the imprecision of literature is unsuitable to express the "facts" of theology; that literature is merely the frothy surface hiding a substrate of true (or false)—that is, logically verifiable (or discountable)—bedrock beliefs.

This highlights a fundamental polarity that will surface regularly in this volume: the antagonism between those such as MacDonald who view imagination as God's *primary* gift to humans in the service of cognition and epistemology, and those such as McCrie who is of the opinion that:

> The same considerations that made [pre-Reformation] literature an admirable herald of the Bible and of the Reformation, render it a dangerous pioneer of doctrine that is likely to overthrow them both.[3]

Put differently: imagination is a useful, if capricious, force that may provoke change but offers a poor theological foundation. In response to this charge, I briefly outline some considerations that will help us to approach MacDonald's literary opus as theologians with less cynicism.

---

2. McCrie, *Religion of Our Literature*, 287, 289.
3. McCrie, *Religion of Our Literature*, ix.

To engage in theology is, in a fundamental sense, to become a worshipper. God cannot be the object of human investigation for this would require an impossible perspective "outside" of being; rather, investigation into the nature of God can only be the result of personal interaction with God, should God so permit—a permission, it would appear, granted only to those who are humble; to those who recognize their dependency on, and subordinacy to, God—the "babes" of Matthew 11:25 to whom, uniquely, are revealed the secrets of the kingdom of heaven. In MacDonald's language, true theology is understood, practiced, and expressed only by the child, one who embodies this submissive, worshipful attitude. Three further considerations are evident: first, that since theology's "object" is not only infinite but personal, it can never be fully known; second, that such knowledge is essentially "storied" in that the truth regarding a person cannot be established by factual statements, however verifiable or logically correct; third, that truth is imprecise since subjectively perceived.

One might counter this by suggesting that theology is essentially a second-order, objective reflection on such personal stories, notably the gospel narratives' articulation of Christ, but, in light of the "personality" or person-based nature of truth, literature may be viewed as not only a source of personal or imaginative fuel for subsequent reflection, but as itself a means of theological reflection and articulation. One thinks, for example, of Augustine's *Confessions*, Dostoevsky's novels,[4] or the works of Dante. Speaking of Dante's *Commedia*, for example (a poem that has significantly shaped European theology), Vittorio Montemaggi proposes that truth is always the fruit of "human encounter" (truth, in other words, is always in some sense embodied) and that—in recognition of this—literature such as Dante's draws the reader into a personal encounter with the author, others, and ultimately God. In Montemaggi's words: "Dante's text requires us to read it not only objectively but also by consciously situating our interpretation of it in the context of our subjective, first-person experience."[5] MacDonald is similarly driven by a conviction that theology involves more than the objective, academic analysis of presenting facts; rather, subjective engagement is required with the source of those facts—God. To this end, he writes imaginatively, demanding an interpretation based on personal, conscious engagement with the text—and

---

4. See especially Williams, *Dostoevsky*.
5. Montemaggi, *Reading Dante's Commedia as Theology*, 36.

therefore with himself as writer. This is most evident in *Lilith*, in which we are invited to "read" MacDonald's mind.

For Montemaggi, Dante's poem is theology.[6] This volume, likewise, approaches MacDonald's work—notably his novels—as theology; as the exploration and articulation of the human encounter with God. Such encounters may be fictional, but, as Montemaggi notes regarding the prevalence of human characters in Dante's fiction:

> Human particularity and encounter destabilize easy distinctions between truth and fiction. A nonfictional story that fails to awaken us to the infinite value of human particularity can from this perspective be considered less true than a fictional one that succeeds.[7]

This tension between "real" theology and that expressed in literature is a fundamental concern of MacDonald. Inasmuch as the former is the fruit of "adult" endeavor—that is, of formal academic training in the discursive arts—it is suspect; only the more subjective and intuitive approach of the child, MacDonald asserts, is capable of engaging with, and expressing, the "personality" of truth. This is a claim we explore here. While certainly not a systematic or dogmatic theologian, it will be argued that MacDonald, whether in essays or novels, is making strong theological claims; not least, that he himself is such a child and therefore a medium of true theology. In this light, we will consider how his novels are not merely illustrative but *constitutive* of what he thinks; that even the most imaginative novels (fantasy works such as *Phantastes* and *Lilith*, for example) must be approached as theological works. We will also consider how MacDonald's preference for imaginative story-telling represents a conscious methodological choice reflecting the view that theology has less to do with imparting factual information as awakening imaginative perception with a view to encouraging that personal encounter with the divine that is its essence. His pastoral goal in writing is the animation of childhood in us, for the Father can only embrace children. In what follows, it is assumed that since MacDonald is writing primarily as a theologian intent on leading his flock towards Christ,[8] that the best way to read it is as theology, which, as Montemaggi suggests (and I have taken the liberty of substituting MacDonald for Dante) is:

---

6. Montemaggi, *Reading Dante's Commedia as Theology*, 21.
7. Montemaggi, *Reading Dante's Commedia as Theology*, 26.
8. See page 130.

to be open to the claims it makes on our active participation in the journey of which it speaks. We might or might not agree with the propositional import of the particular way in which [MacDonald] conceptually and imaginatively articulates his theology in [for example, *Phantastes*]. But if we are to read it *as* theology, and not simply engage in a detached analysis of its theological ideas, we need to allow ourselves, existentially, to interact with the text not simply as an object under examination, but as a living partner in a journey seeking to explore the deepest dimensions of our being, of the cosmos' being, and of the point of encounter between the two.[9]

The Reluctant Congregationalist

Having read natural philosophy (sciences) at the University of Aberdeen, George MacDonald trained for the Congregational ministry at Highbury Theological College, London. Often portrayed as having been ousted from his first pastorate (in Arundel, Sussex) by a diaconate of duplicitous shopkeepers and tradesmen unsympathetic to his liberal "German" theology, the truth may be more prosaic: the loss of living was, it seems, to some extent self-engineered and little lamented. His theology, in any case, was never likely to appeal to a provincial Congregational congregation.[10]

By mid-century he was working primarily as a writer. Friends and acquaintances included Charles Dodgson (who tested *Alice* on the MacDonald children), Charles Kingsley, John Ruskin, Lady Byron, and Alexander John Scott, later principal of Owen's College, Manchester.[11] He became a critic of the world he had left behind but unlike disenchanted

---

9. Montemaggi, *Reading Dante's Commedia as Theology*, 33.

10. Greville MacDonald emphasizes "constructive dismissal" (*GMAW* 177–87). However, contemporaneous letters suggest that his father's heart was elsewhere. From Highbury he writes, "I am not very happy myself [due to] wrong and painful thoughts," and soon after accepting the pastorate confesses that his "greatest desire is . . . to go out itinerating"; "I mean to take another mode of helping men" (Sadler, *Expression of Character*, 26, 50, 54).

11. On *Alice*, see *GMAW* 342. Kingsley's *Water Babies* was a response to *Phantastes*. See Manlove, "MacDonald and Kingsley," 143. MacDonald arranged clandestine meetings between Ruskin and Rose La Touche in his house, against the wishes of her parents, and according to Greville MacDonald, Ruskin, along with A. J. Scott, was "one of the closest friends of my father" (*GMAW* 330, 191–92). Lady Byron praised MacDonald's first poem *Within and Without*, subsequently financing family wintering in Algiers. See *GMAW* 265.

Evangelicals of the era such as George Eliot, Francis W. Newman (brother of John Henry), or Edmund Gosse whose trajectory was away from faith,[12] MacDonald remained "evangelical." He published and lectured in a quest to promote Christianity in an era increasingly uncomfortable with traditional religion. His work might be summarized as a rejection of childishness (petulant, stubborn worship of a misconceived God) in favor of childhood (genuine submission to, and relationship with, the Father).

While C. S. Lewis was of the opinion that MacDonald always had an enduring respect for his childhood religion,[13] Chesterton dryly remarks that he said things "that were not in the least like the Calvinists" and suggests his contribution to theology might be significant: "As Protestants speak of the morning stars of the Reformation, we may be allowed to note such names here and there as morning stars of the Reunion." "I fancy," says Chesterton, "that he stands for a rather important turning-point in the history of Christendom."[14] His relative obscurity, however, and absence from current theological discourse is perhaps testimony to the opposite. However, his "obscure" ideas have found their way into popular culture, especially through *The Lord of the Rings*.[15] C. S. Lewis also credits him for leading him to faith, describing him as his "master"[16] (perhaps more so as a mentor in fantasy writing than theology). I shall argue that, in some measure, Chesterton was right: that MacDonald was "a morning star of the Reunion" by providing a *via media* between conservative and liberal Evangelicalism, and by helping those of faith to reconnect with pre-Reformation roots.

Kerry Dearborn suggests that MacDonald's proviso for accepting ideas from eclectic sources was that they were "consistent with the

---

12. Hempton, *Evangelical Disenchantment*.

13. Lewis, *George MacDonald*, 12. Lewis notes MacDonald's repudiation of Calvinist doctrines yet suggests that he sees "elements of real and perhaps irreplaceable worth in the thing from which he is revolting."

14. GMAW 13.

15. There is a ring-wielding villain in *David Elginbrod*, the ring being inscribed in an undecipherable foreign tongue. In the short story, *The Castle*, there is a lost ring which "had for ages disappeared from the earth, but which had controlled the spirits, and the possession of which made a man simply what a man should be, the king of the world" (POS 175–76).

16. Lewis, *George MacDonald*, 20. See also Lewis, *Surprised by Joy*, 179–81, 225, 226.

Trinitarian faith."[17] However, universal salvation (including that of Judas and Satan) and a purgatorial hell, to give but two examples, are ideas which might indicate otherwise (if for "Trinitarian" we read "Evangelical orthodoxy"). His theology is a syncretistic amalgam of ideas, happily exploring, for example, evolution and Eastern mysticism. Such leanings lead one scholar to remark that he has "a view of human experience *quite different* from that of much of historic Christianity," another, that his faith amounts to a "private religion," and according to Chesterton, "He evolved out of his own mystical meditations a complete alternative theology leading to a completely contrary mood." During his lifetime, those such as McCrie accused him of starting "some new scheme of Christianity."[18] These comments cannot, in my view, be justified. It seems, rather, that MacDonald's work reflects (as one contemporary put it) "the noble protest of men like Maurice and Kingsley and [F. W.] Robertson, with whom the recovery of the central truth of Christianity, that God is love, came as almost a new gospel."[19] His views are—as we explore in this chapter—firmly embedded in contemporary thinking, and, as he himself observes: "No man could sing as he has sung, had not others sung before him."[20] However, it is apparent that he has more in common with Emanuel Swedenborg (who imaginatively journeys into heaven and hell),[21] Jacob Boehme (whose mystical theology is produced despite the censure of church authorities, and whose humble station in life as a shoemaker probably appealed to MacDonald's Romantic leanings), or Gregory of Nyssa (with his focus on *epektasis*—the soul's progressive journey towards God) than any of the progenitors of the Westminster Confession.[22]

Much of MacDonald's writing is a thought-experiment which tests the boundaries of the Evangelical orthodoxy of his day. It explores two

17. Dearborn, *Baptized Imagination*, 177.

18. Hein, *Harmony Within*, 53 (emphasis mine); Reis, *George MacDonald's Fiction*, 32; GMAW 12; McCrie, *Religion of Our Literature*, 287.

19. Moore, "Influence of Calvinism," 334.

20. EA 3.

21. Note 48, page 22.

22. The similarity between Boehme's cosmology and MacDonald's is discussed in chapter 5. Resonances with Gregory are discussed in the final chapter, page 261. William Raeper singles out Swedenborg and Boehme as influences (GMWR 240) and one suspects MacDonald had Boehme in mind when he cast a cobbler as the hero of *Salted With Fire*.

related questions. What did Jesus mean when he challenged his followers to become "as children"? How might this work out in practice? Questions that must take account of the distortions, limitations, and power structures of a world where the choice to be a child appears misguided—particularly when one has to deal with a vampire. MacDonald explores the nature and implications of that choice. This theological enquiry evaluates MacDonald's answers to these questions and explores their implications and contribution to theology.

George MacDonald's Theology—Key Ideas and Influences

The enduring, and ambiguous, influence of Scotland is perennially evident in George MacDonald's work. On the one hand, the liminal realm of *Faerie* exercised its magic power:

> Tales . . . of mountain, stream, and lake; of love and revenge; of beings less and more than natural—brownie and Boneless, kelpie and fairy; such wild legends also, haunting the dim emergent peaks of mist-swathed Celtic history.[23]

This was a colorful world contrasting with the blacks worn to Sunday service. Scotland, for MacDonald, was a land of paradox with "the sweetest songs in its cottages, and the worst singing in its churches, of any country in the world."[24]

On the other hand, then, was an inflexible Calvinism, a counterpoint providing both foil and foundation for his thought, an inflexibility of which MacDonald's immediate predecessors and mentors had fallen foul. In his childhood, for example, A. J. Scott's and John McLeod Campbell's licenses had been revoked by the General Assembly of the Church of Scotland in 1831 for suggesting that Christ had died for all, not just the elect (an issue that, in the seventeenth century, had split the Baptists into "general" and "particular"). One of Scott's accusers, the leader of the Evangelical party, Andrew Thomson, considered Scott and his circle to have:

> propagated doctrines which belie the word of God most odiously—which reason repudiates as inconsistent and mistaken—which break the constitution of the gospel into pieces, and

---

23. *MA* 3:88.
24. *DE* 3:99.

substitutes for it freaks of fancy and unwholesome paradoxes—and which introduce into religion all that is silly and bigoted and presumptuous.[25]

With such shadows hanging over him, it is unsurprising that the enduring respect for Calvinism that Lewis detected in MacDonald is not immediately apparent:[26] Calvinism is invariably, almost obsessively, disparaged, leading one contemporary critic to complain: "His Calvinistic characters . . . are nearly all fanatics, cranks or oddities [yet they are presented as] the legitimate products of Calvinism"; in truth, however, they are representative of only "two or three wizened, juiceless crabs from some out of the way lightning-smitten bough."[27] In MacDonald's mind, however, that "lightning-smitten bough" equated to most established religion, leading an earlier critic to observe that "his quarrel is therefore with all the Evangelical Churches at home and abroad."[28] That said, non-Evangelical religion does not escape: the "fashionable sheep" of Anglicanism are mocked;[29] there is also an early critique of "Pentecostal" emotionalism, observing that "scream will call forth scream, as vibrant string from its neighbour will draw the answering tone."[30]

In MacDonald's view, hard Calvinism is the worst idolatry. First, it defames the character of God. Its God "car[es] not for righteousness, but for his rights,"[31] dramatized by Murdoch Malison, the "Scotch schoolmaster of the rough old-fashioned type" in *Alec Forbes of Howglen*:

> His pleasure was law, irrespective of right or wrong, and the reward of submission to law was immunity from punishment. He had his favourites in various degrees, whom he chose according to inexplicable directions of feeling ratified by "the freedom of his own will."[32] These found it easy to please him, while those

---

25. Newell, "Unworthy of the Dignity," 250.
26. Lewis, *George MacDonald*, 11–12.
27. Wilson, *Theology of Modern Literature*, 272–73.
28. McCrie, *Religion of Our Literature*, 305.
29. *DE* 3:178, 182.
30. *MA* 3:59.
31. *US3* 161.
32. This phrase of John Locke (Locke, *Second Treatise of Civil Government* 6.63) concerns a child coming of age, now governed by "reason" instead of trustees, and is probably a dig at Calvin's voluntarism. See "'Morality' of God," page 139.

with whom he was not primarily pleased, found it impossible to please him.[33]

Such negative views of God result from the dominance of a juridical model in Western theology which lead to a theological grammar of lord and servant or master and slave.[34] According to Veli-Matti Kärkkäinen, it results from "the biblically, historically, dogmatically and ecumenically unfounded and counter-productive tendency in some conservative Protestant traditions to make the forensic framework not only the dominant one but also the exclusive one" while neglecting the many other New Testament soteriological metaphors.[35] This concern was shared by F. D. Maurice who, like Coleridge before him, placed Christ at the heart of his theology and of his understanding of the *imago Dei*.[36] It is thus that, following his mentor, MacDonald offers a very contrasting image of God as "easy to please but hard to satisfy."[37] Conceiving of God as the ideal Victorian father he writes:

> That no keeping but a perfect one will *satisfy* God, I hold with all my heart and strength; but that there is none else he cares for, is one of the lies of the enemy. What father is not pleased with the first tottering attempt of his little one to walk? What father would be satisfied with anything but the manly step of a full-grown son?[38]

MacDonald's second concern was the reduction of faith (a relational and obedient response to God) to belief (merely intellectual assent to "correct" dogma).[39] It is evident that negative childhood experiences led to sympathy with popular polemics against the "miserable, puritanical, martinet" God,[40] such as the broadside of Herbert Spencer in 1884:

---

33. *AF* 1:239–40.

34. Stockitt, *Imagination and the Playfulness of God*, 138.

35. Beilby and Eddy, *Justification*, 124. Walter Schmithals identifies ten NT soteriological metaphors (Brown, *Dictionary of NT Theology*, 1:437–79). See also McIntyre, *Faith, Theology, and Imagination*, 60–61.

36. Maurice, *Kingdom of Christ*, 97.

37. A phrase used by Lewis and Chesterton. See Lewis, *George MacDonald*, 41; *GMAW* 12.

38. *US2* 10–11.

39. See McGrath, *Heresy*, 22.

40. *US3* 161.

> The visiting on Adam's descendants, through hundreds of generations, dreadful penalties for a small transgression which they did not commit; the damning of all men who do not avail themselves of an alleged mode of obtaining forgiveness, which most men have never heard of; and the effecting a reconciliation by sacrifice of one who was perfectly innocent are modes of action which, ascribed to a human ruler, would call forth expressions of abhorrence; and the ascription of them to the Ultimate Cause of things, even now felt to be full of difficulties, must become impossible.[41]

Such issues provoked a theological response (in this particular case, a sermon)[42] with a strong leaning towards theodicy.

As Brian Cummings notes, having started with the goal of justifying humanity to God, by the time Milton was writing *Paradise Lost* the Reformation had come full circle with Milton finding it necessary to "assert Eternal Providence, and justifie the wayes of God to men."[43] MacDonald felt himself to be in the same position. Foremost was the paradox of an omnipotent God of love and grace who, apparently, was content to eternally damn the majority of the creatures made in God's image—being either unwilling or unable to save them—as articulated by the false gospel of Calvinism, "founded on the pagan notion that suffering is an offset for sin";[44] a religion that "would have us love Christ for protecting us from God, instead of for leading us to God."[45]

MacDonald found resolution by aligning himself with a more imaginative, Romantic approach to theology. In contrast to a "profoundly anti-intellectual and anti-aesthetic" Evangelicalism,[46] he found solace, for example, in Swedenborg. A letter to his father expresses a measure of emancipation and reflects a Coleridgean view of faith as organic, rather than static:[47]

> I grow younger and happier. I see an outlet now from miseries of the mind, unknown to any which form portions of my earliest recollections, and have grown with my growth—but which by &

---

41. Spencer, "Religious Retrospect and Prospect," 345.
42. The sermon is titled "The Truth in Jesus." See *US2* 233–64.
43. Cummings, *Literary Culture of the Reformation*, 421.
44. *HG* 81.
45. *DG* 28.
46. Prickett, *Romanticism and Religion*, 253.
47. Prickett, *Romanticism and Religion*, 54.

by I shall quite outgrow. Swedenborg says that the angels are always growing younger. In this saying, which is *logically* absurd, there is a very deep meaning. Oh I know a little now . . . what Christ's deep sayings mean about becoming like a child.[48]

This early discovery of "childlikeness" underlines the influence of "German" (European) mysticism. Prior to this, while in the north of Scotland, there is evidence from his fiction that he read mystics such as Novalis and poets such as Goethe.[49] Whenever and however discovered, the issue is that he found an alternative, imaginative approach to faith. This letter, written shortly before his departure from Arundel, is indicative of this epiphany, and his unease at Highbury was no doubt down to excessive dogmatism quenching such mystical leanings.[50] The influence of English Romantics such as Coleridge, Wordsworth, and Shelley (and a Romantic reverence for Shakespeare)[51] cemented this very imaginative approach to epistemology. It represents a strong alignment to Romanticism and a suspicion of Enlightenment rationalism.

The Influence of Romanticism

Imagination and childhood preoccupied the Romantics, and in Coleridge—"one of the first British theologians to assert that all of creation shared in the gift of life given by God"[52]—MacDonald found the foundation for his theology of imagination. Chapter 13 of *Biographia Literaria* begins with lines from *Paradise Lost* affirming human being as the pinnacle of God's created order:

> To intellectual!—give both life and sense,
> Fancy and understanding; whence the soul
> REASON receives, and reason is her being,
> Discursive or intuitive.[53]

---

48. Sadler, *Expression of Character*, 58–59.
49. POS 37–38.
50. See page 32.
51. Especially evident in Coleridge. See, for example, Coleridge, *Collected Works*, 2:19.
52. Stockitt, *Imagination and the Playfulness of God*, 33.
53. Coleridge, *Collected Works*, 1:295.

MacDonald took on board Coleridge's understanding of "reason" (cognition) as being both "discursive or intuitive" and echoed his famous division of imagination into primary imagination, secondary imagination, and fancy, the former being "a repetition in the finite mind of the eternal act of creation in the infinite I AM" and therefore the spark of the divine presence in the human mind.[54] On this basis, MacDonald insists that imagination is the prime cognitive faculty that *leads* "reason":

> The imagination labours to extend [the intellect's] territories, to give it room. She sweeps across the borders, searching out new lands into which she may guide her plodding brother. The imagination is the light which redeems from the darkness for the eyes of the understanding.[55]

Crucially, however, after Coleridge, the "light" referred to in this last sentence is divine. Human imagination is not simply *like* God's but "a repetition in the finite mind"—it *is* God's direct presence in human consciousness. As MacDonald put it:

> But God sits in that chamber of our being in which the candle of our consciousness goes out in darkness, and sends forth from thence wonderful gifts into the light of that understanding which is His candle. Our hope lies in no most perfect mechanism even of the spirit, but in the wisdom wherein we live and move and have our being.[56]

Human imagination is the divine gift uniting the poles of being—God in nature and God in consciousness. The imagination leads in "finding out the works of God"; the "intellect" must follow:

> What we mean to insist upon is, that in finding out the works of God, the Intellect must labour, workman-like, under the direction of the architect, Imagination.[57]

The distinction between imagination and fancy is evident. In Coleridge, fancy is "emancipated from the order of time and space," however this does not imply a similarly transcendent dimension: it deals with "fixities and definites" and "must receive all its materials ready made

---

54. Coleridge, *Collected Works*, 1:304–5.

55. *Orts* 14.

56. *Orts* 25; cf. "When the light of sense / Goes out, but with a flash that has revealed / The invisible world" (Wordsworth, *Selected Poems*, 372).

57. *Orts* 11.

from the law of association."[58] That is, fancy transcends spatio-temporal constraints but is nevertheless earth-bound, a human capacity. Robin Stockitt summarizes thus: "The exercise of choice that is open to Fancy is deliberate and intentional but the raw materials available to it are limited to what the human mind can remember or has experienced."[59] MacDonald reflects this in his advice to those who would foster imagination in the young. The good teacher should

> point out to him [the pupil] the essential difference between reverie and thought; between dreaming and imagining. He will teach him not to mistake fancy, either in himself or in others, for imagination, and to beware of hunting after resemblances that carry with them no interpretation.[60]

As Cardinal Newman remarked, it was through such philosophical engagement that Coleridge, a "very original thinker," had "made trial of his age, and succeeded in interesting its genius in the cause of Catholic truth,"[61] praise centered on the recognition that, unlike Kant's reverse Copernican revolution in philosophy, Coleridge's quest was to center meaning back on God. Newman, however, qualified his accolade by observing that Coleridge "indulged in a liberty of speculation, which no Christian can tolerate," a comment to be borne in mind here as we evaluate MacDonald's ideas, particularly as those more skeptical of Coleridge, such as F. J. A. Hort, described him—in an age with a predilection for taxonomy—as

> that which refuses to be classified. An author whose opinions will not range with those of any recognised party, or whose works never seem quite rightly lodged in any one division of a well-regulated library, occupies in general estimation what was once the place of a zoophyte or platypus,—an uncanny creature, possibly of demoniacal origin. Such a divine monster was Coleridge.[62]

Is MacDonald also "an uncanny creature, possibly of demoniacal origin"? Certainly his work represents a protest against religious taxonomy: his

---

58. Coleridge, *Collected Works*, 1:305.
59. Stockitt, *Imagination and the Playfulness of God*, 66–67.
60. *Orts* 41.
61. Newman, *Apologia Pro Vita Sua*, 97.
62. Prickett, *Romanticism and Religion*, 3.

thoughts "never seem quite rightly lodged in any one division of a well-regulated library"—as will become clear when we read *Lilith*.

F. D. Maurice, like Newman, mediated Coleridgean ideas to the Victorian church.[63] His influence, however, was not confined to Anglicanism: through writers such as R. W. Dale, James Baldwin Brown, and MacDonald, his influence on nonconformity (especially Congregationalism) was considerable. "In fact," writes F. J. Powicke in the 1870s about his student days at Spring Hill College, "a Maurician cult grew up, and probably did more to shape our theology than the lectures of the principal, Dr. [David Worthington] Simon."[64] "Maurice's influence on MacDonald," says William Raeper, "cannot be stressed too strongly."[65] Through the mouth of the hero in *David Elginbrod*, MacDonald paid tribute:[66]

> I seldom go to church . . . but when I do, I come here; and always feel that I am in the presence of one of the holy servants of God's great temple not made with hands. I heartily trust that man. He is what he seems to be.[67]

Maurice singled out his debt to Coleridge, writing, for example, that *Aids to Reflection*—a book that particularly appeals to "childlike men and women"—"is [a book] to which I feel myself under . . . deep and solemn obligations,"[68] and that with regard to the history of the Bible, he had "said very little indeed of which [Coleridge's] thought was not the germ," confessing to have stolen "many other thoughts."[69] Geoffrey Rowell identifies three in particular: "that eternity was independent of duration; that the power of repentance is not limited to this life; and that it is not revealed whether or not all will ultimately be saved."[70] As well as his father's Unitarianism, Rowell also notes the impact of the "teaching of the Scottish divines, Erskine of Linlathen and McLeod Campbell; the Cambridge Platonists; the mystical tradition of Jacob Boehme and

---

63. See Prickett, *Romanticism and Religion*, 120–75.

64. Johnson, *Dissolution of Dissent*, 142.

65. *GMWR* 240.

66. "Many people assumed [this] was meant to represent F. D. Maurice" (Amell, "On MacDonald and Maurice," 26).

67. *DE* 3:196. MacDonald named one of his sons "Frederick," asking his namesake to be godfather (Amell, "On MacDonald and Maurice," 27).

68. Maurice, *Kingdom of Christ*, 11, 10.

69. Maurice, *Kingdom of Christ*, 12.

70. Rowell, *Hell and the Victorians*, 83.

William Law; all these left their mark on Maurice's theology"[71]—and MacDonald's, through whom they were mediated to a wider audience.

Jeremy Morris notes a focus on the *imago Dei*. Maurice particularly objected to Pusey's idea that at Baptism the candidate received a new *nature*, the implication being that the old nature was at best suspect, at worst evil—in other words, a doctrine that undermined the goodness and "grace" of creation and the universality of the impact of the Incarnation.[72] Maurice stressed that the Articles of the Church of England

> did not begin, as was the case with Calvinism, from a conviction of human sinfulness which then became the basis for a theological system, but from a restatement of the "Catholic foundation" of the Trinity, the Incarnation, the being of God, the Scriptures, and the Creeds.[73]

Other themes we find in Maurice include a focus on the kingdom of God in contrast to human self-focus, a self-centeredness that is the essence of sin:

> And it is the Kingdom of God because men are brought into it that they may see themselves, their fellow creatures, the whole universe, as He sees them; not partially, or each in reference to a separate centre, as they naturally do.[74]

The fatherhood of God is also contrasted with "schemes for our deliverance":

> We have theories of sin, of justification, of apostolical succession, schemes of divinity Protestant, Romish, semi-Romish, Anglican, Dissenting. But where is God in them all? Not first at least, not a Father; but merely the provider of a certain scheme for our deliverance.[75]

On this view, faith is not to be found in "correct" dogma (Maurice was particularly suspicious of doctrines that distinguished between "correct" or "incorrect" belief, notably Evangelicalism and Tractarianism) but instead focused on "complete fidelity to God's will"[76]—obedience. Stephen

---

71. Rowell, *Hell and the Victorians*, 62.
72. Morris, *Maurice and the Crisis*, 63.
73. Morris, *Maurice and the Crisis*, 90.
74. Maurice quoted in Morris, *Maurice and the Crisis*, 154.
75. Maurice quoted in Morris, *Maurice and the Crisis*, 150.
76. Morris, *Maurice and the Crisis*, 56, 61.

Prickett identifies a corresponding preference for "aesthetic rather than discursive forms of apprehension," and that this "poetic" methodology necessarily led to a distrust of systems. Instead, truth must be perceived organically, the latter concept not only emphasizing the need for holistic vision able to discern "organic," symbolic truth, but drawing attention to the subjective, fluid, and developmental nature of revelation.[77] All these ideas are evident in MacDonald.

MacDonald, then, is part of a Romantic tradition tracing its heritage back through the Lakes poets to European writers such as Schelling, Goethe, Kant, and Rousseau. In addition, we find the likes of Novalis (Georg Philipp Friedrich Freiherr von Hardenberg), Heinrich Heine, Friedrich Schiller, and Friedrich Schleiermacher providing chapter epigrams for MacDonald's first published novel, *Phantastes*. Add to this the influence of Jacob Boehme, Dante, and Emanuel Swedenborg and a picture emerges of a mystical and imaginative approach to faith privileging "feelings"—understood not as the means to discern religious truth, but as the *result* of viewing truth from a holistic and imaginative perspective.[78] Wordsworth's mediation in this respect is clear. We simply note at this point that—commenting on "Lines Written a Few Miles Above Tintern Abbey"—MacDonald praises the poet's ability to express how the imagination unites the poles of being: "the result of the conjunction of the mind of man, and the mind of God manifested in His works; spirit coming to know the speech of spirit."[79]

The term "imagination" in this volume will be used (until further clarified) in this Romantic sense (as I believe MacDonald understood it) to refer to the high level cognitive ability to intuitively discern the meaning of symbols; a bridge uniting the "poles of being," that is, a divine gift providing the means to discern the presence of God in the soul and in nature—the bridge to transcendence.

The Victorian Backdrop—A Divided Evangelical World

Such views placed MacDonald on a collision course with a conservative Evangelicalism that, following Calvin, saw human imagination as essentially corrupt. We find Samuel Law Wilson, for example, complaining

---

77. Prickett, *Romanticism and Religion*, 124–27.
78. Prickett, *Romanticism and Religion*, 148.
79. *Orts* 250.

that MacDonald's Romantic leanings lead to "theological perversities" and a "sentimental piety" considered superior to "ordinary Evangelical religion"; that he reduces conversion to a "slight and facile process," ignoring "the awful controversy caused by sin" and the need for redeeming grace. Furthermore, "natural influences in the process of man's salvation" are given undue prominence, marginalizing the Spirit of God.[80]

While critical of MacDonald's artistic misrepresentation, Wilson's real target is unsound theology. He has no time for a partnership between nature and the inward working of the Spirit that negates the need for an infallible Bible interpreted by an "official" church. For example, the conversion (or at least the reformation) of two alcoholics in *Alec Forbes*—accomplished by the working of "one good and strong spirit—essential life and humanity [, the] spirit was love"[81]—is for Wilson a travesty:

> Thus "the spirit of essential life and humanity" it will be observed, is all the spirit that is needed to effect the saving change in this brace of sinners, and there is more virtue in "love" to redeem and reform than in all the moral appliances of Evangelical religion.[82]

Wilson is unable to concede that "love" is more effective in saving souls from eternal damnation than "the moral appliances of Evangelical religion," but behind this lies the more fundamental issue of the liberal challenge to Evangelical conservatism against a backdrop of social ferment.

The latter third of the nineteenth century, when MacDonald produced most of his work, was perhaps that century's most volatile period. In the first half of the century, unchecked capitalism, the Irish famine, Asiatic cholera, urbanization, and industrialization (to highlight merely some of the social challenges) had produced a highly unbalanced society with endemic deprivation. Revolution was in the air.[83] Conditions, especially in the industrial north where thirteen-year-old children worked seventy-two hours a week and died at the age of fifteen,[84] provoked Marx to write *The Condition of the Working Class in England* (first published in

---

80. Wilson, *Theology of Modern Literature*, 284. Wilson, an Irish Presbyterian professor at Assembly's College Belfast, was particularly "concerned about the impact of insights derived from higher criticism upon ordinary believers" (Holmes, "Biblical Authority," 358).

81. *AF* 3:129.

82. Wilson, *Theology of Modern Literature*, 286.

83. Hilton, *Mad, Bad, Dangerous People?*, 334.

84. Hilton, *Mad, Bad, Dangerous People?*, 574, 589.

1845 in German) and Engels, *The Condition of England* (1844). Ruskin complained that treating humans this way was to

> smother their souls within them ... to make the flesh and skin ... into leathern thongs to yoke machinery with.... [England's] multitudes [are] sent like fuel to feed the factory smoke, and the strength of them is given daily to be wasted.[85]

R. W. Dale, "probably one of the most influential Nonconformist theologians of the nineteenth century,"[86] paints a picture of a fast-changing world full of both danger and promise, but emphasizes the former:

> We are living in a new world ... Immense development of the manufacturing industries, the wider separation of the classes in the great towns—a separation produced by the increase of commercial wealth—the new relations which have grown up between the employers and the employed, the great spread of popular education, the growth of a vast popular literature, the increased political power of the masses of the people, the gradual decay of the old aristocratic organization of society, and the advance, in many forms, of the spirit of democracy—have urgently demanded fresh applications.[87]

By mid-century, social awareness—"the spirit of democracy"—was growing. Evangelicals sensed a new dawn: that mere toleration might finally give way to social equality, that the Church might finally be disestablished, and that Christ would begin to establish his kingdom among the "dark satanic mills." Dale's call for "fresh applications" from the religious community was salutary. It is as if the Ruskinian image of the poor being used as factory-fodder is stirring the religious conscience—revealing the paucity of the theological platitudes supporting social oppression—in a way that pre-industrial-revolution exploitation of the poor could not, masked as it was by scenes (if only imaginary) of pastoral contentment. It is the driving force behind Carlyle's polemics about "the condition of England": work in factories, in his view, was not equivalent to honest artisan labor, but merely slavery. He, like Dale, demanded a religious response from the "ancient guides of Nations, Prophets, Priests" that had lost contact with reality, mocking their apostasy and delusion:

---

85. Ruskin, *Stones of Venice*, 162.
86. Johnson, *Dissolution of Dissent*, 4.
87. Johnson, *Dissolution of Dissent*, 5.

> Ye have forgotten God, ye have quitted the ways of God, or ye would not have been unhappy. It is not according to the laws of Fact that ye have lived and guided yourselves, but according to the laws of Delusion, Imposture, and wilful and unwilful *Mistake* of Fact; behold therefore the Unveracity is worn out; Nature's longsuffering with you is exhausted; and ye are here![88]

We must not allow Carlyle's typically Jeremianic invective to detract from its perspicacity: theological shift was needed. It came in the form of a transition from the "age of atonement"—"a time when the dominant mode of thought [was] an amalgam of enlightenment rationalism and Evangelical eschatology, and its core or 'hinge' was the Christian doctrine of the Atonement"[89]—to the "age of incarnation." The preoccupation with personal salvation became increasingly a *social* quest to wake humanity to the knowledge that the race was *already* part of the family of God under the headship of the incarnate Christ; and since it was optimistically assumed that evolution was moral as well as biological, hopes rose for a golden future under King Jesus. There was a corresponding rise in postmillennialism[90] and an increasing Maurician emphasis on the social implications of Christ's "spiritual society."[91]

This shift had a direct impact socially, particularly on the relationship between nonconformity and the State.[92] The theological emphasis on the incarnation—one aspect of which was that Christ's intervention in human history had *already* united all under the headship of Christ—fueled the nonconformist quest for equality. It led to a stronger emphasis on sanctification (holy living in community) rather than simply justification (the personal "insurance policy").[93] Those such as Edward Miall were convinced that the disestablishment of the Church of England was imminent. This, combined with increasing nonconformist wealth and education, led to a corresponding increase in political engagement driven by a theology emphasizing the Christian's duty to engage with this life rather than simply focus on the afterlife, facilitated by the weakening of the Anglican establishment.

---

88. Carlyle, *Past and Present*, 24. See also Morrow, *Thomas Carlyle*, 75–103.

89. Hilton, *Age of Atonement*, 3.

90. The belief in a millennial golden age before the second advent. See Bebbington, *Dominance of Evangelicalism*, 130–32.

91. Maurice, *Kingdom of Christ*, 206.

92. A significant theme in Johnson, *Dissolution of Dissent*.

93. Johnson, *Dissolution of Dissent*, 22–23.

However, when MacDonald was writing, these long-term implications were only incipient. Despite strides made to address social deprivation, the "brotherhood of man" theology had yet to systematically impact social ills,[94] partly due to an almost hallucinatory belief in human goodness and a corresponding naivety, perhaps blindness, relating to the true state of society, in part because that society was considered ordained by God. This goes some way to account for the unconvincing social settings and characters that populate MacDonald's fiction. If one adds to this the general problem of Romanticism's ambiguity in relation to evil,[95] then we have perhaps uncovered some of the root issues which need to be explored in relation to MacDonald's thought.

In mid-century there was also fierce debate centered around three issues: the doctrine of future punishment for the wicked (as opposed to "the larger hope" that all might be saved), the infallibility and inspiration of the Bible (and whether "higher criticism" was acceptable), and the implications of scientific advances. Such issues divided Evangelicals. Increasing unease about the moral implications of conservative theology led to the prevalence of more liberal ideas and the need for faith to bend with cultural change gained more traction. The central moral dilemma concerned the nature of God: was God really like Murdoch Malison, the sadistic schoolmaster?[96] Darwin suggested "yes." Unlike Goethe's Romantic vision of nature as God's numinous robe favored by Carlyle and MacDonald, Tennyson's nature, "red in tooth and claw," Darwin pondered, must have been invented by a demon: "What a book a Devil's Chaplain might write on the clumsy, wasteful, blundering low and horridly cruel works of nature."[97] Doubt was in the air about both "Nature" and God, leading Tennyson to ask:

> Are God and Nature then at strife,
> That Nature lends such evil dreams?
> So careful of the type she seems,
> So careless of the single life . . . ?[98]

---

94. Hilton suggests that there was no public or political consensus on civic culture until after mid-century. See Hilton, *Mad, Bad, Dangerous People?*, 311.
95. Watts, *Dissenters*, 3:9.
96. Note 33, page 20.
97. Watts, *Dissenters*, 3:19.
98. *In Memoriam*, 78 (sec. 54).

MacDonald was "liberal" in that he chose to engage with such questions. Liberals saw conservatives as stubborn and petulant children refusing to modify their views in the light of contrary revelation. Conservatives, for their part, considered such "revelation" as fundamentally flawed and accused liberals of rebellion against the hard-won truths of their forebears. Judgements against liberals from conservatives such as Wilson and McCrie who accuse MacDonald of inventing a new religion (like the recent conclusion of John Piper and Timothy Keller that MacDonald was "not a Christian")[99] were not uncommon. Charles Haddon Spurgeon typified the reaction to liberalism when he remarked in 1877 that "a new religion has been initiated which is no more Christianity than chalk is cheese,"[100] and accused liberals of "toying with the deadly cobra of 'another gospel' in the form of 'modern thought.'"[101]

MacDonald's migration towards liberalism was not untypical. William Hale White, for example, a fellow Congregationalist who had studied at Highbury College's reincarnation as New College, found himself unable to accept the inflexible dogmatism on offer and was expelled for questioning whether the Bible should be read as one book (he became a civil servant).[102] He writes:

> The theological and biblical teaching was a sham. . . . So it came to pass that about the Bible . . . we were in darkness. It was a magazine of texts, and those portions of it which contributed nothing in the shape of texts, or formed no part of the [Calvinistic] scheme, were neglected.[103]

Thomas Toke Lynch (whose Romantic poetry was perceived as a threat to orthodoxy) left active ministry to become a writer, and within nonconformity numerous voices questioned traditional claims. Many column inches were devoted to religious debates, becoming front page in the 1870s and 1880s when events surrounding the Congregational Leicester Conference (1877) became public knowledge, and when Spurgeon went into print to complain about the "down grade"—the liberalization—of his

---

99. See page 135.

100. Watts, *Dissenters*, 3:65.

101. Charles Haddon Spurgeon quoted in Johnson, *Dissolution of Dissent*, 205.

102. Watts, *Dissenters*, 3:3–4; Johnson, *Changing Shape of English Nonconformity*, 65.

103. Hale White, *Autobiography*, 12, 14. Mark Johnson observes that "Colleges like Highbury, which had generated Revival preachers, tended to be theologically narrow and intellectually secluded" (Johnson, *Dissolution of Dissent*, 67).

own Baptist denomination leading to acrimonious exchanges with liberal colleagues such as John Clifford culminating in his secession from the Baptist Union in 1887.[104]

The general picture in the third quarter of the nineteenth century is one of increasing impatience with inflexible conservative Evangelical doctrines and a consequent migration towards liberalism or secularism.[105] The flow was not, though, in one direction: many continued to find refuge in the "old truths." The result was fragmentation more than migration, and (reminiscent of the situation during the interregnum of the seventeenth century when Church and State censorship ceased to function) it was felt that the abandonment of "first principles" was precipitating a rise in "the vain speculations of romancing rationalists."[106]

Conservatism and Liberalism

MacDonald and his mid-century contemporaries faced a dilemma. Sixteenth-century Enlightenment thinking had fostered a more rational approach to Christianity which tended to equate truth with verifiable facts and was suspicious of the unverifiable. The architects of the Reformation had constructed a Christian edifice built on the "factual" foundation of a divinely-inspired inerrant text and a historical Jesus who worked miracles to prove his authenticity. As the Methodist theologian Marshall Randles noted, for example, in his *First Principles of Faith* (1884), "theism is essentially founded in reason." As Dale Johnson notes, he "built his entire case on the argument from causality."[107] The dilemma was that the same principles that had given rise to a new, more vibrant, more

---

104. Hopkins, *Nonconformity's Romantic Generation*, 193–248. In 1877, much controversy ensued when a splinter group of Congregational leaders organized a fringe meeting of the Leicester Conference seen to be promoting liberal values.

105. I am using the term "conservative" primarily in this inflexible sense to mean those fundamentally opposed to revising received views, noting that other conservative views were being sharpened by the debates of the day.

106. Christopher Hill notes regarding the seventeenth-century situation: "To the argument that individual interpretations of the Scriptures and congregational autonomy would lead to religious anarchy, radicals retorted that the inner light is one, and can be recognised by the children of light. *Areopagitica* [Milton] assumes that, given freedom of debate, all men's reason must naturally lead them, sooner or later, to recognise the same truths" (Hill, *World Turned Upside Down*, 81). The situation then, and in the nineteenth century, proved Milton and the radicals to be mistaken.

107. Johnson, *Changing Shape of English Nonconformity*, 130.

"reasonable" expression of Christianity—the fruit in part of the emphasis on the logical and therefore investigable nature of God's creation—led to erosion of those "factual" foundations and cracks were appearing in the superstructure.[108] In other words, the Reformers had constructed a religion based on the view that the logical investigation of God's creation would reveal truth, however sixteenth-century conclusions were now being undermined by that same methodology.

Although Evangelicalism did not, and does not, equate to Calvinism (as Evangelicalism was also forged in the fire of the Great Awakening with its mystical overtones and Arminian theology), Calvinist thinking was deeply embedded in the resulting system—especially so in MacDonald's Scotland—a system vulnerable, as it were, to self-harm on two counts: not only was its internal logic corrosive to its foundational beliefs, but the focus on the defense of those "correct" beliefs led to increasing fragmentation. As the eighteenth-century biographer of Jacob Boehme had expressed it (with some perspicacity):

> Learned Reason's Influence and Operations in the Sanctuary [has] split all Christendom into numberless Parties; each as sure of it's [sic] own Rectitude, and of it's [sic] Neighbour's Deficiency.[109]

The Reformation quest for truth was, of course, a laudable endeavor; however, it was driven by a fundamental distrust of human imagination that, in the short term, led to a diagnosis of "iconolatry" leading to fervent iconoclasm, which, in the long term, bequeathed to Reformed religion a profound anti-aestheticism and a lingering iconophobia. Iain McGilchrist puts his finger on the issue:

> What is so compelling here is that the motive force behind the Reformation was the urge to regain authenticity, with which one can only be profoundly sympathetic. The path it soon took was that of the destruction of all means whereby authenticity could have been recaptured.[110]

It is unsurprising, therefore, that MacDonald expressed unease and was depressed by his experience at Highbury since such nonconformist

---

108. Jonathan Sacks argues that the structural weakness in Christianity caused by the contamination of "Jerusalem" with the logic of "Athens" goes back to the Apostle Paul. See Sacks, *Great Partnership*, 62–66.

109. Okely, *Memoirs*, ii.

110. McGilchrist, *Master and His Emissary*, 316.

colleges set out to produce effective preachers of fixed dogma, not critical thinkers. The colleges were "'factories for preachers and pastors,' in the phrase of the Presbyterian W. G. Elmslie, as opposed to shrines of culture or centers of scholarship and erudition";[111] they championed the principles of dissent but did not allow people to be dissenters.[112]

MacDonald recognizes the paradoxes in the religion of his day. He summarily dismisses views he considers based on falsehood while holding in tension conflicting conservative and liberal claims, refusing to be drawn towards over-dogmatic conclusions. His Maurician ability to live with paradox reflects his mentor's view that truth is larger than specifics and is "organic" in the sense discussed above.[113] Although notionally wedded to Reformed factual foundations such as a miracle-working Jesus, his general approach to the received wisdom from tradition and sacred text is that both may be questioned and must be interpreted imaginatively.

The Nature of MacDonald's Response

Both conservative and liberal Evangelicals viewed the cosmos as created by God and that there existed beyond it a supernatural realm. The key difference concerned the view of that cosmos and the sacred text. The supernatural theism of conservatives regarded creation as entirely separate from God and essentially corrupt having been irrevocably damaged by the Fall. The cosmos, like "un-elect" humanity, was destined for the fire; it would be recreated, rebellious humanity would not. The sacramental doorway to the more "real" transcendent realm was the Bible—the inerrant interpreter of history and human experience; it was the unchanging reference point in a world of flux.

Conversely, liberal incarnational theology focused on God's immanence leading to a sacramental view of observed reality; a Romantic optimism that nature, despite its flaws, revealed God. The Bible was a product of human history; history should be used to interpret the Bible, not the other way round. The view, however, of both Bible and cosmos was that both were sacramental despite the damage caused by human

---

111. Johnson, *Changing Shape of English Nonconformity*, 63. The view was: "What was Evangelical was old; what was new was not Evangelical" (Johnson, *Changing Shape of English Nonconformity*, 65).

112. Johnson, *Changing Shape of English Nonconformity*, 78.

113. Prickett, *Romanticism and Religion*, 126–27.

sin; both were inspired by God; inerrancy in Scripture and perfection in creation were not prerequisites for sacrality.

The view of the Bible as inerrant and the oft-repeated cry "THE BIBLE, AND THE BIBLE ALONE, IS THE RELIGION OF DISSENTERS"[114] reflected a longing for epistemic certainty in a changing world, but, as P. T. Forsyth was to observe at the end of the century, this was a certainty that came with a high price tag:

> "The whole Bible or none," it was said. "Take but a stone away and the edifice subsides." This came of the Bible having been reduced to a fabric instead of an organism. And how many sceptics that course has made! . . . If I were a Secularist I would not touch by assault the doctrine of plenary verbal inspiration and inerrancy. I should let it work freely as one of my best adjutants.[115]

For conservatives, security was sought in the incontrovertible "evidences" of biblical miracles and Paley's natural religion. Liberals also appealed to verifiable facts. The issue between them was not so much methodology as the "factual" starting point. Conservatives, for example, insisted on a literal Adam and Eve, a "young" earth, and that sin was a perennial obstacle. Liberal John Clifford, in contrast, was of the opinion—based on his understanding of Henry Drummond's *The Ascent of Man*—that humans were evolving morally and spiritually, and that "Man . . . is altruistic in the soul of him, in a world that is founded on altruism."[116] Such liberal optimism was dealt a severe blow by Darwin's observation that if God was the architect of nature, God must be "demonic."[117]

In this climate, MacDonald's quest to rehabilitate God relies not on challenging the foundations of truth, but, following Newman and Maurice, on redefining truth in aesthetic terms; that truth is a "symbol" that must be holistically discerned rather than a proposition to be believed. The child—imaginatively exploring a universe of uncertain novelty and mystery with fresh eyes—serves this agenda by offering a counterpoint to the hubris of certainty. He thus insists that "the truth *of a thing* is the blossom of it."[118] It is the aesthetic "surface" of reality that speaks truth to the perceptive child; reality is a metaphor perceived—not primarily

---

114. J. A. James quoted in Moore, *Sources*, 132.
115. Forsyth, *Positive Preaching*, 85.
116. Hopkins, *Nonconformity's Romantic Generation*, 182.
117. See page 31.
118. *US3* 69.

deductively or inductively—but "abductively" (intuitively) by the power of childlike imagination.[119] This is why conservatives—despite the fact that MacDonald consistently calls himself a follower of Christ, affirms his reverence for the Bible as inspired, and preaches obedience to Christ—are so suspicious of MacDonald's "new religion": he is challenging the nature of truth and its factual foundations. Being a firm rejection of the inflexible logic of his forebears such as Samuel Rutherford who concluded that infants would be sent to hell[120]—and therefore of a subsequent Evangelicalism that had failed to exorcise such doctrines despite efforts to become "softer"—MacDonald's Christianity *does*, for those who subscribe to such views, amount to a "new religion." There are, however, strong resonances with traditional themes, evident, for example, in his focus on faith as practical obedience rather than theoretical belief. The latter, he argues, reduces Christianity to mere intellectual assent, whereas obedience to perceived truth resulting in moral improvement is the mark of the faithful.

Such views reflect the medieval understanding of "faith."[121] Modernity was preoccupied with faith as *assensus*—intellectual assent to certain "enshrined" propositions (that is, idolatrous concepts)—leading to the definition of a Christian as "someone who believes the right things." This is constantly challenged by MacDonald, overtly in sermons such as "Justice" and "Righteousness" (*US3*), and covertly through the demolition of fictional hypocrites.[122] He repeatedly emphasizes the need to be an obedient child, reflecting the three other medieval understandings of faith as *fiducia*—practical trust in God as the "rock of our salvation" as opposed to being worried about tomorrow, *fidelitas*—loyalty and allegiance to God as opposed to infidelity, and *visio*—a way of seeing "with the eyes of faith." The latter, rather than seeing the world adversarially as a place of threat resulting in a defensive posture or indifferently as a neutral place unconcerned about human being, views the world as life-giving, nourishing, and gracious, and embraces metaphor. Perhaps this "medievalism" reflects the tendency of Romantics to look back at the golden age of chivalry rather than forward to a millennial utopia. However, I will argue that this is not simply nostalgia for a lost ideal, rather it is a rejection

---

119. See page 127.

120. Torrance, *Scottish Theology*, 101.

121. I am indebted to Marcus Borg for sowing the seeds of these ideas. See Borg, *Heart of Christianity*, 28–37.

122. Such as Robert Bruce in *AF*.

of present "unchildlikeness" and the sense that humanity is becoming increasingly disconnected from transcendence. As John Pridmore perceptively remarks:

> Childhood in Wordsworth is recollected. For MacDonald childhood is what is promised. Where Wordsworth is solaced by memory, MacDonald is upheld by hope. Childhood is not a lost estate to be mourned but a condition to which we must aspire.[123]

One might say that MacDonald is redefining "orthodoxy" in the medieval sense of "right worship" rather than in the modern sense of "right belief" as these three concepts of faith emphasize the need for an active response. *Visio*, central to Romantic theology, is especially important since it concerns the ability to see truly. In the *Curdie* novels, for example, light and vision are perennial themes connected to faith. The young princess Irene ("peace"), lost on the mountain, glimpses the great-great-grandmother's lamp in the distance. The grandmother, a theophany ("the Mother of Light")[124] whose lamp is an image of faith, had earlier said to Irene:

> I will tell you a secret—if that light were to go out you would fancy yourself lying in a bare garret, on a heap of old straw, and would not see one of the pleasant things round about you all the time.[125]

When the princess asks why more people do not investigate this very obvious phenomenon (it shines in the neighborhood), it is because they dismiss it—"take it for a meteor, wink their eyes, and forget it again." Now, desperate to find her way home:

> The light that filled her eyes from the lamp, instead of blinding them for a moment to the object upon which they next fell, enabled her for a moment to see it, despite the darkness. By looking at the lamp and then dropping her eyes, she could see the road for a yard or two in front of her.[126]

Faith does not simply provide light, but gives one "good eyes." The grandmother herself (God) is only visible to those with "good" eyes. As she remarks to the other protagonist, the young miner Curdie:

123. Pridmore, "George MacDonald," 34.
124. *PC* 51.
125. *PG* 119 (an image that Lewis uses in *The Last Battle*).
126. *PG* 141.

> it is one thing what you or your father may think about me, and quite another what a foolish or bad man may see in me. For instance, if a thief were to come in here just now, he would think he saw the demon of the mine, all in green flames, come to protect her treasure, and would run like a hunted wild goat. I should be all the same, but his evil eyes would see me as I was not.[127]

This passage illustrates a central thesis: that those with unchildlike "evil eyes" have an erroneous vision of God as a "demon," a vision (in both senses of the word) that needs to be exorcised from contemporary Christianity.

In Greville MacDonald's view, the main difference between his father and John Ruskin was his father's gift of "fairy vision." Speaking of his father's leaning towards the imaginative rather than the rational, he writes:

> That instinct . . . was his exalted fairy vision, the light that in lighting every man reveals the secrets of all.
>
> Far from its being the image of his own mind, as Ruskin whimsically said, that my father saw in the sky, it was, I think he would answer, only when man is purified of faith in the material—"the cloak and cloud which shadows me from Thee"—that he will see God.[128]

MacDonald's vision was, one might say, a fiduciary hermeneutic of a world which he saw as infused with "bright shoots of everlastingness."[129] He chose to look at the world with the eyes of faith. That MacDonald sees differently to those such as Ruskin is not in question; what we do need to consider, however, is whether MacDonald is seeing truly. Is he, as Ruskin suggested, merely seeing a projection of his own fantasies in the sky? To phrase the question more precisely: does his work reveal aesthetic truth or aesthetic fantasy?

This introduction to MacDonald's thought has outlined the influence of, and resonances with, historical and contemporary currents. We have also identified key ideas and questions. The task before us is to construct a coherent summary of MacDonald's theology, a task that, because of his

---

127. *PC* 56.
128. *GMAW* 339. The reference is to "The Cock Crowing" by Henry Vaughan.
129. *GMAW* 339.

methodology and aversion to "systems," involves assembling a mosaic from scattered fragments. The picture of the child, it will be argued, is the dominant image, as it were, on the lid of the puzzle holding the key to its reassembly. However, before a close reading of MacDonald it is necessary to consider the Victorian child.

2

The Victorian Child—
Social and Theological Attitudes

CONCEPTS RELATING TO CHILDHOOD in Victorian times were full of paradox and enigma and it is helpful to explore these as benchmarks against which to compare MacDonald's contrasting image (chapter 3) as a precursor to considering how he uses it (chapters 4–8). Since children are representative of the race (that is, children are human, not merely potentially so), the "theology of childhood" is central to Christian anthropology. It is therefore, as Karl Rahner observed, curious that there is no definitive articulation of such a theology.[1] Theological musings on the subject do, nevertheless, abound. They are the focus here and are far from inconsequential.

Sin and Innocence

We begin by considering an example of the implication of certain "theological musings." Western theology, since Augustine, has been preoccupied with the doctrine of original sin, a doctrine contested by Pelagius (and MacDonald): one side insisting that the child is essentially corrupt, the other that it is innocent.[2] Taking these emphases to their

---

1. Rahner, "Ideas for a Theology of Childhood," 33.

2. John Milbank notes that Augustine does *not* say that all humans are guilty of original sin. Rather, we are guilty, like the hands of a murderer, for the sin of the race. See Milbank, *Being Reconciled*, 10.

absurd conclusions with respect to child-rearing, we have, on the one hand, Coleridge's "hands off" approach, leaving Hartley to be mothered by nature. On the other (rejecting the idea that nature, human or otherwise, is in any way benign) we have Jonathan Edwards's daughter, Esther Edwards Burr, writing in the 1750s that she has begun to use the whip on her ten-month-old daughter.[3] It is immediately apparent that MacDonald's assertion that God is a child is likely to raise significant questions for the later descendants of Jonathan Edwards.

For most of the nineteenth century, the Puritan view dominated: childhood was considered a necessary evil, a stage in life to be left behind as soon as possible (despite some insisting that childhood extended to the age of thirty).[4] Though such views had thawed somewhat by mid-century, attitudes to childhood were predominantly negative, especially in a religious community suspicious of childhood passion and vice—evidence of original sin. The ascendancy of evolutionism did little to emancipate childhood: the burden of original sin was simply exchanged for that of collective racial memory as the "little savages" in their cots were deemed to not only recapitulate the dawn of humanity, but carry collective memories of a natural history which, unlike the benign vision of the Romantics, was red in tooth and claw. It led to *fin de siècle* pessimism, such as that of Thomas Hardy's *Jude the Obscure*; a vision of children burdened with inchoate ancestral memories, predetermined by heredity, and unmoved by free will. *Jude* graphically expresses the logical outcome of evolutionary determinism, particularly—according to Sally Shuttleworth—the depressingly pessimistic version of Schopenhauer. Thus the category of childhood, viewed as a period of innocence and naivety, is waning by the end of the century, if not abolished.[5] For Hardy, all children are "old," dramatized most clearly in the child nicknamed Father Time who, according to Hardy, was "Age masquerading as Juvenility, and doing it so badly that his real self showed through the crevices."[6] For Hardy, childhood is illusory. Father Time, a conflation of deity and humanity, is here packed onto a train by his birth mother with a poor box of belongings and sent to stay with an unknown father who has not been told he is coming. He sits, saucer-eyed, in the third-class carriage, "an

---

3. Esther Edwards Burr quoted in Bunge, *Child in Christian Thought*, 327.
4. Shuttleworth, *Mind of the Child*, 20.
5. Shuttleworth, *Mind of the Child*, 353.
6. Hardy, *Jude the Obscure*, 261. See also Shuttleworth, *Mind of the Child*, 340.

enslaved and dwarfed Divinity." Father Time, aged before his time and expelled from his creation, is travelling into the void to an uncertain fate and taking humanity with him.

MacDonald's suggestion that God is a child—a claim we will unpack in due course—is, therefore, a radical challenge to theology and forces reconsideration of the value of childhood. MacDonald, like Hardy, conflates age and youth but he reverses the analogy, underlining the eternity, as well as the childlikeness, of God: it is adulthood with its pretentious cultural accretions, its selfishness, and its power-lust that is false; the goal of humanity is not to leave childhood behind as soon as possible, but to embrace it and emulate the God that is, using Hardy's language, "Juvenility masquerading as Age." The goal of life is divine childlikeness. It is adulthood, not childhood, that is synonymous with sin.

Whether viewed positively or negatively, the child was at the heart of the Victorian world. Sally Shuttleworth summarizes thus:

> The figure of the child lies at the heart of nineteenth-century discourses of gender, race, and selfhood: a figure who is by turns animal, savage, or female, but who is located not in the distant colonies, nor in the mists of evolutionary time, but at the very centre of English domestic life.[7]

Early- and Mid-Nineteenth-Century Attitudes to Childhood

Natural Religion and the Romantic Inheritance

At the outset we note, with Ann Wierda Rowland, that "the history of children and the history of childhood are two different things"; that the child as a social construct has a somewhat tangential, tenuous relationship to the lived experiences of real children.[8] Lamentations regarding the loss or erosion of childhood have more to do with the former.[9] This distinction goes some way towards accounting for Judith Plotz's complaint that Romantic ideas did little to contribute to reform. Her work, nevertheless,

---

7. Shuttleworth, *Mind of the Child*, 4.

8. Rowland, *Romanticism and Childhood*, 7.

9. A recent example might be Rowan Williams's observation that the space called "childhood" is being eroded by a society bent on exploiting its children. See Williams, *Lost Icons*, 20.

reveals the weakness of developing philosophical ideas at some distance from social context. Wordsworth, for example, stands accused of using his Romantic idealism to justify parental neglect,[10] and that this distortion of reality—the conceptual, poetic separation of the child from both the adult and the real world—is prescient of later Romantic texts that set a lone child against the world (see below). Plotz is not impressed:

> This separation of adult from child defines the Wordsworthian child. It is not innocent radiance or joy, but an aesthetically embalmed apartheid that constitutes Wordsworth's major contribution to the nineteenth-century literature of childhood.[11]

Theoretically at least, however, childhood for the Romantics *was* a state of "innocent radiance or joy" where the infant mind was not only attuned to nature's ministrations, but "trailing clouds of glory" as if still semi-conscious of its divine origin. Wordsworth's manifesto on childhood, "Ode: Intimations of Immortality from Recollections of Early Childhood," suggested that such awareness progressively waned, such that:

> At length the Man perceives it die away,
> And fade into the light of common day.[12]

Prior to adulthood, the child mind, with its innate receptivity to divine things, is tutored by a sacramental nature. Thus, writing in 1781, a Scottish writer (strikingly at odds with his Calvinist compatriots) optimistically observed, "Children are especially susceptible of instruction with regard to natural religion. The being of a God, and the worship due to him being engraved on the mind, make a branch of our nature," concluding: "It is easy to fortify in children the belief of a Deity, because his existence is engraved on the human heart."[13] Anticipating mid-Victorian criticism of religious education, the author expresses a MacDonaldian sentiment:

> Religious education thus carried on, instead of inspiring gloominess, and despondence, will contribute more than any other means to serenity of mind and cheerfulness of temper.... Surely

---

10. Rowland, *Romanticism and Childhood*, 62.
11. Rowland, *Romanticism and Childhood*, 63.
12. Wordsworth, *Selected Poems*, 142.
13. "Education with Respect to Religion," 149.

any frightful notion of the Deity, must have a dismal effect on a tender mind, susceptible of every impression, of fear above all.[14]

Rowland credits Scottish Romanticism with providing much of the foundation for the Romantic discourse on childhood, noting that the work of Adam Smith and John Millar did much to reinforce the equation of antiquity with childhood. Emphasizing the developmental nature of society, the ancient savage was seen both as a childhood figure at the dawn of civilization and as an "elder"—a repository of ancient wisdom. Such views informed the view of the child mind as ancient well before ideas of evolutionary recapitulation. Most writers in the wake of Locke, Rowland argues, "embrace a theory of infancy and development that allow them to compare child and savage." Primitive man is a "big baby," and childhood language is that of the savage.[15]

"Savage" childhood language and behavior implied two things: first, inexperience, meaning that new words had to be invented (or old ones recycled) every time a new experience was encountered; and second, emotional displays unchecked by the constraints of civilization. Thus imagination was "closely associated with the ignorance and inexperience of infancy," and was something that civilized people grew out of.[16] In a phrase that MacDonald would have applauded, Rowland observes: "Infancy thus represents an embodied imaginative state."[17]

The Romantic Theology of Childhood

Those such as Presbyterian Samuel Law Wilson concluded that they and MacDonald worshipped different deities.[18] Do the claims of Romanticism (and the child in particular) justify such a conclusion?

Judith Plotz thinks so—that the Romantic obsession with the ideal nature-communing child led to its deification. Schiller (an influence on MacDonald),[19] she argues, contributed to this by insisting on the child's mediatory role through its affinity with a nature conceived as virgin and untainted by culture—a mediation "affording us a retrospective view of

14. "Education with Respect to Religion," 149
15. Rowland, *Romanticism and Childhood*, 81, 88.
16. Rowland, *Romanticism and Childhood*, 91.
17. Rowland, *Romanticism and Childhood*, 95.
18. See pages 27–28.
19. *Rampolli* contains nineteen pages of Schiller in translation.

ourselves, and revealing more closely the unnatural in us."[20] Aligning the child mind with nature, beyond the vicissitudes of history and the corruption of culture, places it in a virgin territory of immutability and timeless antiquity. Age and infancy are again conflated. Coleridge's musings in "Frost at Midnight" over the young Hartley sleeping at his side reflect this: the baby merges with nature, "wander[ing] like a breeze by lakes and sandy shores," listening to the "eternal language which thy God utters."

While Coleridge is firmly wedded to a Christian God, Plotz is unsure about his successors. She points to a common Romantic trope of a make-believe kingdom presided over by a child-redeemer. Whether the creations of children or adult authors,[21] The Child, instead of merely connecting to a higher power, becomes that power, a permeating life-giving force—an idolatrous concept transplanted into the real world. "As an imaginary kingdom," she writes, "it is almost always figured as a lost garden paradise presided over by a child-redeemer or child-idol: 'Infancy is the perpetual Messiah which comes into the arms of fallen men, and pleads with them to return to paradise.'"[22]

In Plotz's view, it is but a short step from adulation of the concept of the quintessential child to worship of *The* Child—a being "who figures powerfully in Golden Age children's literature, especially male-authored fantasy literature."[23] The Romantic discourse on childhood

> made it easy, unavoidable almost, to assume the living reality and splendor of such an essential being as *The* Child, who is unmarked by time, place, class, or gender but is represented as in all places and all times the same.[24]

We will consider later what relationship MacDonald's Child-God has to the child of Romanticism, but I suggest that Plotz's theology of *The* Child seems somewhat overstated: practical belief in "the living reality and splendor of such an essential being as *The* Child" seems unlikely. It seems more reasonable to accept Rowland's evaluation of the "ideal

---

20. Friedrich von Schiller quoted in Plotz, *Romanticism*, 7.

21. De Quincey, Thomas Malkin, Hartley Coleridge, the Brontës, and James Barrie are listed. See Plotz, *Romanticism*, 3.

22. Ralph Waldo Emerson quoted in Plotz, *Romanticism*, 3.

23. Plotz, *Romanticism*, 4.

24. Plotz, *Romanticism*, 5.

child" as a motif for expressing interiority and innocence—it evokes a "natural" state, and an interior, remembered existence.[25]

The preoccupation with childhood (at least in print) was very much a middle- and upper-class affair. Plotz's main case is that Romanticism was characterized by a higher-class aloofness from real social issues combined with an incorrigible idealism. This was no doubt true, but it seems excessive to accept Alan Yue's claim that "there are no children in Wordsworth's poetry"[26] or that the Romantics were bereft of any real understanding of childhood. Plotz does, however, remind us that the Romantic child is essentially a literary symbol, idealized and colored by class prejudices. This explains why many of MacDonald's child characters appear to hover improbably above their surrounding grime, and is a reminder not to summarily dismiss them without considering their symbolic value.

Class, Gender, and the Child-Mind

The realm of the nursery was female—where even young boys were dressed in petticoats—with little connection with the thrusting male world of commerce and empire. Men knew little of this sequestered "dark heart" of the home which, as evolutionary theories took hold, was seen as a savage place where infant language mirrored that of primeval "man" (or animals), or where (perhaps justifiably) folklore and old wives' tales held sway over education.[27] It was a woman's place—her highest destiny—and therefore she had little need of education, not least because any energy diverted to her brain was sure to undermine her reproductive ability.[28] Fathers were advised to foster a sense of veneration in their daughters on the grounds that "the intimacy bred of taking liberties is a fatal exchange for the deep sense of trustful reverence." The husband was the "family's monarch" and advised to "allow his girls to listen to the conversation without expecting to be included in it."[29]

25. Plotz, *Romanticism*, 26.
26. Plotz, *Romanticism*, 85.
27. Rowland, *Romanticism and Childhood*, 204–5.
28. Shuttleworth writes: "At its most extreme, Clouston and Maudsley and others insisted that the exertion of intellectual energies would seriously impair female reproductive development" (Shuttleworth, *Mind of the Child*, 210).
29. "Essays on Practical Education," 46.

Childhood studies dawned in this world of gender and class division, fueled by strong religious sentiment. Who was this creature at the heart of the nursery that was riddled with original sin or (later in the century) burdened with racial memory, that could speak the language of animal and human ancestors, that was at once innocent and irretrievably corrupt?

It is, perhaps, surprising that childhood studies as a discipline had not developed earlier, considering the Romantic obsession with the child.[30] Nevertheless the Romantics did bequeath to the Victorians ideas about the child mind which, at least in the view of Plotz, were entirely misguided. The Romantic obsession with childhood connectedness to nature led to the valuing of *dis*connectedness from adult society. It was considered laudable to shield a child for as long as possible from quotidian reality in order to foster a sense of holism. Plotz, however, citing the work of twentieth-century Swiss psychologist Jean Piaget, argues that this prevents the development of a healthy sense of self, observing that "Piaget labels as [mental] defects the very attributes the Romantics cite as excellences."[31]

Romantic notions of childhood innocence contrasted, in Victorian times, with a preoccupation with original sin and its later correlate, savage racial memory. The child became an accident waiting to happen, and mothers, nurses, and tutors were admonished to watch for signs of incipient decline. Babies, and even the fetus *in utero*, were deemed to be susceptible to madness,[32] the first post-natal sign of which was prattling nonsense and an over-fertile imagination, and that uncontrollable malady of *passion* which was to be early nipped in the bud. John Haslam, apothecary to Bethlehem Hospital, who included in his *Observations on Madness and Melancholy* (1809) a chapter on "Cases of Insane Children,"[33] highlights not only the hereditary nature of insanity, but its roots in faulty education—particularly one deficient in morality, here defined as failing to subjugate passions—

---

30. The science of child development is normally traced to Darwin's "A Biographical Sketch of an Infant" in the journal *Mind* in 1877. See Shuttleworth, *Mind of the Child*, 221.

31. Plotz, *Romanticism*, 28.

32. Shuttleworth, *Mind of the Child*, 21.

33. Shuttleworth, *Mind of the Child*, 23.

which often plant in the youthful mind the seeds of madness which the slightest circumstances readily awaken into growth. It should be as much the object of the teachers of youth, to subjugate the passions, as to discipline the intellect.[34]

While the prevailing view was that childhood make-believe and play (or the even more dreadful secret sins of lying and masturbation—sexual "precocity") heralded insanity or even death, some had more tolerant views. The *Cambridge University Magazine*, for example, reports as early as 1841 that "the common idea of the imagination is, we believe, far below its true elevation," and traces misconceptions to "too slight attentions to the real operations of the mind," and a propensity to divide mental processes artificially. It advises:

> Away with this cold "cutting up" of that glorious *unity* called MIND; of whose several kinds and species of *operation* are so inseparably linked together, and harmoniously blended.[35]

These sentiments presage, as we shall see, later Victorian liberalism. Nevertheless, the subjugation of the passions and the discipline of the intellect is a familiar refrain permeating the early Victorian narrative and was the primary goal of education.

Mid-Century Debate and Religious Education

By mid-century, secularization and the growing awareness of child psychology were influencing educational debates. Questions were raised about whether Sunday schools should teach secular subjects, whether state schools should teach religion, whether children should be forced to learn quickly or allowed to "flower" naturally, or, indeed, whether schooling (for the poor) was necessary at all. On the basis that "the whole theological world" was in disarray, in 1875, the religiously skeptical *Westminster Review* questioned the wisdom of "enthralling children's minds with the fetters of doubtful doctrine."[36] This polemic against the "religionists," caricaturing educational practices over the previous decades, reveals popular views.

---

34. Shuttleworth, *Mind of the Child*, 23
35. "Literature and Imagination," 58.
36. "Religious Education of Children," 377.

Anglicanism is targeted by considering E. B. Ramsay's *Manual of Catechetical Instruction*. The methodology is forensic, even inquisitorial, with rote learning seen as the route to forming much-needed "precise and correct ideas." Ramsay claims that three of the questions "involve an abstract of the whole theory of Coleridge's 'Aids to Reflection.'"[37] Noting that the work is aimed at seven- to ten-year-olds, this draws a predictably sarcastic reaction:

> Those who are conversant with this eminently philosophical work will be able to estimate the adaptability of the "Manual" to the mental calibre of the young.[38]

There is "a total disregard of the principles of psychology," and children are left with "the impression that salvation depends on correctly remembering words that convey no possible meaning."[39] Ramsay, admitting that "it must appear as if directed to the head," nevertheless wants to foster "tender feeling [in] his young pupils, and to call forth the emotions of the heart,"[40] but the *Review* is quick to point out that it is liable to have the opposite effect. Passages concerning guilt and damnation are especially injurious to young girls of a nervous disposition who are apt to "dwell much on anything which might raise a misgiving or an anxiety." Expressing George MacDonald's view, the conclusion is: "The power of imagination is not sufficiently taken into account in dealing with the young."[41]

The negative psychological effects of the religious indoctrination of children were a topic of current debate. The *Review* cites a medical report claiming that religious fervor accounted for 3 percent of admissions to mental asylums,[42] leading to the conclusion that learning half-understood statements concerning the awful consequences of disobedience leads to mental breakdown in the young.[43] This catechetical approach, however, was more likely to produce boredom and frustration than madness. The liberal Unitarian journal *The Theological Review* notes in passing, while discussing Sunday schools, that:

---

37. Ramsay, *Manual of Catechetical Instruction*, xvii.
38. "Religious Education of Children," 377.
39. "Religious Education of Children," 379.
40. Ramsay, *Manual of Catechetical Instruction*, xix.
41. "Religious Education of Children," 381.
42. "Religious Education of Children," 383n.
43. Crichton Browne's paper (note 32, page 48) lists, among others, "theomania." See Shuttleworth, *Mind of the Child*, 38.

> Some of those who have come over from orthodoxy . . . evidently conceive of religious instruction as identical with the inculcation of theological dogmas, and associating these with their painful remembrance of catechisms and creeds, reach a decided conclusion against bringing young scholars, at any rate, under any sort of religious training.[44]

Many parents, it seems, who had suffered under Ramsay's *Manual*, had—for ten years at least—simply refused to subject their children to the same ordeal.

The second example given, however, was more likely to result in madness.[45] In *Sermons for the Very Young* (1864), "the Deity is habitually represented as an angry judge ready to inflict endless, unutterable tortures upon the trembling and despairing sinner," and psychological pressure is used to effect conversion by describing "the most horrible scenes [of hell] which cruelty and fanaticism could devise."[46] It carries heart-breaking and gruesome tales of God visiting vengeance on sinners, such as the residents of Sodom and Gomorrah, who, after retiring one night, are woken by an apocalypse:

> What a rumbling sound wakes them from their slumbers? What glare of light breaks into their chambers? Whence the fearful cry—the shriek of horror? The wrath of God is upon them. Do they repent now of their sins? It is too late.[47]

It is preceded by the advice: "Think, little child, of the fearful story."

The *Review* notes that since it is repeatedly stressed that God does not hear the prayers of sinners, and that "even when we wish to do right there is something wrong in it,"[48] the child is left with no option but to consider itself eternally damned.[49] It illustrates the theological belief that a "state of hopeless degradation [is] the normal condition of children," and results in the destruction of "self respect," "a sense of guilt," and "consciousness of an Unseen Power full of anger . . . armed with a fearful

---

44. "Sunday-Schools," 79.

45. The mental strain produced by fervent evangelism is discussed further on pages 176–78.

46. "Religious Education of Children," 382.

47. "Religious Education of Children," 383.

48. "Religious Education of Children," 384–85.

49. Charles West (founder of Great Ormond Street Hospital for Children) reports, "Some of the most painful death-beds which I have ever witnessed" were the result of such theology (West, *On Some of the Disorders*, 119).

system of punishment"—all of which act negatively on "sympathetic feelings," "higher aspirations," and "the moral tone."⁵⁰

Finally, psychological manipulation of a more "hysterical" nature is exemplified by "The Happy Child and the Wicked Mother" in *Familiar Talks with the Children* (1870), a volume of sentimental tales where saintly, weeping children sacrifice their young lives on behalf of reprobate parents who, in consequence, weep themselves (mothers) or turn from alcohol (fathers).

This article in the *Westminster Review*, though sarcastic and clearly biased, reveals a continuing felt need (among "religionists") to save the child from itself—to deliver it from its essence, its childlikeness, in processes reminiscent of exorcism. In all these schemes, childhood is valued for its potential, not for its essence—a necessary evil prior to adulthood. Whether couched in commercial or religious terms, the goal of childhood was to escape from it as soon as possible in order to become either a commercial contributor to society (or a fecund mother) or a consenting adult destined for heaven. In the catechetical approach, the goal is for the child to find refuge from itself in the mother Church; the child's imagination is acknowledged but then virtually ignored, the goal being to supplant childish fancy with adult rationality. The last two methods reflect the Evangelical pressure for a "decision"—an essentially "contractual" act also, ironically, normally reserved for adults. In these cases, the imagination is engaged, but then abused. The "decision" is to turn away from one's corrupt nature, to renounce oneself. In the words of a mid-century Wesleyan, for example:

> It must be remembered that the fault of human nature is not merely weakness—it is *corruption*; and that a renewal cannot spring from any change that intellectual cultivation may effect.⁵¹

Moreover, as we are here discussing the education of children, we are reminded that:

> The only armour which is hell-proof is—"*It is written.*" ... Our wisdom is to wrap the family of man as early as possible in that impenetrable mail.⁵²

---

50. "Religious Education of Children," 385.
51. "Shall Religion Be Separated?," 344.
52. "Shall Religion Be Separated?," 348.

Notwithstanding the child's immaturity and inherited defects (from Adam, the apes, or merely parents), we are reminded, somewhat ominously, that while the law might regard children as exculpable minors, God does not:

> [The Bible's] best promises are made to young people. It tells us of "little ones" who are admitted into covenant with the Lord. It details judgements that have been inflicted on children.[53]

In contrast, however misguided the Romantics were about the nature of childhood, they nevertheless valued it both as a physical state and a social construct. Although Coleridge does muse poetically over the sleeping Hartley about what he might *become*, there is nevertheless a celebration of who the baby *is*. This contrasts with the (especially male) Victorian impatience with, and distance from, childhood, an impatience which translated into schools bent on forcing their young charges towards premature flowering, "hot-houses" which not only produced early flowering and fruiting, but often an early death. The mid-Victorian years were full of debate as to whether such practices should be tolerated.[54]

In summary, the early- and mid-century consensus among "religionists" was that childlikeness equated to irrationality, emotional instability driven by a surfeit of passion (especially in girls), immorality due to an unregenerate soul (evidenced particularly by the sins of lying and masturbation, both especially feared as they were beyond the sphere of adult control),[55] and unproductiveness (both commercial and sexual) and therefore of little commercial or social value. In addition, the nonconformist pressure for a "decision" for Christ not only illustrates the negative view of childhood itself, but blurs the boundary between childhood and adulthood:[56] not only must children make "adult" moral decisions, they must also suffer the penalties for not doing so. Such negative views of childhood, combined with the idea that education should take into account God's pre-ordained social class divisions,[57] form the

---

53. "Shall Religion Be Separated?," 348. Of note here is the confusion between covenant and law. See, for example, the discussion in Wright, *Justification*, 71–77.

54. Shuttleworth, *Mind of the Child*, 107.

55. Shuttleworth, *Mind of the Child*, 65–66.

56. According to Rowan Williams, a perennial issue. See Williams, *Lost Icons*, 30–31.

57. The Exeter Diocesan Board, for example, felt the need to improve the education of the poor "by making it more efficient in preparing persons for the duties assigned to them by Providence" ("Education on Church Principles," 299). From a Dissenting

backdrop to MacDonald's work. As we will explore, he firmly challenges the former but has a tendency to idealize the latter.

Post-Darwin and *Fin de Siècle* Attitudes to Childhood

The Wesleyan article cited above is a polemical broadside against encroaching secularism peppered with Bible verses flung in anger. It illustrates the vehemence of mid-century debates whose temperature was raised even higher when Darwin published *Origin*. A major front in the battle concerned childhood and children, especially their education, reflecting increasing unease with the doctrine of original sin and growing awareness of child psychology.

Judith Plotz's complaint that Romantic theory had lost touch with reality might well be leveled at much of the Victorian discourse about childhood. The polarity and zealousness of both the Christian and evolutionist/secularist camps is striking when reading Victorian texts. Both sides make strong, often absurd, claims based on scant knowledge of children themselves (the theorists on both sides were primarily male who had little cause to visit the nursery). One thinks, for example, of Adolf Kussmaul's unlikely declaration that infants are born deaf,[58] or Dr. Louis Robinson's experiments, which consisted of suspending newborns from branches as evidence of simian ancestry,[59] or of George John Romanes's claim that seven-week-old infants have the intelligence of a mollusk.[60] It was even suggested that "rock a bye baby in the treetops" offered evidence of our "arboreal ancestry."[61]

The growing child study movement was also, at first, reluctant to engage in the messy business of interacting with real children; there was also a widespread tendency to use fictional characters as source material

---

perspective: "If a man best learns his duty by studying the Scriptures, he certainly must improve his disposition to fulfil his task in 'that state of life to which it has pleased God to call him'" (I. P., "Thoughts" 219).

58. Kussmaul, *Untersuchungen*, 10, 13–14. See also Shuttleworth, *Mind of the Child*, 223.

59. Shuttleworth, *Mind of the Child*, 274.

60. A chart published by Romanes in 1883 showed the human baby as achieving the intelligence of a mollusk at seven weeks, a reptile at four months, and at fourteen weeks to have reached the level of higher Crustacea. Shuttleworth, *Mind of the Child*, 255.

61. Shuttleworth, *Mind of the Child*, 363.

for "scientific" child studies, and to accept decidedly apocryphal accounts of child behavior at face value. The latter included a widely-disseminated eighteenth-century account of the "insane baby" that had to be held down by four nurses to prevent it climbing up the nursery walls (evidence of insanity in infants),[62] and (as late as 1911) a report in a work called *Child Nurture* claimed that "scientific fathers in Germany" had taken to dropping infants from first-floor windows to see if they would land on all fours like a kitten.[63] Even the otherwise reasonable James Sully seemed to accept the 1779 account of the famous four-year-old, Christian Heinrich Heineken of Lübeck, as a credible "prodigy of learning":

> Handed over to his tutor whilst still a baby, the infant was said to have mastered the Old Testament by the age of one, the history of the ancient world, universal geography, and Latin by the age of two and a half, and the deeper mysteries of dogmatic theology and ecclesiastical history by the age of four, by which time his fame had spread across Europe.[64]

The use of fictional *literary* texts to provide case histories was also widespread, leading to a symbiotic relationship between scientists and authors with each fueling the others' output. It is unsurprising that under such conditions strange theories developed, often surrounding the paranoia towards sexual "precocity" that inevitably had a negative effect on the lives of children and included, for example, Isaac Baker Brown performing clitoridectomies on girls as young at ten to cure them of insanity.[65] However misguided, such theorizing and practice demonstrates awareness and exploration of this newly-discovered continent called "childhood" embedded in the heart of society. The child was a hot topic.

Saint, Sinner, or Savage?

The eighteenth-century Romantic notion of the child mind as a blank slate on whose virgin surface nature writes divine truth created the saintly child; a positive, if naive, construction of childhood. The ascendancy of the Puritan emphasis on original sin among Protestant Evangelicals

62. James Crichton-Browne quoted in Shuttleworth, *Mind of the Child*, 22.
63. Shuttleworth, *Mind of the Child*, 246.
64. Shuttleworth, *Mind of the Child*, 146.
65. Until 1866, when expelled from the Obstetrical Society. See Shuttleworth, *Mind of the Child*, 36.

in the nineteenth century created the sinner child, placing a social burden on children, now constantly watched by their guardians for signs of incipient sin (or insanity), and drilled by the Catechism or its nonconformist equivalent, memorizing Bible verses. MacDonald's literary image of the sadistic schoolmaster dramatizes the pressure on children. Henry Maudsley, in a chapter entitled "Insanity in Early Life" in *The Physiology and Pathology of Mind* (1868)—"one of the first accounts that placed childhood mental disorders in an evolutionary perspective"[66]—records the imprisonment of a schoolmaster for beating a child to death (in his view an insane child),[67] and notes occurrences of mania linked to religious fervor:

> A boy of about eleven years of age who came under my care . . . moved about restlessly, throwing his arms about and repeating over and over again such expressions as—"The good Lord Jesus," "They put Him on the cross," "They nailed His hands," &c: it was impossible to fix his attention for a moment.[68]

Clearly the pressure on real children from this philosophical page-turn was not positive.

Despite making confident medical pronouncements, Maudsley's work reveals a more ambivalent attitude to the *cause* of immoral behavior, as if feeling his way in the uncertain territory opened up by Darwin. On the one hand, childhood insanity is caused by original sin or demons:[69]

> To talk about the purity and innocence of a child's mind is a part of that . . . poetical idealism and willing hypocrisy by which a man ignores realities. . . . By nature sinful above everything, and desperately wicked [Jer 17:9], man acquires a knowledge of good through evil.[70]

66. Shuttleworth, *Mind of the Child*, 181.
67. Maudsley, *Physiology and Pathology of Mind*, 328–29.
68. Maudsley, *Physiology and Pathology of Mind*, 313–14.
69. Quoted is an account, from one "Griesinger from Kerner," of a girl of eleven, a "pious Christian child," who, in "a deep bass voice . . . kept repeating the words, 'They are praying for thee.' . . . On the evening of the 22nd January another voice, quite different from the bass one, spoke incessantly while the crisis lasted . . . now and then interrupted by the former bass voice regularly repeating the recitative. . . . What, however, gave a distinctive character to its expressions was the moral or rather immoral tone of them—pride, arrogance, scorn, and hatred of truth, God, Christ, that were declared. The situation was resolved when a voice cried out [from the girl]—'Get thee out of this girl, thou unclean spirit'" (Maudsley, *Physiology and Pathology of Mind*, 317–18).
70. Maudsley, *Physiology and Pathology of Mind*, 322.

In other words, God will use evil such that humans evolve morally. On the other hand, he recognizes the role of hereditary and evolutionary factors: the infant has "the latent power of an actual evolution which no monkey ever has; in it is contained . . . the influence of all mankind that has gone before."[71] Whether inherited from Adam or the apes, depravity was nevertheless seen as the nascent state of the child.

Imagination and Insanity in Childhood

Mid-century child psychology saw "adult sanity [as] dependent on the ruthless control of imaginative visions within childhood."[72] Maudsley, Shuttleworth argues, compounded the negative views of childhood imagination by associating it with animal savagery. Using Coleridge's terminology but rejecting his theology, he equates childhood fantasy with animal passions:

> The instincts, appetites, or passions, call them as we may, manifest themselves in unblushing, extreme, and perverted action; the veil of any control which discipline may have fashioned is rent; the child is as the animal, and reveals its animal nature with as little shamefacedness as the monkey indulges its passions in the face of all the world.[73]

Elsewhere Maudsley makes it clear that childish passion is no more than an animal reaction to an external stimulus:

> Children and savages best exhibit in a naked simplicity the different passions that result from the affectation of self by what, when painful, is deemed an ill; when pleasurable, a good.[74]

The terms "unblushing," "indulging passions in the face of all the world," and "naked simplicity" clearly reinforce the association of sexual curiosity with mental disease (apparently ignoring the fact that young children have very little interest in sexuality). There is also the blurring of the boundary between normal and pathological childlike behavior: Maudsley appears to equate normal childhood—certainly infancy—with

71. Maudsley, *Physiology and Pathology of Mind*, 333.
72. Shuttleworth, *Mind of the Child*, 45.
73. Maudsley, *Physiology and Pathology of Mind*, 322. See also Shuttleworth, *Mind of the Child*, 182.
74. Maudsley, *Physiology and Pathology of Mind*, 150.

insanity. Some thirty years later, Havelock Ellis suggested that criminals were those trapped in a savage evolutionary stage by arrested development: in a case of guilt by association, children were now viewed (at least potentially) as insane *and* criminal. Shuttleworth remarks that:

> Ellis, building on these theories, argued that moral insanity in the child, exhibited through eccentricity, lying, bad sexual habits, and cruelty to animals, was the first stage of "instinctive criminality." As for Maudsley, children were closer to the animal or savage state than adults, and the insane child even more so.[75]

Charles West (founder of Great Ormond Street Children's Hospital) offered a more benign view of childhood imagination. Noting the terror experienced by children facing death that had been over-zealously catechized or evangelized, he sympathizes with their emotional turmoil:

> The dark grave is realised, or, at least, imagined more vividly than its conqueror; and the little child [is] driven to look within for the evil which it does not know, and cannot find, but vaguely dreads, and would be sorry for if it knew it.[76]

Undeveloped reasoning powers in a child, he argues, lead to "exaggerated . . . perceptive faculties [and] a vividness of . . . imagination." Because of this, "the griefs of childhood may be, in proportion to the child's power of bearing them, as overwhelming as those which break the strong man down,"[77] leading to a plea for compassion:

> These facts deserve special attention; they prove how much more the susceptibility and sensitiveness of children need to be taken into consideration than is commonly done. This keenness of the emotions in children displays itself in other ways, and has constantly to be borne in mind in our management of them.[78]

West closes his lecture by suggesting that the only thing which offers any hope for the suffering child is that Jesus welcomed children into his arms despite their not having learned the Creed or professed faith.

West's criticism as a Catholic of what we would now call fundamentalist Christianity, his Romantic leanings, his qualified acceptance of Darwinism while insisting on "a perfection to be attained not here,

---

75. Shuttleworth, *Mind of the Child*, 183n8, 206.
76. West, *On Some of the Disorders*, 119.
77. West, *On Some of the Disorders*, 127.
78. West, *On Some of the Disorders*, 128.

but higher,"[79] represent a liberal middle road which contrasts with the polarized views discussed. Of note is the rejection of inherent depravity in childhood, however caused, replacing this with a more nuanced understanding of the causes and power of childhood passions, underscored by a belief in a benevolent God.

The Nineteenth-Century Child

We have considered the Victorian child as a social construct, a literary device, and a theological metaphor. None may directly bear on the biological and psychological state we call childhood, but all contribute to a theological anthropology and, inasmuch as the child bears the *imago Dei*, in some measure touch on views regarding God's nature. Protestant Evangelicalism, however, tended to focus on the distortion, even obliteration, of that *imago*. The focus on original sin and the corresponding development of a religious "forcing apparatus" to drive this out of the child is, in some measure, a denial of the humanity of the child. It says that the child is something "other" which, without intervention, will grow into something subhuman.

A contrast has emerged between Romantic views of a benign nature nurturing the innocent child-mind and Puritan ideas disdainful of such optimism. However, it must be noted that these two opposing ideologies were always present: "Most scholars agree that Evangelical ideology held firmer sway in the early years of the century while the romantic gradually gained influence, yet both existed at the same time to varying degrees."[80] In the next chapter we will consider more closely the Victorian theology of childhood and MacDonald's particular contribution to the debate.

---

79. West, *On Some of the Disorders*, 133.
80. Sutphin, "Victorian Childhood," 54.

3

George MacDonald's Contribution to Childhood

THE DISCUSSION SO FAR has revealed the Victorian child to be a saint, sinner, or savage, depending on the theological or ideological leanings of the exponent. For each position, it is also apparent that there appears to be a somewhat cavalier attitude to presenting evidence, particularly the acceptance of fictitious accounts at face value and a tendency to theorize rather than engage with real children. We have identified the reason for this: the category "child" refers to social, ideological, and theological concepts that have deeper roots and wider application than anything to do with physical human juveniles.

There is a certain irony, though, that in an age with a predilection for verifiable facts, in the growing field of child studies much of the debate took place in the literary realm—that of speculative imagination. Echoing Montemaggi's claims regarding the place of literature in the development of ideas (discussed in the context of reading Dante), Sally Shuttleworth insists that this was *the* major forum where social (and many theological) ideas were developed and where the figure of the child was central.[1] John Pennington and Jean Webb point to the realist novel as being the literary expression of positivism and that fantasy novels such as Lewis Carroll's *Alice* or MacDonald's *North Wind* expressed a mid-century return to metaphysics.[2] For Pennington, metaphysical literature represents "a reaction against literary trends and conventions, and metafictionists

---

1. Shuttleworth, *Mind of the Child*, 3.
2. Pennington and McGillis, *Behind the Back*, 53, 175.

often undercut and parody these conventions to suggest that our sense of 'reality' is tenuous."³ This certainly characterizes MacDonald's work and was the reason that George McCrie felt so threatened: his world view was being challenged. MacDonald regularly challenges convention, particularly so in tales such as *North Wind*, a novel that invites the reader to explore the world through the eyes of a child.

Colin Manlove, earlier in his career, saw MacDonald's fantasy-writing in negative terms as a "self-protecting silencing of his intellect"; later, however, he concedes that it is an attempt to demonstrate that God is beyond rational, theological systems, and that "MacDonald believed that Christianity had much more to do with lived than proved truths."⁴ This is no doubt the case, but is MacDonald therefore guilty of being anti-intellectual? Irrational? Is the child protagonist of *North Wind*, for example, too good to be true? Or do we side with him when he remarks that *nothing* can be too good to be true?

> "There are very few things good enough to be true," said Diamond; "but I hope this is. Too good to be true it can't be. Isn't true good? and isn't good good? And how, then, can anything be too good to be true?"⁵

With these issues in mind, we close this chapter by exploring *North Wind* in relation to childhood and metaphysics—especially since the protagonist is described as "a true child in this, that he was given to metaphysics."⁶ It is, of course, to be expected that there will be disagreements between secularists and "religionists" and for the moment we must lay to one side those who considered the child a savage. Instead, we focus on the tension between "saints" and "sinners." In order to get a better perspective, before reading *North Wind*, it is helpful look more closely at the kind of theology against which MacDonald was reacting.

Childhood Sins, Adult Sinners—A Tractarian Perspective

A preoccupation with original sin, rather than the *imago Dei* (which one might term "original blessing"), distinguished "harder" Evangelicals

---

3. Pennington and McGillis, *Behind the Back*, 53.
4. Pennington and McGillis, *Behind the Back*, 150.
5. *NW* 307.
6. *NW* 89.

from their more flexible counterparts; however, this was not confined to Evangelicalism. Here we consider how High Churchman H. E. Manning (later Cardinal of Westminster) made the doctrine of sin central to his theology, and how MacDonald responded to such theology. Manning represents the high moral tone of Tractarianism which considered itself ineffectual if not offensive to the morally corrupt and complacent general public.[7] We consider Manning's 1848 sermon, "The Sins That Follow Us." Taking as his text 1 Timothy 5:24—which in his KJV reads: "Some men's sins are open beforehand, before going to judgement; and some men they follow after"—the Archdeacon discusses blatant sinners "who stand in the face of the Church, and in the sight of God, self-accused," but is more concerned with secret sins which will only be exposed on the day of judgement. Noting briefly that the context concerns "the high and dangerous work of ordaining pastors for the flock of Christ," he nevertheless insists that "we need not dwell on context" on the grounds that the words "enunciate a great law in God's kingdom, and describe an awful fact in the administration of His perfect justice."[8] In other words, there is a universal, inescapable, application.

Manning emphasizes that we may be unconscious of the "sins that follow us," that these may well have been committed in childhood, and that such is the *unconscious* "state of thousands."[9] We are reminded that *we* may forget the life-long accumulation of sins that we draw in our wake, but God does not: "our forgetfulness [cannot] blot the book of His remembrance."[10] Childhood sins will come back to haunt us:

> As the sins of the fathers upon the children, so the sins of childhood on youth, and youth on after years. How little did we know what we were laying up for ourselves. How little did we think at that day, in the hour of our transgression: This will find me out when I am in middle life, or in my old age; though it tarry never so long, it will come at last.[11]

Furthermore, sin "when at its worst . . . is the least perceived," and most of it relates to "the indulgence of particular sins in youth or childhood." It is a theme constantly repeated. "Our early sins of willfulness, irreverence,

---

7. Reardon, *Victorian Age*, 109n1.
8. Manning, *Sermons*, 73.
9. Manning, *Sermons*, 76–77.
10. Manning, *Sermons*, 79. One might note that God also chooses to forget and forgive sins (e.g., Isa 1:18; Dan 9:9; Mark 2:7).
11. Manning, *Sermons*, 80.

self-worship, have followed us"; our present infirmities are due to "the sins of our past life, following us in chastisement"; and on judgement day, "Sins [one has] forgotten as never truly to repent of, shall be then gathered in array."[12]

Unfortunately, the only solution offered for this unconscious alliance with evil is the oxymoronic concept of conscious repentance. It begs the inevitable question posed at the end of the sermon: having done one's best to repent, Manning asks, "Are you so sure that you do repent?" If you answer in the affirmative,

> then you have one great reason to mistrust yourself; I mean, because you are so sure. If you were less satisfied, you might be surer; because you are so sure, you have the most reason for misgiving.[13]

It is a message at the core of which is doubt which can never lead to assurance of forgiveness. Doubt, as we will explore, is also central to *North Wind*, the difference here is that sin is the theological foundation and focus. The justice of God is not only untempered by love, but love is missing. MacDonald describes such theology as "undivine," that is, pagan:[14]

> A theology which would explain all God's doings by low conceptions, low I mean for humanity even, of right, and law, and justice, then only taking refuge in the fact of the incapacity of the human understanding when its own inventions are impugned as undivine.[15]

In such religious schemes, he argues, "hell is invariably the deepest truth, and the love of God is not so deep as hell. Hence, as foundations must be laid in the deepest, the system is founded in hell."[16] It is a theology which has negative consequences for a child's self-understanding. MacDonald explores this through the young hero of *Robert Falconer* (often considered MacDonald's most faithful self-portrait):[17]

---

12. Manning, *Sermons*, 81, 82.
13. Manning, *Sermons*, 88–89.
14. See page 140.
15. *RF* 1:152. These comments, aimed at Scottish Calvinism, follow the autobiographical account of MacDonald's fierce grandmother's burning of her son's violin because of its corrupting influence. See *GMAW* 29.
16. *RF* 1:152.
17. See, for example, *GMWR* 32, 37–38.

> The first article in the creed that Robert Falconer learned was, "I believe in hell." Practically, I mean, it was so; else how should it be that as often as a thought of religious duty arose in his mind, it appeared in the form of escaping hell, of fleeing from the wrath to come? For his very nature was hell, being not born in sin and brought forth in iniquity, but born sin and brought forth iniquity.[18]

In contrast, MacDonald advocates a theology based on F. D. Maurice's "abyss of love." While accepting that "there is an abyss of Death, into which I may sink, and be lost," Maurice had insisted that:

> Christ's Gospel reveals an abyss of Love, below that; I am content to be lost in that. I know no more, but I am sure that there is a woe on us if we do not preach this Gospel, if we do not proclaim the name of the Father, the Son, and the Spirit,—the Eternal Charity.[19]

MacDonald, similarly, argues that the deepest in God is not power, "for power could not make him what we mean when we say *God*," but love: "In one word, God is Love. Love is the deepest depth, the essence of his nature, at the root of all his being."[20] Furthermore, the child, carrying the image of the God of love, is the beneficiary of "original blessing" and expresses "the deepest heart of humanity," the divine heart. The marriage of these two "depths" is a rejection of the doctrine of original sin. For just as Jesus received the "child in the midst":

> when we receive the child in the name of Christ, the very childhood that we receive to our arms is humanity. We love its humanity in its childhood, for childhood is the deepest heart of humanity—its divine heart; and so in the name of the child we receive all humanity. Therefore, although the lesson is not about humanity, but about childhood, it returns upon our race, and we receive our race with wider arms and deeper heart.[21]

There is a fusion here of the divine and human centered on childhood, that is, the presence of the "child-God" resides in "the deepest heart of humanity." The child, embodying the *imago Dei* as well as the *imago hominis*, rather than being a barrier to God and cursed with original sin

---

18. *RF* 1:152–53.
19. Maurice, *Theological Essays*, 442–43.
20. *US3* 8.
21. *US1* 16.

becomes a gateway to God and a mediator of God's presence. It is this that MacDonald explores in *North Wind*.

A Reading of *At the Back of the North Wind*

North Wind is a multi-layered narrative which, to use a clichéd term, is clearly aimed at those who read to children as much as children themselves. Multiple readings have been offered,[22] and applauded by MacDonald on the basis that: "If [the reader] be a true man, he will imagine true things: what matter whether I meant them or not?" Since a truly artistic work employs God-given images, he argues, an author "cannot help his words and figures falling into such combinations in the mind of another as he had himself not foreseen."[23] That noted, we focus here on *North Wind* as an articulation of MacDonald's theology of "the child." Although early in his canon, it clearly presents ideas which never left him. I suggest there were three motivating factors in MacDonald's mind as he put pen to paper.

First, the narrative clearly challenges sin-centered theology such as that of H. E. Manning, especially in relation to childhood; instead it presents a vision of childhood innocence. A strong theme is doubt, here equated with hope rather than fear.[24] Unlike the doubt of Manning, which short-circuits faith, for MacDonald, doubt is the soil in which faith grows:

> A man may be haunted with doubts, and only grow thereby in faith. Doubts are the messengers of the Living One to rouse the honest. They are the first knock at our door of things that are not yet, but have to be, understood; and theirs in general is the inhospitable reception of angels that do not come in their own likeness. Doubt must precede every deeper assurance; for uncertainties are what we first see when we look into a region hitherto unknown, unexplored, unannexed.[25]

---

22. There are sixteen essays in Pennington and McGillis, *Behind the Back*.

23. *Orts* 320.

24. Manlove suggests that *North Wind* is unique among MacDonald's work in "putting doubt at its core beside faith" (Manlove, "Reading," 152). However, the juxtaposition of doubt and faith recurs in MacDonald's opus, usually distinguishing the faithful (who have honest doubt) from the faithless (secure in their "fundamentalist" convictions).

25. *US2* 201.

God, he argues, would rather have honest doubt than dishonest faith:

> But God is assuredly pleased with those who will neither lie for him, quench their dim vision of himself, nor count *that* his mind which they would despise in a man of his making.[26]

So instead of triumphant theological certainty (MacDonald holds the view that "the more ignorant a man is, the more capable is he of being absolutely certain of many things—with such certainty, that is, as consists in the absence of doubt"),[27] this narrative is redolent with ambiguity and uncertainty. MacDonald deliberately leaves questions unanswered and loose ends untied: the reader must exercise faith.

Second, flowing from this vision of innocence, it presents a narrative of childhood death as something to be embraced rather than feared. Childhood death was a vexing contemporary issue. It is conceivable that *North Wind* was a response to a poem by Dinah Craik in a Christmas gift book, *Home Thoughts and Home Scenes* (1865), concerning the imminent death of a child. If not a specific response to this book, it is certainly informed by the sentiments expressed. Illustrated by the picture of a mother cradling a dying infant, surrounded by anxious children and an impotent doctor, the accompanying poem reads:

> How trembling the children gather round,
>   Startled out of sleep, and scared and crying!
>   "Is our merry little sister dying?
>   Will they come and put her underground
>
> "As they did poor baby on that May day?
>   Or will shining angels stoop and take her
>   On their snow-white wings to heaven, and make her
> Sit among the stars, as fair as they?
>
> "But she'll have no mother there to kiss!
>   We are sorely frightened," say the children,
>   "Thinking of this death, so strange bewildering:
>   Tell us, only tell us what death is?"[28]

---

26. EA 328.

27. MA 3:133; cf. Augustine, "*Si comprehendis, non est Deus.*"

28. Ingelow et al., *Home Thoughts* 31. This is discussed further in Sutphin, "Victorian Childhood," 63.

In *North Wind*, MacDonald is clearly endeavoring to answer this question.

Third, it dramatizes ideas presented a few years earlier in the essay "The Imagination, Its Function and Its Culture,"[29] an essay insisting that imaginative perception, rather than logical evaluation, is God's primary gift for assessing truth, that is, the true nature of the presenting state of affairs we call "reality." It therefore articulates aspects of MacDonald's cosmology. It is helpful to consider the proposals made in this essay before reading *North Wind*, not least because it articulates the theory of imagination that underpins the methodology and content of all of MacDonald's work.

"The Imagination: Its Function and Its Culture"

Victorian education, as noted in chapter 2, was focused on producing commercially productive, logical adults and was highly suspicious of imagination. It led Dickens, in *Dombey and Son*, for example, to denounce the educational "forcing apparatus" that crammed children prematurely full of mere facts.[30] In "The Imagination, Its Function and Its Culture," MacDonald, likewise, denounces those who say:

> "Are there not facts? . . . Why forsake them for fancies? Is there not that which may be *known*? Why forsake it for inventions? What God hath made, into that let man inquire."

To which he responds:

> We answer: To inquire into what God has made is the main function of the imagination. It is aroused by facts, is nourished by facts; seeks for higher and yet higher laws in those facts; but refuses to regard science as the sole interpreter of nature, or the laws of science as the only region of discovery.[31]

MacDonald is not rejecting rational thought, simply recognizing, as he remarks elsewhere, that "fact at best is but a garment of truth, which

---

29. Orts 1–42. The essay was first published in 1867. See Manlove, "Reading," 169.

30. Dombey senior, not interested in his child except as the future "& Son," dispatches him to a "school" whose mistress was "quite scientific in her knowledge of the childish character." Her method was "not to encourage a child's mind to develop and expand itself like a young flower, but to open it by force like an oyster" (Dickens, *Dealings with the Firm*, 100, 102). See Shuttleworth, *Mind of the Child*, 109–121.

31. Orts 2.

has ten thousand changes of raiment woven in the same loom."[32] After affirming in Coleridgean terms that human imagination is "that faculty in man which is likest to the prime operation of the power of God," MacDonald identifies the main ontological/epistemological problem that is the focus of *North Wind*:

> We must not forget, however, that between creator and poet lies the one unpassable gulf which distinguishes—far be it from us to say *divides*—all that is God's from all that is man's; a gulf teeming with infinite revelations, but a gulf over which no man can pass to find out God, although God needs not to pass over it to find man; the gulf between that which calls, and that which is thus called into being; between that which makes in its own image and that which is made in that image.[33]

Put simply, God may be beyond reason, but not beyond discovery: there are "infinite revelations" in nature. However, another kind of cognition is needed; creation should be viewed as an artwork:

> [God] begins with the building of the stage itself, and that stage is a world.... He makes the actors, and they do not act,—they *are* their part. He utters them into the visible to work out their life—his drama. When he would have an epic, he sends a thinking hero into his drama, and the epic is the soliloquy of his Hamlet.[34]

In this theatrical analogy, MacDonald is emphasizing that "[God's] imagination is one with his creative will. The thing that God imagines, that thing exists"; "God's fiction . . . is man's reality":[35]

> As the thoughts move in the mind of a man, so move the worlds of men and women in the mind of God, and make no confusion there, for there they had their birth, the offspring of his imagination. Man is but a thought of God.... Indeed, a man is rather *being thought* than *thinking*.[36]

This Novalis-like vision of God's "dream" being human reality is central to MacDonald's idealist ontology and is predicated on the necessary condition that God is the *source* of all things, and thus the divine creative

---

32. *WMM* 1:69.
33. *Orts* 2.
34. *Orts* 4.
35. *US3* 24; *Orts* 223.
36. *Orts* 4.

energy—as electric current through a diode—may only flow in one direction: "a gulf over which no man can pass to find out God, although God needs not to pass over it to find man." The obstacle to knowing God directly is that the gulf between humanity and God is "teeming with infinite revelations" that the finite mind will never fully grasp, not only because the object of enquiry is infinite, but because the human mind has its source in that "object"—the divine mind.

Since God is thinking his "stage" into being, to know God one must read nature using the God-given imagination, for "God has made the world that it should thus serve his creature, developing in the service that imagination whose necessity it meets."[37] Anticipating objections that human imagination is peripheral to cognition, he observes:

> If [imagination] be to man what creation is to God, we must expect to find it operative in every sphere of human activity. Such is, indeed, the fact, and that to a far greater extent than is commonly supposed.[38]

But are not our God-given *intellectual* abilities (that is, rationality and logic) best suited to investigate creation (the Deist position)? MacDonald responds by arguing that it is more reasonable to expect the imagination of God to partner directly with human imagination rather than condescend to work with its lesser correlate, human intellect: "The work of the Higher must be discovered by the search of the Lower in degree which is yet similar in kind." However, he concludes by echoing the sentiment expressed in the *Cambridge University Magazine* for a more holistic approach to cognition.[39] "Intellect" must not be ignored; it must, however, be led by imagination:

> Let us not be supposed to exclude the intellect from a share in every highest office. Man is not divided when the manifestations of his life are distinguished. The intellect "is all in every part." There were no imagination without intellect, however much it may appear that intellect can exist without imagination. *What we mean to insist upon is, that in finding out the works of God, the Intellect must labour, workman-like, under the direction of the architect, Imagination.*[40]

---

37. *Orts* 5.
38. *Orts* 7.
39. See page 49.
40. *Orts* 11 (emphasis mine).

The Ambiguous Setting and Cast of *North Wind*

To explore these conceptual proposals, in *At the Back of the North Wind* (as in many of his narratives) MacDonald places an innocent child—here Diamond, an androgynous, fragile, prepubescent boy with, apparently, learning difficulties—in a world that is ambiguous both ontologically and morally. It is a fluid narrative with blurred boundaries, questioning notions of reality and challenging conventional stereotypes. Against this fluid background, Diamond, the son of a poor coachman, provides the focal point as he copes with various challenges—his father's illness, taunts about being "God's baby," driving his father's cab (without permission) to dangerous areas of London, and so on. The narrative implies that Diamond himself is ill, both mentally and physically, and his talk about having met North Wind, God's agent in the narrative, is interpreted as madness by his mother. He is therefore discarded by society as unfit for either education or work. The text is thus a reverse *Bildungsroman*: rather than the protagonist changing and maturing through exposure to life experiences, Diamond is a figure of stasis who dies in the same childhood state as in chapter one. He not only represents but mediates God's "unmoving" fire at the center of reality. As in the narrative of *Sir Gibbie*, which we consider later, the action circles around him; it is others who change.

So although, in many respects, Diamond is "ambiguous," the narrative proposes that the ambiguity has more to do with this confusing world of paradox and mystery that is beyond "reason"; instead, childlike imagination is needed, especially in its role as the bridge to transcendence. The narrative explores "mysteries"—evil, childhood death, gender, sexuality, class, education, and social deprivation—through the eyes of a child. It suggests there is a "thin door" between this world and the next,[41] but rather than being adjacent realities, MacDonald is exploring an ontology of intersection—the entwining of "fairyland" with the grim realities of London. Early in the narrative, for example, Diamond is whisked from his bed by a personified North Wind and swept across the skies of London. Having blown tiles from the roof above his bed, she "lifted him from the roof—up—up into her bosom, and held him there," later winding him in her hair for safety.[42] From this vantage point

---

41. In the poem "The Lost Soul," death knocks at MacDonald's "thin door." See page 164.

42. *NW* 76.

he watches as with her "great besom" she sweeps filth from the city, the wind howling down streets and alleyways. The apparent movement of the streets below is set against the stasis experienced by Diamond. Until this point the reader assumes Diamond is dreaming, but abruptly, at his request, North Wind sets him down to help a poor crossing-sweeper of his acquaintance, Nanny, struggling with her own little broom in the rising wind. Diamond eventually has to find his own way home on foot. In another scene, Diamond hears two horses having a conversation, one of which claims to be an angel, all of which leaves the reader questioning the nature of reality (and whether, perhaps, Diamond is hallucinating).

In particular, the narrative challenges materialistic, immanentist, geocentric views of reality that are blind to transcendence. Being the son of a poor coachman, Diamond lives in the stables and his bedroom is the hayloft immediately above his namesake, the horse. The "thin door" between Diamond and death is the decaying wall of the stable:

> He had not the least idea that the wind got in at a chink in the wall, and blew about him all night. For the back of his bed was only of boards an inch thick, and on the other side of them was the north wind . . . in many places they were more like tinder than timber.[43]

As illustrated in *Lilith*, MacDonald is suggesting that what we consider to be a robust, hermetically-sealed, safe quotidian reality is located within the wider reality of God's "dangerous" presence, and that, although unaware of it, the wind of God's Spirit gets in through chinks in what amount to very flimsy walls, and "blows about us all night." The image of Diamond's vulnerability in a cold world presages his death—the fate of 20,000 children in London annually[44]—the direct result of the coldness (that is, sin) of his father's employer, the "black" (untransformed) Mr. Coleman who, indifferent to Diamond's welfare, ignores the need to repair the coach house forcing his mother to paste paper over the holes.[45]

The image challenges our notions of what is "inside" and what is "outside." Diamond, surrounded by bales of hay (the image of a very temporary shelter, a manger housing this young savior whose father's name is also Joseph)[46] thinks he is inside, but soon he hears North Wind whisper-

43. *NW* 12.
44. Baldwin, "History of the Hospital."
45. *NW* 13–14.
46. For Colin Manlove, Diamond "is a Victorian Christ" (Manlove, "Reading," 172).

ing on the other side of the thin partition accusing the boy of blocking up her window, a knot-hole in the wood, with straw.

> "What window?" asked Diamond.
> "You stuffed hay into it three times last night. I had to blow it out again three times."
> "You can't mean this little hole! It isn't a window; it's a hole in my bed."
> "I did not say it was *a* window: I said it was *my* window."
> "But it can't be a window, because windows are holes to see out of."
> "Well, that's just what I made this window for."
> "But you are outside: you can't want a window."
> "You are quite mistaken. Windows are to see out of, you say. Well, I'm in my house, and I want windows to see out of it."[47]

For MacDonald, "nature" (played by North Wind) is closer to the center of reality (God) than our temporary shelters that alienate us from it and provide a false sense of security. Resonances with the Incarnation reinforce this reading. However, the insular realm of quotidian reality is punctured by "windows" that allow access for divine agents and for the "sun-glory" of God himself to enter human history.[48] This text suggests that one of those windows is a child.

In the moral realm there is parallel ambiguity. "Mother nature," the nurturing robe of God that is also red in tooth and claw, is played by North Wind who one moment gently caresses a flower, the next, sinks a ship. She is also a shape-shifting being who to those who are "good" appears as a beautiful woman, but may incarnate herself as a wolf to the morally depraved;[49] she is a being of immense power but nevertheless benign. Diamond, in his innocence, that is, sinlessness and faith, simply accepts her for who she is. When, for example, North Wind warns him to trust her even if she should appear in hideous guises such as a bat, a serpent, or a tiger—that is, as a manifestation of evil—she asks: "Do you understand?" He simply replies: "Quite well."[50] This "insane," naive trust is interpreted by others as just that:[51] he has a "tile loose," is nicknamed "God's baby," and confesses that he "never can tell what they call

---

47. *NW* 14.
48. *US3* 53–54.
49. *NW* 43.
50. *NW* 22.
51. *NW* 140–41, 174, 195, 304, 306.

clever from what they call silly."[52] MacDonald's thesis in *North Wind* is expressed by Diamond's benefactor, a Mr. Raymond: "I suspect the child's a genius . . . and that's what makes people think him silly."[53] The genius of true faith, it is proposed, looks like madness to those who claim sanity.

At every page-turn, the reader is confronted with ambiguities that challenge conventional thinking. In a novel about death, for example, there is no grim reaper; instead, nature herself, North Wind, plays the angel of death. Furthermore, in a literary world where God and his priests were inevitably male, this divine agent is decidedly female. In contrast to stereotypical female tropes such as the meek Victorian housewife, she is not only a being of immense power, but a powerfully erotic figure who frequently presses Diamond to her "bosom," an eroticism reinforced by the sensuous woodcuts of Arthur Hughes.

Illustrations from *At The Back of the North Wind*
by Arthur Hughes[54]

52. *NW* 355. The boy is often called "silly." MacDonald suggests that, in the archaic sense of the word they were correct. See *NW* 356. "*Silly* did not originally refer to the absurd or ridiculous—in fact quite the opposite. The word derives from the old English word *seely*, meaning happy, blissful, lucky or blessed. From there it came to mean innocent, or deserving of compassion, only later mutating this sense of naive childishness into a more critical, mocking term, signifying ignorance, feeble-mindedness, and foolish behaviour" (British Library, "Silly").

53. *NW* 221.

54. *NW* 373, 375.

Despite her role as a divine agent, North Wind is not omniscient. Her work is choreographed by an unseen higher power whose song, she says, originates "outside this air in which I make such a storm," whose promptings she must obey, but who remains mysterious:

> I am always hearing, through every noise, through all the noise I am making myself even, the sound of a far-off song. I do not exactly know where it is, or what it means.[55]

She is thus unable to account for her actions: "I have to do ten thousand things without being able to tell how"[56]—God may be in nature but remains hidden. She, like human members of the cast, is mystified by evil and catastrophe. When Diamond asks her, on sinking the ship, how such an event is good for those drowned, she points to universal, eschatological resolution:

> "Somehow, I can't say how, [the song] tells me that all is right; that it is coming to swallow up all cries. . . . It wouldn't be the song it seems to be if it did not swallow up all their fear and pain too, and set them singing it themselves with the rest. I am sure it will."[57]

Although she is the doorway to the afterlife (Diamond must walk through her body to access the land behind her), she is not permitted to enter it: the north wind, MacDonald reminds us, can only blow southwards; death has no place in eternity.

As well as that relating to content and morality, there is also ambiguity in relation to the style and methodology of the narrative itself. We encounter dream narratives (from Nanny and Diamond) which include dreams within dreams and stories within the story. One chapter is devoted to the tale told by a philanthropist visiting the children's hospital, and extended nursery rhymes also provide nested narratives. The reader is left bewildered. It has been suggested that this disorientation is because MacDonald has over-padded his narrative at the expense of plot focus,[58] but equally it might be read as a further destabilizing device.[59] Is periph-

---

55. *NW* 83–84.
56. *NW* 71.
57. *NW* 84.
58. See Robb, "Fiction for the Child," 30.
59. Knoepflmacher, *Ventures into Childland*, 229.

eral material as peripheral as it seems? MacDonald is saying: "You, the reader, must decide what is real, what is important."

Finally, regarding methodology, we note that the narrative opens with the words, "I have been asked to tell you about the back of the north wind," but it leaves the reader wondering who is doing the asking.[60] The narrator is not the standard omniscient narrator of fiction: he often ponders what certain things mean and claims ignorance of others, and yet at the same time narrates scenes which can only be the fruit of omniscience. Towards the end of the tale he confesses to having befriended Diamond and persuaded him to tell him about the back of the north wind. Perhaps Diamond is real? John Pennington summarizes:

> Thus MacDonald creates a highly original and complex work that challenges the reader's narrative assumptions, breaks them, and provides the reader with a higher reality—death—which becomes, ironically, peaceful and beautiful.[61]

Challenging Convention—Good Death

The inherent ambiguity in *North Wind* forces a re-evaluation of what is considered morally and ontologically normal and acceptable; it challenges societal mores and conventions. As noted, this was a particularly Romantic preoccupation driven by the view that learned, social conventions were essentially contrived and "false," especially when contrasted with the natural innocence of the nature-communing child. This is very evident in *North Wind*, and it is here that MacDonald is particularly subversive, notably as he contrasts the "transparent" innocence of Diamond with the somewhat ambivalent philanthropy of his benefactor, Mr. Raymond—names clearly chosen for a reason.

Although ostensibly named after his father's favorite horse, old Diamond,[62] MacDonald is proposing that such seemingly random acts have divine genesis and significance; here, Diamond's naming foretells his ordained destiny as an Aaronic priest.[63] He is not only transparent

---

60. See Manlove, "Reading," 157.
61. See Pennington, "Alice at the Back," 58.
62. *NW* 10.
63. *NW* 21; cf. Exod 28:18. The reference here is not simply to Aaron's priestly "breastplate of judgment," representing God-ordained authority; it draws attention to how such authority has become warped. The divine symbol is no longer on the

(that is, totally open to the presence of God) and immutable, despite forces ranged against him, but reflects and refracts eternal light in a dark Victorian town. He is Dia-mond ("dual-world")—not only does he inhabit, and bridge, upper and lower social spheres, he is also a citizen of both earth and heaven.[64] Ultimately, his light is entirely dependent on its divine source: as his earthly life wanes, his face is repeatedly described as white until on his deathbed he is translucent alabaster. The implication is that his true nature is only revealed in the post-mortem embrace of God's loving fire, a positive experience only for those whose hearts are diamond-pure and transparent:

> The man who loves God, and is not yet pure, courts the burning of God. . . .
>
> The man whose deeds are evil, fears the burning. But the burning will not come the less that he fears it or denies it.[65]

Falling into the latter category, the philanthropic children's author who secures the future of Nanny and Diamond and his family is Mr. Raymond—"light of the world." His light, however, is suspect, perhaps more "worldly light":[66] although he visits the children's hospital it would appear that this has more to do with market research than compassion,[67] a philanthropy that is more about him than the poor of London.[68] His gaze, like Milton's Satan, is drawn downwards by wealth making him blind to transcendence, something that is reinforced as the narrative draws to a close where we find Nanny and her friend Jim, rescued street children,

breastplate of those who claim to judge in the name of God; instead, it becomes a tool of judgment in God's hand on those who claim to wear such a breastplate.

64. See Manlove, "Reading," 172.

65. *US1* 46.

66. See Manlove, "Reading," 161. Manlove discusses the significance of other names, such as Diamond's father's employer, a Mr. Coleman and the angel-horse, Ruby, noting that the colors black and red relate to the stages of alchemical transformation in the quest for the Philosopher's Stone. Manlove suggests that such alchemical symbolism forces us to look below the "surface" of London to its deeper, more ancient (and more corrupt) roots; that even the "obvious" appearance of reality is deceptive.

67. Knoepflmacher, *Ventures into Childland*, 258.

68. Knoepflmacher suggests that Raymond exemplifies the bourgeois benevolence of such as Dodgson and Ruskin and calls into question the motives and efficacy of middle-class philanthropy. See Knoepflmacher, *Ventures into Childland*, 256. This seems a more plausible reading than John Pennington's view that Raymond—who reads to the children "The Little Lady and the Goblin Prince" (an allusion to MacDonald's forthcoming *The Princess and The Goblin*)—is MacDonald himself. See Pennington, "Alice at the Back," 57.

living in Mr. Raymond's country residence with Diamond and his family. The house, called The Mound, "stood upon a little steep knoll, so smooth and symmetrical that it showed itself at once to be *artificial*."[69] This image of Mr. Raymond's country retreat as a newly-dug grave implies that his attitude to the country, that is, to divine nature, is fundamentally adversarial—an attitude that soon rubs off on the street children to whom he has given refuge. The Mound equates to a fortification against transcendence but neither this, nor his attempts at philanthropic mitigation, can insulate him from death—in his case, not a death to be embraced, as evidenced by Diamond's face which is increasingly beatified as his days grow short, but a vain attempt to stave off the fearful death resulting from trusting in money rather than North Wind. Death comes to us all; how we experience it depends on our ability to be imaginative. The contrast between Mr. Raymond's denial and Diamond's embrace of death is a strong theme in the narrative. The former, by ignoring death and focusing on the mundane, becomes increasingly deathly; in contrast, by embracing death Diamond finds true life.

This narrative proposes that innocence, not depravity, is the natural state of an uneducated ("uncultured") child and that fear of death is a false emotion that has to be learned; it is both *rational*, therefore false because unimaginative, and *irrational* since it is based on false premises. On meeting the "angel of death" for the first time, Diamond "was not yet frightened, for he had not yet learned to be."[70] Fear of death, as Mr. Raymond illustrates, comes from a refusal to embrace it. Early in the narrative, "death" holds out her arms to the child:

> "Will you go with me now, you little Diamond? I am sorry I was forced to be so rough with you," said the lady.
> "I will; yes, I will," answered Diamond, holding out his arms.

But this intuitive embrace is checked by a rational thought: Diamond suddenly realizes he is only wearing his nightgown. North Wind consoles him:

> "Oh, never mind your clothes. You will not be cold. Nobody is cold with the North Wind."
> "I thought everybody was," said Diamond.[71]

---

69. *NW* 352 (emphasis mine).
70. *NW* 13.
71. *NW* 19–20.

This is a direct challenge to the theology that led to the death-bed angst of children.[72] North Wind remarks that she is known by many names which hide her true nature: "Evil Chance, sometimes Ruin; and they have another name . . . which they think the most dreadful of all,"[73] but death should not be thought of as cold:

> That is a great mistake. Most people make it, however. They are cold because they are not with the North Wind, but without it.[74]

MacDonald stresses that the boy never feels the cold when he is traveling with her: held to her breast or wrapped in her hair, he is traveling at her speed, embracing her agenda; the wind is felt only when resisted. Clothes which keep out the cold are symbolic—as is the thin stable wall—of human denial of death and false comfort in material things:[75] the coldness is felt only by those who are "not with the North Wind, but without it," and is an adult, learned response to death. The child, in contrast, simply "stretches out his arms":

> If Diamond had been a little older, and had supposed himself a good deal wiser, he would have thought the lady was joking. But he was not older, and did not fancy himself wiser, and therefore understood her well enough. Again he stretched out his arms.[76]

As the narrative closes, Diamond appears increasingly disconnected from quotidian reality: now that his practical ministrations are over, he has become an appendage, a child who does not need education (since he is now a page boy in the house) and who is increasingly called "silly." "Mr. Raymond advised his father to give him plenty of liberty"[77] and soon we find him "dressed in a suit of blue, from which his pale face and fair hair came out like the loveliest blossom."[78] His duties in the house are merely nominal, indeed "Mrs. Raymond confessed that she often rang her bell just to have once more the pleasure of seeing the lovely stillness of the

---

72. Such as that described by Charles West. See note 49, page 51.
73. *NW* 377.
74. *NW* 20.
75. On the other side of Diamond's thin bedroom wall is "Mr. Dyves's garden," a reference to the rich man in Hades in Luke 16 (*NW* 18). Diamond, in contrast, is in "Abraham's" bosom.
76. *NW* 20.
77. *NW* 351.
78. *NW* 353.

boy's face, with those blue eyes which"—as windows to transcendence—"seemed rather made for other people to look into than for himself to look out of." Even his old street friends, Nanny and Jim, "appeared to regard him as a mere toy, except when they found he could minister to the increase of their privileges or indulgences, when they made no scruple of using him—generally with success."[79]

We have here a child who has outlived his usefulness in the eyes of those he is closest to. He is now a toy, kept for decoration and amusement. At the beginning of his life he is considered "simple" and given little to do except babysitting, now—after a short productive season of provision for his family—he once again finds himself unemployed since those around him consider him unemployable. Keeping a child as a "toy" dressed in finery was a growing trend in Victorian middle-class society, but MacDonald here is painting a picture of a child who is too good for this world and will *never* fit into a conventional role: his true destiny lies beyond death.[80]

When Diamond finally succumbs to death—an event full of ambiguity since he has practically invited it by leaving windows open so that North Wind can visit him—he is found lying white and cold in his room. The closing sentences of the narrator are:

> I walked up the winding stair, and entered his room. A lovely figure, as white and almost as clear as alabaster, was lying on the bed. I saw at once how it was. They thought he was dead. I knew that he had gone to the back of the north wind.[81]

The choice of the word "alabaster" which is "almost clear" is reminiscent of the broken box of perfume poured over the feet of Jesus: Diamond's life has been poured out, not only to save his friends, but as an oblation offered to the unseen eternal power behind North Wind's actions. Is he really dead? Or alive somewhere else? The narrator may be confident—"I saw at once how it was"—but the reader is left feeling unsure, wondering instead whether to side with those who "thought he was dead."

---

79. *NW* 359.

80. For Lisa Hermine Makman, *North Wind* "presents the new toy-child but, strikingly, replays in its narrative the progressive development of the fantasy that children are toys" ("Child's Work is Child's Play," 109). I suggest it is a critique rather than a replay.

81. *NW* 391.

Specific Theological and Social Proposals found in *North Wind*

We conclude this reading of *North Wind* by looking more closely, and critically, at MacDonald's "theology of childhood" as expressed in this narrative—issues which, far from being merely theoretical, lead to incisive criticism of Victorian social attitudes, especially towards children and women.

Childlike Imagination and Obedience

Perhaps in an attempt to reflect his understanding of typical human religious experience, MacDonald has Diamond overtly encountering North Wind early in his life and at his death; in the meantime—the middle section of the book—North Wind is primarily absent implying that Diamond is "walking by faith rather than sight" (and that he is physically healthy), and "faith" is portrayed as an obedient, intuitive, *imaginative* response to situations that, to those around him, appears as folly. When his father is ill, for example, Diamond amuses the baby by singing it a song which, he claims, "baby and I learned out of North Wind's book."[82] The reference is to a book that he and his mother had found lying on a beach, a mysterious volume left there by North Wind with its leaves fluttering in the breeze, containing rambling poems which made no sense to his mother, who simply "thought it might amuse him, though ... couldn't find any sense in it" (rationally meaningless) but which Diamond intuitively understands (imaginatively perceived).[83] Earlier in the narrative, the pages of a dropped Bible also flutter in the wind to reveal the truth of Diamond's name.[84] The message is that both nature and the Bible may only be read truly when their leaves are fluttered by imaginative spiritual discernment—the wind of the Spirit that "blows where it wishes" (John 3:8). Subsequently, in the squalid London lodging, the recollection and recitation of a further poem inspires the diminutive child to harness old Diamond and make a significant amount of money driving (without permission) his father's cab.[85] The message is that such "childish" action—in this case dangerous and naive—is nevertheless "sensible" in that it results

---

82. *NW* 224.
83. *NW* 145.
84. *NW* 21.
85. *NW* 224–27.

from imaginative and intuitive understanding of North Wind's will, a will that is "hidden ... from the wise and prudent" and "revealed ... to babes" (Luke 10:21).[86]

Diamond, the perfect child, is imaginative and obedient with a trust that precedes or overrides risk-assessment. His actions are illogical, naive, and unwise, but MacDonald insists that North Wind (God) protects those who thus trust her. He decides, for example, to walk alone into a dangerous slum to rescue Nanny, despite being warned off by a policeman; intervenes in a case of domestic abuse, and so on. In each case the reader is tempted to side with those who consider him insane, and yet in every case he experiences miraculous preservation and makes a positive impact on his world. MacDonald is dramatizing Paul's claim that "the foolishness of God is wiser than men, and the weakness of God is stronger than men," and that "the wisdom of this world is foolishness with God" (1 Cor 1:25); and, as illustrated by the financial ruin of Mr. Coleman (who had invested all his capital in the ship sunk by North Wind), that "he catches the wise in their own craftiness" (1 Cor 3:19).

But is this merely naive optimism? Certainly here, as elsewhere, God's perfect protection of the perfect child is implied, but I suggest that primarily MacDonald is asking: If death is essentially benign, why do we fear it? Is it not better to take risks and die on the basis that "whoever seeks to save his life will lose it" (Luke 17:33)?[87] As he remarks elsewhere:

> Happy he who, as his sun is going down behind the western, is himself ascending the eastern hill, *returning through old age to the second and better childhood* which shall not be taken from him. For he who turns his back on the setting sun goes to meet the rising sun; and he who loses his life shall find it.[88]

The Implications of MacDonald's Portrayal of Childhood Imagination and Obedience

As noted, Alan Yue once remarked that there are "no children in Wordsworth's poetry."[89] This is, in a sense, a trivial observation since no fictive

---

86. Discussed further on page 141.

87. Cf. Matt 10:39; 16:25; Mark 8:35; Luke 9:24; John 12:25.

88. *DG* 9 (emphasis mine). A scene captured by Arthur Hughes's *Knight of the Sun*, the knight being MacDonald. See Sutherland, "George MacDonald," 216.

89. Plotz, *Romanticism*, 85.

child is "real,"[90] but it does raise an important question: In what sense is Diamond "real"? The next chapter explores this further, but we note here that characters such as Nanny and Jim (the rescued street children) appear more real than Diamond. Their cynicism and worldly wisdom resonates with our experience of real children and contrasts with the "unreal" sentimentality of Diamond, but no character is "real." These are symbols used to challenge, rather than confirm, conceptions of reality. As we look "through" this artwork we find ourselves looking at Diamond's fictive world through his eyes. We are then drawn to view our world as an artwork that mediates divine truth with sight suspicious of the prescriptive pretensions of "adulthood."

Diamond, furthermore, embodies those mental states—a child mind prone to insanity and dreams—most feared by adult Victorians as they were inherently *unknowable*, beyond both rationalization and control. This text proposes that it is "adult" certainty that is illusory rather than the "insanity" and dreams of childhood; thus doubt is to be welcomed since it precipitates fresh vision. The reader must decide whether, and on what grounds, the immediate, "irrational" obedience exemplified by Diamond is reasonable or advisable. Is Christian faith "reasonable or advisable"? MacDonald is dramatizing fundamental theological questions concerning the essential unknowability of God, the shortcomings of human logic, the problem of evil, and the imprecision of human cognition. There is, nevertheless (as in all of MacDonald's work), profound optimism interwoven with profound doubt—a phrase which might summarize Christian faith.

Is Diamond's irrational obedience reasonable? To accuse him of irrationality (or insanity) is to side with those who call him "God's baby," an accusation which MacDonald makes clear is the result of spiritual insensitivity and an inability to perceive the wider picture. The answer must be affirmative if we accept MacDonald's "ontology of imagination" for, as an *ideal* child, as "God's baby," Diamond's imagination is perfect, a pure reflection of its source. His apparently naive confidence has a divine foundation. Thus when, defying rational logic, he decides to rescue Nanny from certain death in a most undesirable part of London and is surrounded by attackers, he is unsurprised when the policeman who had warned him not to carry out his quest becomes his rescuer:

---

90. See page 47.

"You had better have let me come with you, little man," he said, looking down in Diamond's face, which was flushed with his resistance.

"You came just in the right time, thank you," returned Diamond. "They've done me no harm."

"They would have if I hadn't been at hand, though."

"Yes; but you were at hand, you know, so they couldn't."

Perhaps the answer was deeper in purport than either Diamond or the policeman knew.[91]

Diamond's unquestioning obedience to imaginatively perceived divine cues, if taken to its logical conclusion, means that whatever happens he is in the hands of God—an omniscient and sovereign God who foresees and protects those who are obedient. It is a theme repeated throughout the narrative as Diamond experiences one "coincidence" after another.

Four Immediate Objections to this Conclusion

At this point we will consider four objections to this conclusion, with particular attention to the fourth since this sheds light on MacDonald's ontology and methodology.

The first and most trivial objection is that humans are *not* ideal. Recognizing this, this text must be read as an encouragement to live more imaginatively rather than as a demand for unquestioning obedience to perceived truth. While it could be argued that MacDonald has underplayed the need for rational skills in *North Wind*, this does not detract from the core message that obedience is the main requirement of those who claim faith. Faith cannot remain merely theoretical.

A second objection relates to human cognition and epistemology: reflective of his Evangelical upbringing, MacDonald has underplayed the role of community in human discernment, and that in two senses. First, divine truth is not only evident in the Bible and nature as objective truth to be "read," but is the presence of Christ in the Christian community. Perhaps MacDonald's ignoring of this dimension reflects his profound suspicion of the contemporary church which will become more evident as we proceed. That said, MacDonald, with his emphasis on "original

---

91. *NW* 215–16.

blessing," would, in my view, extend this concept to the wider human family carrying the image of God. Diamond's epistemic distance, as it were, from his mother is somewhat worrying in that one would expect God to be influencing Diamond's life through his unique, intimate relationship with her, as well as through other relationships, but this is not evident. Related to this is the biblical insistence that truth is discerned communally. Diamond's stubborn faith that he is "right" is troubling.

A third, less trivial objection concerns the genuineness of human free will. Does the policeman incident simply reflect an omniscient God's foreknowledge, or does God "pre-program" the destiny of individuals? There is a paradox in that MacDonald's emphasis on the need for individual perception (that the role of art, including God's artwork, nature, is to awaken rather than impart meaning) is nevertheless championing a theology that suggests that truth is defined in terms of God's unique will for that individual, a destiny unmodified by individual action. (This is not to say that individual action is inconsequential; on the contrary, *North Wind*'s core message is that there are very negative life outcomes for those who choose to ignore God's will for their life, but such negative outcomes are indicative of "kicking against the goads" of a predetermined life trajectory which does not, apparently, modify God's pre-ordained will or "truth" for that person.) One answer might be to remind ourselves that on the divine side of the "gulf" is a God "teeming with infinite revelations"—that the individual trajectory towards God has infinite possibility, but this does not address the issue of divine micro-management. While MacDonald is rejecting simplistic predeterminism, it would appear from this narrative that the will of a sovereign and omniscient God is nevertheless inexorable and that the best course of human response is to discern and obey.

How God relates to God's creation and God's creatures leads to a fourth question concerning the validity of MacDonald's thought experiment. He is asking: What happens if we place a sinless ideal child in a fallen world? This concept is doubly flawed. First, to be human is to be born into an "impure" environment, the word preferred by David Kelsey to describe our proximate context, and that the "processing" of impurity—how one deals with it—is part of what it means to be fully human. However, such "processing" cannot be considered simply a reaction to *external* stimuli: it necessarily involves dealing with *internal* impurity consequent upon being embedded in an impure quotidian environment. Just as Diamond is androgynous, one could argue he is also morally questionable in having a pre-Edenic innocence that is no longer an option for those born into the real world. David Kelsey argues at length that the quotidian environment is "distorted"—evil and sinful—noting that whereas sin has to do with willful, culpable human behavior (moral distortion is not the normative state of God's good creation), the former may simply result from the finitude of a universe with limited resources: what we *call* "evil" may have its source in God who has chosen to work in a creation which is finite.[92] While MacDonald would counter this objection by insisting that the sector of reality in which we live is merely a moment in God's infinite being, a being to which we have full access, the reality is—and this is fully recognized by him—that to all practical intents and purposes our quotidian world appears finite to us. If MacDonald did not support this view he would be less fixated on escape, through death, to another realm. In other words, the pressure from a finite and impure external world means that even Diamond's perfect response to divine cues may have evil consequences.

Furthermore, from the "internal" perspective, a pre-Edenic child is an impossibility: "impurity" is intrinsic to human nature because of its embeddedness in a distorted world. So while MacDonald might try to distinguish between "being born *in* sin and brought forth in iniquity" and "being born sin and brought forth iniquity,"[93] the distinction is not as black-and-white as he imagines but speaks more of theological focus as exemplified by the contrast between Maurice and Manning. It calls into question MacDonald's supposition that to be made in the image of God necessarily implies inherent goodness. Put differently, a good case might be made for rejecting the doctrine of original sin as a hereditary concept, but this does not mean that humans are immune to quotidian distortions and impurity.

We may conclude, with Kelsey, that—as biblical Wisdom literature emphasizes—the normal everyday human being is normative of God's creation, not some ideal future superhuman (or past state of perfection). Kelsey summarizes thus:

> The real human person is God's good creature precisely in his or her quotidian everydayness and finitude, and not because they satisfy some one, universally applicable, ideal of a human person completely—that is, "perfectly," actualized in all respects. The

---

92. Kelsey, *Eccentric Existence*, 207.
93. *RF* 1:153 (see page 64).

status of "real" human person is not constituted by transcending the quotidian, any more than it is a degraded (i.e. "fallen") version of a historically once or future human perfection.[94]

This is not to say that moral degradation (sin) is normative of God's creatures. Rather, the objection here is that MacDonald, in his attempt to create the ideal child, has created a child which is *not* ideal since it lacks a fundamental aspect of human nature which would make it fully human. He has, it could be argued, broken his own guidelines on moral congruence for in creating a fantasy world he has forgotten that when it comes to morality, the writer "must obey—and take [moral] laws with him into his invented world as well."[95]

A second aspect of this fourth objection concerns Diamond's premature, prepubescent death. Having never reached the age of majority, and therefore not, in the eyes of society, morally accountable, Diamond has never had to deal with adult issues. One must ask, therefore, whether he is in any sense *ideal*, except as an artistic device.

Un-idealizing the child

MacDonald's contribution to the evolution of childhood would not be complete without considering other children portrayed in *North Wind* who, ironically, serve to undermine the Victorian idealization of the child, particularly with regard to sexuality. The portraits of "real" children such as Nanny and Jim help us to form a more holistic picture of MacDonald's understanding of children and childlikeness.

"Cripple Jim" is an abused child whose "mother broke his leg when he wur a kid."[96] Crossing-sweeper Nanny is taken with Jim early in the tale: "I love Jim dearly," she says, "I always keeps off a penny for Jim—leastways as often as I can,"[97] and observes that "Jim was very fond of looking at the man in the moon"[98]—he is drawn by the Spirit towards transcendence; understandably, as a disabled and abused slum-dweller, he longs for escape. As Nanny draws closer to Jim she distances herself from Diamond; eventually the pair of them grow more and more critical,

94. Kelsey, *Eccentric Existence*, 207.
95. *Orts* 316.
96. *NW* 197.
97. *NW* 197.
98. *NW* 313.

"often [saying] to each other that Diamond had a tile loose."⁹⁹ Jim only speaks four words in the narrative. During a thunder storm, as Diamond exults in the transcendent experience, Jim comments about the lightning:

> "It might kill you," said Jim.
> "Oh, no, it mightn't!" said Diamond.¹⁰⁰

The gravitational pull of the moon—offering escape from poverty, disability, and "artificiality"—is now ignored. Jim is visionless and earthbound. Despite being surrounded by nature in his country lodgings with Mr. Raymond, he can only be factual about lightning. MacDonald is suggesting that environment is of less consequence than will and orientation (Jim's entrancement with the moon begins in a slum); that Jim's choice to side with Nanny and focus entirely on the "facts" of reality has robbed him of transcendent vision. And Nanny, whose first address in the slum was "Paradise Row . . . next door to the Adam and Eve"¹⁰¹ is, despite the improvement in her lot, still living in a fallen state. In her eyes, "Jim was a *reasonable* being, Diamond . . . at best only an amiable, over-grown baby, whom no amount of expostulation would ever bring to talk sense, not to say think it."¹⁰² In Nanny and Jim we have a foil for Diamond's goodness, demonstrating that childlikeness is not always an attribute of children.

We noted earlier the Victorian fear of childhood sexuality. Perhaps Diamond exemplifies Plotz's Child, a splendid being "unmarked by time, place, class or gender" typical of male-authored fantasy literature.¹⁰³ Perhaps he reflects, as Helen Sutherland suggests, the Pre-Raphaelite practice of deliberately painting androgynous other-worldly figures with ambiguous expression to underline their ideality. Burne-Jones, for example, remarks:

> I mean by a picture a beautiful, romantic dream of something that never was, never will be—in a light better that any light that ever shone—in a land no one can define or remember, only desire—and the forms are divinely beautiful.¹⁰⁴

99. *NW* 358.
100. *NW* 364.
101. *NW* 193.
102. *NW* 346 (emphasis mine).
103. See page 46.
104. Helen Sutherland notes that MacDonald was acquainted with the Burne-Jones family and had an intimate working relationship with Arthur Hughes who so successfully captured the spirit of *North Wind*. Sutherland, "George MacDonald," 222.

Both views might apply to Diamond, but does this mean that MacDonald is uncritical of contemporary attitudes to real children?

It is clear from *North Wind* and other texts that sexuality is never far from the surface in MacDonald's work. In *The Light Princess*, for example, the prototype of the story of *Little Daylight* in *North Wind*,[105] the princess is cursed with weightlessness and may only experience gravity when swimming; she swims at night, and one night a prince comes upon her naked form in the water:

> He soon reached the white object, and found that it was a woman. There was not enough light to show that she was a princess, but quite enough to show that she was a lady, for it does not want much light to see that.[106]

Ruskin objected, prior to publication, that it would "not do for the public in its present form" on the grounds that it was "too amorous throughout."[107]

Victorian middle-class adult male attitudes to children and sexuality are, certainly to post-Freudian eyes, questionable. Ruskin was infatuated with the sixteen-year-old Rose La Touche, his "mouse pet," an infatuation that the MacDonalds "were a little troubled about,"[108] and Charles Dodgson's correspondence with the MacDonald family consists mainly of letters to his daughters,[109] and he frequently took Mary, then ten, to the theater in London.[110] It is tempting to read Diamond's prepubescent state as avoiding the need to confront the disturbing implications of sexual awareness. Sally Shuttleworth would probably agree, noting that the Victorian focus on childhood innocence exhibited an ambivalence marked by a paranoia that the opposite might indeed be the case:

> Was childhood, for the Victorians, less an entity or experience in itself than a gloriously empty space, defined pre-eminently by the fact that it did not partake of the sexual feelings which complicated puberty and adult life? Ideas of childhood innocence

---

105. *The Light Princess* appeared first in the novel *Adela Cathcart* (1864).
106. *Fairy Tales* 32.
107. Ruskin, "July 22, 1863."
108. *GMAW* 333.
109. In the two volumes of Carroll's letters (Cohen, *Letters of Lewis Carroll*) there are none addressed to George but many to Louisa and the girls.
110. Sadler, *Expression of Character*, 264.

gained their hold precisely due to equally powerful, underlying fears that the very reverse might be true.[111]

This ambivalence is expressed in *North Wind*.

Despite Diamond's asexuality, there is, as noted, strong eroticism in his encounters with North Wind. Although portrayed as innocent and maternal, the strength of the imagery implies something deeper. At the beginning of the storm scene, North Wind lifts him from the roof "into her bosom . . . like an inconsolable child." He clearly finds consolation as he "[nestles] closer to her grand bosom."[112] Soon he is laughing, "leaning against her bosom"[113] while the storm around rages:

> But so sheltered was he by North Wind's arm and bosom that only at times, in the fiercer onslaught of some curl-billowed eddy, did he recognise for a moment how wild was the storm in which he was carried, nestling in its very core and formative centre.[114]

Here he is at the "core and formative centre" of "mother nature," and after a brief weaning they are reunited: "Diamond nestled to her, and murmured into her bosom,—'Why did you leave me, dear North Wind?'"[115]

For U. C. Knoepflmacher, this is clear evidence that MacDonald has never fully reconciled himself to being prematurely weaned,[116] but, perhaps more significantly and certainly more positively, a firm rejection of the "hideous emblems of maternity" found in the *Alice* books and the gynophobia implied by the all-male cast of Ruskin's *King of the Golden River*.[117] Whereas Ruskin and his peers preferred female passivity, MacDonald's celebration of female sexual power may be read as a rebuttal of the gynophobia of Carroll and Ruskin and of the middle-class attitudes that they represented. This is most strikingly revealed in the short story *Little Daylight* (chapter 28 of *North Wind*) which Mr. Raymond tries out on the children of (presumably) Great Ormond Street Hospital, a story freighted with sexual meaning.

---

111. Shuttleworth, *Mind of the Child*, 195.
112. *NW* 76.
113. *NW* 81.
114. *NW* 82.
115. *NW* 88–89.
116. Knoepflmacher, *Ventures into Childland*, 241; cf. 122.
117. Knoepflmacher, *Ventures into Childland*, 230–31.

Prefacing the chapter with the comment, "I do not know how much of Mr. Raymond's story the smaller children understood," the story is a reworking of *The Light Princess* and concerns a beautiful princess "with the sunniest hair and the loveliest eyes of heavenly blue" who has been cursed by a bad fairy to wake only at night; the curse will only be broken when she is kissed by a prince. Her beauty waxes and wanes with the phases of the moon. Contrasted with her beauty, "so much more painful and sad was the change as her bad time came on. The more beautiful she was in the full moon, the more withered and worn did she become as the moon waned." A voyeuristic prince, chancing upon the radiant girl dancing in the full moon, is entranced by her beauty, but in the power of her "waxing" state, she despises his approaches and he is left to wander the forest, disconsolate. One moonless night he stumbles upon an old hag moaning in the darkness. He finds her repulsive, but, fearing she is about to die, instinctively kisses her, at which point she is resurrected as the beautiful princess, now free from the curse.

Mr. Raymond, an amalgam of Ruskin and Carroll,[118] is telling a tale which reveals his (and therefore their) revulsion of menstrual women, an aversion which must be overcome and which "repudiates the hankering for ever-pure little girls harboured by his two fellow-fantasists"[119] or the reduction of femininity to "aestheticized female shapes gazed from afar." Knoepflmacher further observes that:

> Princess Daylight's story has much to do with Lewis Carroll's wishful constructions of perennially young dream-children and with Ruskin's confession to MacDonald about the shattering discovery that Effie Gray had become a menstrual woman.[120]

This thinly-coded critique of contemporary attitudes to menstrual women[121] with its implied criticism of those such as Dodgson who pre-

---

118. Knoepflmacher insists on this correspondence as evidenced by the close personal friendship between them and the borrowed motifs found in their respective children's stories. See Knoepflmacher, *Ventures into Childland*, 231, 262.

119. Knoepflmacher, *Ventures into Childland*, 262.

120. Knoepflmacher, *Ventures into Childland*, 266.

121. Colin Manlove suggests that *Little Daylight* is primarily concerned with imagination, and that "night and moon" are "symbols of the imagination" (Manlove, "Reading," 169). However, Knoepflmacher's reading seems more plausible: it is difficult to read it otherwise when, apart from monthly cycles, there is also a reference to the "flow of the tide of life" followed by the observation that "there was no chance of the prince wishing to kiss the princess during that period" (*NW* 274, 288).

ferred the company of MacDonald's ten-year-old daughter to adult females[122] set within a narrative which portrays divine power as primarily female, erotic, and anything but passive, throws light on the character of Diamond and MacDonald's conception of childhood. If nothing else, MacDonald cannot be accused of turning a blind eye to puberty with the implication that Diamond's androgyny is not a disapprobation of sexuality, but a conscious literary choice. What, then, are the implications for MacDonald's contribution to the concept of childhood and attitudes to children?

The erotic relationship between North Wind and Diamond can be read as a plea for a more tolerant attitude towards childhood sexuality; that growing sexual awareness in the prepubescent child is divine rather than demonic. Theologically, it is a rejection of crude conceptions of original sin that equate the Fall with sexual activity.[123] This is most evident in *The Light Princess*, which concerns a princess cursed with weightlessness and therefore unable to "fall." She is also unable to cry, with a

---

122. Dodgson's flirting with young girls continued throughout his life. In 1863 he photographed himself inserted between three of MacDonald's daughters with Mrs. MacDonald kneeling to one side, glaring at the camera (Knoepflmacher, *Ventures into Childland*, 161; *GMAW* 344), and his regular visits to the MacDonald household, judging by the bias of the correspondence (note 109, page 88), appear motivated more by female attraction than philosophical discourse. Furthermore, "Canon and Mrs. Liddell were understandably disturbed by the lavish attentions paid to their stunningly beautiful daughters," and, at the age of sixty, he was boasting of having "girl-friends to brighten, one at a time, my lonely life by the sea: all ages from 10 to 24" (Knoepflmacher, *Ventures into Childland*, 157–58). Ruskin was similarly preoccupied. The obsession with Rose La Touche was preceded by the equally fated marriage with the twenty-year-old Effie Gray, a marriage annulled for his failure to consummate it. In 1864, he wrote jokingly to MacDonald: I "can't bear boys," expressing a preference for girls, of which he has four who "don't expect me to teach them the catechism" (Ruskin, "April 13, 1864"). In Greville's hagiography of his father, the gloss given to Ruskin's flawed relationship with Rose is remarkable for its apparent willful disregard of his father's concerns. He considers it wholly unsurprising, for example, that a man with Ruskin's "normal creative vitality," "love of children," and "adoration of women" should reject the Christian faith on the grounds that it was that faith which had denied him access to Rose. "It is small wonder," writes Greville, "that he cannot conform to the creeds that deny the divinity of those gifts." Even more remarkably, Greville sees this as an example of "the tyranny of worldly wisdom which [his] father had set himself to oppose" (*GMAW* 336–37). And on the annulment: "The story reflects nothing but honour upon Ruskin—unless he lied to my father, or my father to me—one supposition as utterly incredible as the other" (*GMAW* 331). See also Knoepflmacher, *Ventures into Childland*, 139n29.

123. Note 130, page 269.

prelapsarian, shallow personality having never had to face moral choice, and is, by implication, on the verge of puberty and therefore not yet an adult. In this tale, MacDonald makes much of her nocturnal liaisons with the prince who, as he embraces her (implied) naked body, enables her to "fall" into the lake where they swim together. In Romantic symbolism, water was associated with femininity, and MacDonald is clearly equating her fall into the lake with growing sexual awareness, if not union (a fact not lost on Ruskin, precipitating his objections), but what is missing is any negative judgment from MacDonald; rather the opposite as he equates growing sexual awareness with the couple's increasing joy and maturity. The negative judgment is reserved for the princess's parents, the king and queen, who despite their maturity are portrayed as sexually naive (at the beginning of the tale the king asks his wife for a child, apparently unaware of his role in the matter) and unconnected with reality. The narrative thus challenges the common Victorian equation of sex with sin.[124] It may, however, also indicate a wider rejection of Victorian assumptions about the child-mind: that the mystery of the child-mind should be equated with the mystery of divinity rather than with incipient insanity or hidden evil. It also stresses that God is not male.

Little Daylight is a plea for the re-evaluation of male attitudes to femininity, no doubt fueled by the attentions paid by Dodgson to MacDonald's own daughters. Of particular note is the appearance of the princess after the princely kiss. In her hag-like state after the "change" had come upon her, the prince carries the emaciated form towards shelter and help:

> "Mother, mother!" he said. "Poor mother!" and kissed her on the withered lips.
> She started; and what eyes they were that opened upon him! . . . She stood upright on her feet. Her hood had dropped, and her hair fell about her. The first gleam of the morning was caught on her face: that face was bright as the never-aging Dawn, and her eyes were lovely as the sky of darkest blue. The prince recoiled in overmastering wonder. It was Daylight herself whom he had brought from the forest! He fell at her feet, nor dared to look up until she laid her hand upon his head. He rose then.

124. Knoepflmacher, *Ventures into Childland*, 138.

> "You kissed me when I was an old woman: there! I kiss you when I am a young princess," murmured Daylight.—"Is that the sun coming?"[125]

Nocturnal voyeurism has been transformed into the diurnal worship of a female deity of immense power whose face is not only "bright as the never-aging Dawn," but whose eyes—like North Wind's[126] and Diamond's—are windows to eternity, "lovely as the sky of darkest blue," and who is no longer at a distance but, using imagery from Saint John's encounter with the risen Christ (Rev 1:17), kisses her male worshipper. The nocturnal dancer may be read as a projection of male fantasy—an unattainable phantasm—a marked contrast with the transfigured woman now recognized by the prostrate prince as the product of divine "fantasy" and, unlike his own fantasies, eminently real.

Many readings are possible relating to the clandestine, distant, dysfunctional, immature (and so on) attitudes of males towards female sexuality, but from a theological perspective there is a clear message—that girls and women are "divine"; that is, not idealized objects for male gratification, but creatures also made in the image of God. The male response, as illustrated by the prince who "recoiled in overmastering wonder . . . [and] fell at her feet"[127] should be *pure* worship, recognizing that "the deepest, purest love of a woman has its well-spring in him";[128] that only the recognition of female "divinity" can be the basis for genuine relationship between the sexes, with the corollary that, as male *and* female are made in God's image, God is both "male" and "female."

The narrative insists that adult femininity, particularly menstruation, is not to be feared or considered impure but is part of what it means to be truly human. The quest for childlikeness, therefore, does not imply a negation of human maturity or sexuality, despite Diamond's androgyny. If, as Judith Plotz remarks, the "separation of adult from child defines the Wordsworthian [Romantic] child,"[129] this narrative goes *some* way to healing that divorce. Furthermore, the transformation of this princess going through puberty into a "goddess" precludes a reading of MacDonald's notion of childhood as simply a negation of adulthood.

125. *NW* 290–91.
126. *NW* 76, 114.
127. *NW* 291.
128. *US1* 24.
129. See page 43.

Redeeming the Child

MacDonald's project is to redeem the child and make the child the mediator of redemption. His fictional children dramatize the rejection of original sin; instead, the *imago Dei* is the image of a loving father *and* mother. The child is, therefore, a theological concept challenging the foundations of contemporary anthropology. In *North Wind*, MacDonald proposes six attributes that characterize the true child which we now summarize.

The first is imagination: that a childlike imagination is needed not just to perceive the "afterlife," but also *this* life. It is not a rejection of intellection, but a Coleridgean plea for intellect to be led by imagination. The child embodies a pre-adult, almost prelapsarian, state of human development which is closer to the divine image than that displayed by an adult who has falsely learned mistrust and fear—the fruit of decontextualized logic and unthinking convention. But, as the discussion of *Little Daylight* has shown, this should not be read as a trivial denial of adulthood.

The second is trust evidenced by obedience, a proposal that implies God is worthy of such trust—that unquestioning obedience is always rewarded and, if necessary, corrected. It is a rejection of conceptions of God that imply moral uncertainty. That such unquestioning obedience, based as it is on subjective imaginative cues, might be misguided is explored as we consider Diamond's "unwise" choices. Diamond's perfect intuition of God's will, allied with God's perfect benevolence and foreknowledge, always results in his vindication: the "what if" questions concerning imperfect cognition or the place of human will are left for the reader to ponder, but the implication is that—even in the last resort—should death result it is not to be feared.

The third is the humanity of the child—it is already fully human and made in God's image. Diamond's premature death—his failure to reach earthly adulthood—should not be viewed as failure. In a society that valued children for what they would become, MacDonald is celebrating the child for what it already is, a complete human being, acceptable as such in God's sight and representative of the race, but furthermore, that the imaginative, trusting, obedient child is closer to God's image than the potentially misguided but confident adult.

The fourth is priesthood: the child in some sense mediates redemption. Diamond functions not as a savior but as a mediator between heaven and earth. He carries a priestly name that bridges the heights of heaven and the depths of the earth, exposing the darkness of the latter to the light of the former. Like the jewel in Aaron's priestly robe, Diamond is a prism refracting heavenly light. For his Victorian contemporaries the name would also bring to mind those who worked in the mining industry, "diamond crackers" who worked coal, "black diamond."[130] The child is a "window" to transcendence.

The fifth is innocence—sinlessness. In a culture obsessed with childhood depravity resulting from either original sin or simian ancestry, where those such as Henry Maudsley, using words not dissimilar to Ruskin's, accused Romantics like MacDonald of "poetical idealism and willing hypocrisy by which a man ignores realities,"[131] MacDonald portrays this ideal child as being sinless and as having a direct, intuitive connection with God. All these childhood attributes reflect back on the God in whose image humanity is made, notably in relation to the perfect *imago Dei*, Christ.

The final and sixth attribute is doubt: evidence of the lack of "adult" pride—the false security of second-hand, conventional faith. The child accepts the provisionality of its vision and understanding of the world. Those humbly trying to make sense of the world—Diamond, his mother, and even God's agent North Wind—all express doubt. It is those that have no doubts—such as Nanny and Jim, convinced of Diamond's insanity—that are lacking discernment. Doubt is a positive force, "the first knock at our door of things that are not yet, but have to be, understood;"[132] an awareness of limitation and a goad to positive action rather than nascent apostasy. Doubt is the valid obverse of faith, the latter reflecting childlike trust despite the former.

God's child, North Wind ("mother nature") is also feeling her way subjectively in this deceptive world where evil claims to be good and goodness sometimes wears the mask of evil. Conscience must be her guide: "when I do [what the "far-off song" requires] I feel all right, and when I don't I feel all wrong." That "nature" sometimes "gets it wrong" or misinterprets divine intention is worrying, implying that God is not so sovereign after all and an ineffective communicator. As for the origin of that song, North Wind notes that according to rumors spread by East Wind (an unreliable source since "one does not exactly know how much

---

130. Makman, "Child's Work is Child's Play," 110.
131. Note 70, page 56.
132. *US2* 201.

to believe of what she says, for she is very naughty sometimes"), "it is all managed by a baby."[133]

This last phrase indicates the centrality of the child in MacDonald's theology: even God is, in some sense, "a baby." But before (in chapter 5) outlining this theology, it is instructive to meet some of the children in MacDonald's realist fiction.

---

133. *NW* 67.

4

The Child in MacDonald's Realist Fiction

Approaching MacDonald's Realist Fiction

T. S. Eliot observed that:

> The more perfect the artist, the more completely separate in him will be the man who suffers and the mind which creates; the more perfectly will the mind digest and transmute the passions which are its material.[1]

Perhaps C. S. Lewis's observation that in literature MacDonald has "no place in its first rank—perhaps not even its second"[2] stems primarily from his inability to achieve this separation, particularly in his realist fiction, as evidenced by regular authorial intrusions and didacticism. One might also mention poor plot development, stereotypical characters, prolixity, and implausibility (even by the standards of fairyland). However forgivingly one reads many of his novels, the words "good art" seldom come to mind. But this does not mean he has nothing important to say. This chapter explores what that might be.

Without committing the intentional fallacy—evaluating a work on the basis of supposed authorial intent rather than the actual work—we may, nevertheless, legitimately draw conclusions that MacDonald may not have intended. First, he himself encouraged this on the basis that

1. Eliot, *Sacred Wood*, 48.
2. Lewis, *George MacDonald*, 14.

images, symbols, and words carry divine meaning opaque to the writer: "A genuine work of art must mean many things; the truer its art, the more things it will mean."[3] Second, as Schleiermacher observed, the artist is often oblivious to his or her own processes and context, leading to the observation that as critics, "We understand the artful discourses of others better than they do themselves."[4] For these reasons, and those explored in chapter 1, MacDonald's prose should not, therefore, simply be viewed as illustrating an underlying stratum of bedrock theology. As Hans Frei notes regarding narrative writing, we should not ask whether the subject matter or the narrative itself is the most meaningful:

> The question is illegitimate or redundant. For whatever the situation that may obtain in other types of texts, in narrative of the sort in which character, verbal communications, and circumstances are each determinate of the other and hence of the theme itself, the text, the verbal sense, and not a profound, buried stratum underneath constitutes or determines the subject matter itself.[5]

Fiction, Frei stresses, is not *illustrative* of what someone thinks, but *constitutive* of it.[6] We must not, therefore, be overly simplistic in our critical evaluation of MacDonald's narratives, prematurely dismissing them as bad art: they are not just illustrative of his theology as he sees it, but constitutive of it in a manner of which even he may not be aware.

"Few of his novels are good and none is very good," remarked Lewis, but he does allow that "what he does best is fantasy." In a similar vein, Chesterton remarked that MacDonald gave us jewels in a "somewhat uneven setting."[7] Lewis's anthology is a collection of such jewels—aphorisms mined, primarily, from MacDonald's theological essays, a task which Lewis described as "one of exhumation."[8] Such jewels are no doubt valuable, but the critic must also consider that "uneven setting," his fictive ontology. Context is as important as content.

Genre is also as issue. *North Wind* is typical of many of MacDonald's novels that focus on idealized children or childlike protagonists who

---

3. *Orts* 317; cf. 5 (see page 65).
4. Frei, *Eclipse of Biblical Narrative*, 298.
5. Frei, *Eclipse of Biblical Narrative*, 280.
6. Frei, *Eclipse of Biblical Narrative*, 280.
7. *GMAW* 13.
8. Lewis, *George MacDonald*, 14, 17.

seem curiously impervious to the corrosiveness of life and untouched by its squalor. They appear singled out by God for special favors, smile when abused, commune with nature, and, as we discovered when we met Diamond, precociously indulge in "metaphysics." Inspired by such as Novalis,[9] such novels appear at first sight to be *Bildungsromane*, a genre focusing on the maturation of the protagonist through his or her life journey. To speak of a "realist *Bildungsroman*," however, is an oxymoron. Stern observes that the *Bildungsroman*—a style initiated by Goethe and which Frei notes "was to reach its apex in Goethe's *Wilhelm Meister*"[10]—is essentially unreal and rooted in the practices of pietistic confessionary tracts "which cling to the genre throughout its history"; also identified is its didactic nature, noting that it is "designed to let the hero 'eat up the background' and to fill the foreground."[11] Reflecting the observation made regarding Diamond in the previous chapter, the *social* truth of an interdependent self is barely relevant. Instead, as often in MacDonald's fiction, we are faced with individuals such as Diamond who appear disconnected from society and quotidian reality. "The genre," Stern concludes, "is *solipsistic* and *unrealistic*."[12] The distance from realism perhaps accounts for our lack of sympathy for many of MacDonald's idealized child characters, feeling that if not deserving of abuse they are at least in some measure inviting it. We feel little sympathy because they appear unreal.

In contrast, the realist author, Stern insists, must be "*unambiguously committed to the world.*" This clearly does not apply to MacDonald, committed as he is to the afterlife (and fairyland). Furthermore, if we accept Stern's definition of realism as "connoting a way of depicting, describing a situation in a faithful, accurate, 'life-like' manner... [which] necessarily means in some sense faithfully representing the real world,"[13] then clearly MacDonald's realist novels should not be labelled as such. As we approach his "realist" novels, therefore, it is important not to prematurely dismiss

---

9. There are many parallels between *Heinrich von Ofterdingen*, for example, and MacDonald's work. In the latter's "Curdie" stories, for example, as in *Heinrich*, miners sing and use poetry to defeat evil monsters. In *Heinrich*, we also find the prototype of "the oldest man of all" in *The Golden Key*. See Novalis, *Henry of Ofterdingen*, 103–4; cf. *Fairy Tales* 137–38.

10. Frei, *Eclipse of Biblical Narrative*, 211.

11. Stern, *On Realism*, 101.

12. Stern, *On Realism*, 101 (emphasis mine).

13. Stern, *On Realism*, 40, 42.

them as "unreal" on the basis of faulty classification. Lewis observed that MacDonald's novels are at their best when they "depart most from the canons of novel-writing, and that in two directions":

> Sometimes they depart in order to come nearer to fantasy, as in the whole character of the hero in *Sir Gibbie* or the opening chapters of *Wilfrid Cumbermede*. Sometimes they diverge into direct and prolonged preachments which would be intolerable if a man were reading for the story, but which are in fact welcome because the author, though a poor novelist, is a supreme preacher.[14]

With this in mind, we first turn to *Sir Gibbie* and then to *Wilfrid Cumbermede*.

The Innocent Child

If Diamond is a prophet, Gibbie—the hero of *Sir Gibbie* (1879)—is a type of Christ. Not only is he fundamentally innocent and untainted by sin, he is also mute—"as a sheep before its shearers is silent" (Isa 53:7)—and carries a cross on his back, scars cut by the gamekeeper's whip as a result of muteness being misinterpreted as guilt. In some sense he is carrying the sin of humanity.[15]

We first meet eight-year-old Gibbie crouched in a "narrow dirty lane" in Aberdeen ("the grey city") sifting the gutter slurry for a lost earring. Implausibly but triumphantly successful, he "sucked it to clear it from the last of the gutter" and, after thumping through "street after street" on bare feet, returns it to the grateful baker's daughter, receiving no reward for his trouble.[16] The child, it is proposed, will always find what it seeks. *Gibbie* also confirms the thesis in *North Wind*: that exercising faith provides immunity from evil—even the filth of a Victorian gutter; Gibbie does not contract cholera. MacDonald explicitly states his thesis thus: "In proportion to the falsehood in us are we exposed to the falsehood of others,"[17] the implication being that all evil stems from "falsehood."

---

14. Lewis, *George MacDonald*, 17.

15. For a more detailed discussion of Gibbie's innocence, see de Jong, "Innocence of George MacDonald."

16. *SG* 3–5.

17. *SG* 326.

So despite his starvation diet, "Gibbie's health was splendid. His senses were also marvellously acute,"[18] and, although both whipped and later shot by his nemesis the gamekeeper, appears little troubled by his experiences. It is theology which minimizes Jesus's observation that "in the world you will have tribulation" (John 16:33)—trouble that has real, negative consequences.[19] Here, as elsewhere, MacDonald's portrayal of evil is unconvincing (unlike, say, Dostoevsky's abused children):[20] he seems to have an authorial disinclination to face its true horror.

Gibbie is an idea, not a child. He has "notable eyes . . . [of] a deep blue" that, like those of the princess in *Little Daylight*, are windows to a transcendent realm.[21] Contrasting with his muteness, in his eyes "diffused meaning seemed in them to deepen almost to speech." His face is "luminous" and surrounded by "hair which stuck out from his head in every direction,"[22] reminiscent of Wordsworth's daisy, described as a—

> Sweet *silent* creature!
> That breath'st with me in sun and air,
> Do thou, as thou art wont, repair My heart with gladness, and a share
> Of thy meek nature![23]

Gibbie's "meek nature" also "repairs the heart" of others, and MacDonald's Wordsworth essay, which quotes these lines, concludes by reinforcing the view, central in *Sir Gibbie*, that nature is the expression of God's imagination, an expression that is "certainly higher than mere intellectual teaching":

> If the world proceeded from the imagination of God, and man proceeded from the love of God, it is easy to believe that that which proceeded from the imagination of God should rouse the best thoughts in the mind of a being who proceeded from the love of God. This I think is the relation between man and the world.[24]

---

18. *SG* 7.

19. Such as "mockings and scourgings . . . chains and imprisonment" (Heb 11:36-37), and so on.

20. Such as the serf boy thrown to the dogs in Dostoevsky, *Brothers Karamazov*, 1:284.

21. Note 125, page 92.

22. *SG* 1–2.

23. *Orts* 251 (emphasis mine).

24. *Orts* 251, 254.

Gibbie, the perfect *imago Dei*, exhibits these attributes: he "proceeds from the love of God" exhibiting Christ-like perfection, and in his affinity with nature, engages "the imagination of God." He and nature are the narrative's windows on eternity. Like "Dia-mond," he mediates between heaven and earth.

Such affinity with nature is demonstrated, for example, when Gibbie finds sanctuary with an old hill shepherd and his wife. The shepherd accedes to Gibbie being trialed with the sheepdog despite his obvious concern that mute Gibbie "canna speyk to the dog."[25] Happily, however, at their first meeting:

> The dog looked up into his face, noting every glance and gesture, and, partly from sympathetic instinct, that gift lying so near the very essence of life, partly from observation of the state of affairs in respect of the sheep, divined with certainty what the duty required of him was, and was off like a shot.
>
> "The twa dumb craturs un'erstan' ane anither better nor I un'erstan' aither o' them," said Robert to his wife when they came home.[26]

This last sentence reflects the Romantic view that "the more schooling, the less childhood";[27] that real human childhood is "natural" and includes "sympathetic instinct, that gift lying so near the very essence of life." Here, both schooled by nature, Gibbie and the dog have a natural affinity.

However, such scenes are unconvincing and appear to trouble MacDonald. For example, at one point Gibbie finds refuge in a seedy waterfront bar, however, "Evil language and coarse behavior alike passed over him, without leaving the smallest stain upon heart or conscience, desire or will."[28] Evil, for Gibbie, is water off a duck's back. This unlikely state of affairs leads MacDonald to remark:

> If anyone thinks I am unfaithful to human fact, and over-charge the description of this child, I on my side doubt the experience of that man or woman. I admit the child a rarity, but a rarity in

---

25. This Abrahamic couple regard Gibbie as "the son of [their] old age" (*SG* 205).
26. *SG* 138.
27. Plotz, *Romanticism*, 33.
28. *SG* 42.

the right direction, and therefore a being with whom humanity has the greater need to be acquainted.[29]

That MacDonald believes he has been "*faithful* to human fact" is, I suggest, doubtful, otherwise he would not have felt the need to mention it: like the Little Ones in *Lilith*,[30] Gibbie's innocence is not merely sinlessness but an impossible prelapsarian naivety. Rather, this is a "making-strange" in order to force a reconsideration of concepts of reality.[31] Gibbie, like Diamond, is considered an "innocent," "a born idiot," an "odd-looking lad . . . [a] strange-looking creature . . . a mad-like object" by many,[32] yet is brought before us as the exemplary "child in the midst" who has chosen to be obedient to Christ (for his devotion to "the Presence" in nature is synonymous with such obedience).[33] However, unlike Jesus who brings before us an ordinary child, MacDonald brings before us "Jesus" in Gibbie, described and perceived as "a *rarity*." This "divine idiot" (as the narrator calls him),[34] like Diamond, also suggests that godly sanity is perceived as idiocy by the ungodly, but is this "innocent" (that is, sinless and naive) child truly "a being with whom humanity has the greater need to be acquainted" or simply a deceptive and unattainable ideal? Phrasing this question theologically: does this idealized "true child" reflect the biblical call to become "like children"?

This narrative is not realist. It must be considered as either "fairy story" (the absence of fairies notwithstanding), hagiography, or iconography: that is, fantasy that gives us a new perspective on reality, a legendary (semi-fictional) account of a real saintly character (the child is "a rarity" but—he maintains—based on reality), or a sacramental stylized icon pointing beyond itself to transcendent reality. In some measure it is all of these. Either way, we are dealing with art that evokes an aesthetic response, an issue we will consider later, but two theological proposals are clear: first, that it is possible to live "innocently" in the quotidian

---

29. *SG* 43. I am grateful to John Pridmore for drawing attention to some of the issues developed in this chapter, including MacDonald's awareness of Gibbie's implausibility. See Pridmore, "Estimate of Childhood," 69.

30. See page 203.

31. Discussed further in chapter 6, pages 187–91.

32. *SG* 229–30, 241. The faithful shepherdess, Janet, is also disparaged by the pragmatic farmer's wife as a "sort of heaven-favoured idiot" (*SG* 201).

33. Gibbie is tutored by "Mother Nature"—God's "embodied thoughts" (*SG* 58; *Orts* 320).

34. *SG* 250.

context, and second, that those who make such a choice are immune from the consequences of evil. We now consider a third proposition: that "children" are not only immune from the consequences of evil, but help to neutralize it.

Sir Gibbie suggests that all evil is God's blunt instrument to bring about repentance. As a consequence, MacDonald inadvertently champions the doctrine of election (something he explicitly renounces),[35] for the only explanation for Gibbie's superhuman ability to resist and overcome evil is that although "he knew not the Presence," "The Presence, indeed, was with him. . . . Yea, the Presence was in his very soul."[36] Indeed, in perhaps an unfortunate choice of words, "Gibbie was one of those few *elect* natures to whom obedience is a delight."[37]

Thus a widespread flood, that some consider a second Genesis deluge, is not "natural evil" but "natural good."[38] It is one of God's "evil" sheepdogs that worry the wanderer back to the fold (for the good shepherd commands "a terrible set of sheep-dogs," including "pain, fear, anxiety, and shame . . . sacred creatures [that] work[ed] the will of the Father").[39] Ignoring the wider devastation, MacDonald's focus is uniquely on the cathartic effect of this major incident on a small, impotent group huddled for shelter in a Noah's ark of a farmhouse that becomes an island in a sea of floodwater. They are morally challenged: some respond positively, others do not. It is God's mercy on them; good which helps to shape their moral character and therefore eternal destiny. Only Gibbie is empowered to leave the island and rescue others. The picture is one of a divine puppet-master ensuring that "all things work together for good," for the faithful *and* the reprobate, protecting the former from harm and using the negative responses of the latter to contribute to their eventual reformation. Unlike George Eliot's flood in *The Mill on the Floss*, there are no well-meaning Maggies who rescue Toms (convinced God is with

---

35. See, for example, *US2* 244.
36. *SG* 88.
37. *SG* 139 (emphasis mine).
38. *SG* 192–233.
39. "Sermon by Dr. George MacDonald," 30. On returning to the city, Gibbie observes, "The Master was in its streets as certainly as on the rocks of Glashgar [the upland pasture]. Not one sheep did he lose sight of, though he could not do so much for those that would not follow, and had to have the dog sent after them!" (*SG* 249; cf. *US2* 194).

them) only to be embraced by a watery death.[40] It is a Genesis deluge without judgement on the wicked.

Sir Gibbie suggests that *all* suffering is purgatorial—a "necessary evil" to bring about moral reform—but MacDonald makes a more profound theological proposal: he suggests that the suffering of children such as Gibbie, "a copy in small of the good shepherd,"[41] absorbs evil *on behalf of others*; that children suffer vicariously by sharing Christ's suffering, a curious proposal from one who explicitly rejects substitutionary atonement theories. In *The Hope of the Gospel* he makes this clear:

> Very different are the good news Jesus brings us from certain prevalent representations of the gospel, founded on the pagan notion that suffering is an offset for sin, and culminating in the vile assertion that the suffering of an innocent man, just because he is innocent, yea perfect, is a satisfaction to the holy Father for the evil deeds of his children.[42]

This reveals a paradox. On the one hand, MacDonald's focus is very much on sin—evil as human immorality—yet, on the other, Gibbie's suffering is somehow dealing with "evil" on another level as if it were a substance divorced from agency. For example, after being cut by the gamekeeper's whip, Gibbie instinctively staggers to the upland pasture to find refuge. He approaches the cottage of the old shepherd and his wife. As she stands in the doorway, like John before the glorified Christ, he "fell on his face at her feet like one dead" (cf. Rev 1:17), however here the roles are reversed: it is "Christ" who has fallen at the feet of his disciple. On seeing the cross cut into his back, she wonders:

> Could it be that the Lord was still, child and man, suffering for his race, to deliver his brothers and sisters from their sins?—wandering, enduring, beaten, blessing still? accepting the evil, slaying it, and returning none? his patience the one rock where evil word finds no echo; his heart the one gulf into which the dead-sea wave rushes with no recoil; the one abyss of destroying love, into which all wrong tumbles, and finding no reaction, is lost, ceases for evermore?[43]

---

40. "God has taken care of me," says Maggie, "to bring me to you" (Eliot, *Mill on the Floss*, 520).

41. *SG* 139.

42. *HG* 81.

43. *SG* 123.

John Pridmore notes that the words "the one abyss of destroying love" are "rewritten, almost as an afterthought, in the margin of a manuscript repeatedly scored and written across." He observes:

> Something more is being claimed here than that [sic] the notion, that MacDonald more than once entertains, that every child comes to us as Jesus born anew.[44]

This is certainly Gibbie's posture: he "accepts evil, slays it, and returns none." He is not so much *like* Christ as *part of* Christ. In other words, just as natural evil such as floods cathartically purge the landscape and those within it, the suffering of the child purges the world of evil. Pridmore concludes that MacDonald is indeed suggesting that childhood suffering has atoning value.

As the cast are temporarily marooned in the island farmhouse, the farmer's wife, Janet, explores this idea. Reflecting on a statement made by one of her guests—that those such as Gibbie make the world "less like hell"—she ponders on Paul's enigmatic words in Colossians 1:24:

> Were there always innocents in the world, who in their own persons, by the will of God, and unknown to themselves, carried on the work of Christ, filling up that which was left behind of the sufferings of their Master—women, children, infants, idiots—creatures of sufferance, with souls open to the world to receive wrong, that it might pass and cease?[45]

Dostoevsky (or at least Ivan Karamazov) would no doubt question the divine morality of using such innocents as channels "unknown to themselves" to purge the world of evil.[46] Nevertheless, here MacDonald *is* exploring this belief: inasmuch as such "innocents" are part of Christ's earthly body, the community of saints, so they share in this absorbing, purgatorial office. In Janet's words: "little furnaces they, of the consuming fire, to swallow up and destroy by uncomplaining endurance—the divine

---

44. Pridmore, "Estimate of Childhood," 70.

45. *SG* 227. The absence of men from this list suggests that the stereotypical dominant male—that Charles Kingsley proposed should be "like a knight of old" riding forth knowing "that the kingdom of nature, like the kingdom of heaven, must be taken by violence"—is far from "innocent" (Buckland, *Novel Science*, 185).

46. For Ivan Karamazov, children being "punished for their fathers who have eaten the apple . . . is an argument from another world, an argument that is incomprehensible to the human heart here on earth" (Dostoevsky, *Brothers Karamazov*, 1:278).

destruction!"⁴⁷ In other words, childlike innocence is not only impervious to evil, but opposes and destroys it. However, one must distinguish between childhood suffering being contributive to the "fire" that helps *others* to turn from their sin, and suffering being a vicarious offset somehow balancing the universal scales. It is this distinction that MacDonald makes in his criticism of popular atonement theories, and one which, perhaps, Pridmore does not.

That what humans perceive as "evil" is essentially a divine purgatorial fire leads to the view that evil has no purchase on the innocent child since it has no need of reform. The radiating, purifying "energy" of God traverses the diamond-child perfectly; no "heat" is generated as there is no sinful resistance—no "dark matter."⁴⁸ Instead, the child itself becomes a coal in that fire, or rather, a window to the divine furnace, as it embraces God. The fire only burns the unchildlike—a fire of which quotidian "evil" (such as floods) are an expression. It is a perennial theme. In *A Rough Shaking*, for example, we meet a similarly disadvantaged child, Clare Skymer, whose earliest memory is of (perhaps) the Lisbon earthquake, the "Auschwitz of the eighteenth century" when thousands died while worshipping on All Saints' Day in 1755.⁴⁹ It is, however, a sanitized "Auschwitz" in that despite his mother being killed and him being separated from his father, no serious harm befalls Clare since he is the embodiment of "pure righteousness."⁵⁰ Destitute Clare, like Gibbie, is fostered and fed by various surrogate parents and nature until, years later, he is miraculously reunited with his father through a series of improbable "coincidences." God is working hard behind the scenes, once again implying a measure of election.

MacDonald's choice to focus on the positive outcome for this one child, rather than those maimed and killed, is, at best, a lesson that each individual is precious in God's sight and that it is that individual's response to God that counts. At worst, though, it is a caricature of lived reality that strongly suggests MacDonald's theology of evil is flawed.

---

47. *SG* 227.

48. MacDonald, having studied physics, would have been aware of infra-red radiation—the "calorific rays" described by William Herschel to the Royal Society in March 1800—that would heat anything but a perfectly transparent body. Satan is thus conceived as the perfect "black body," "the great Shadow" in *Lilith*.

49. Mary Ann Gillies suggests the story is based on an earthquake that rocked MacDonald's home in Italy in 1887. See Gillies, *Professional Literary Agent*, 189n41.

50. *RS* 206.

Leaving to one side the issue that (if he had Lisbon in mind) thousands died in agony while trusting in God as collapsing churches buried them, Clare's smiles in response to abuse mean that some, as in the cases of both Gibbie and Diamond, "imagined the boy a simpleton."[51] In short, both fictively and in "reality," one must conclude something is not quite "right" with this child or MacDonald's doctrine of evil.

More worryingly, perhaps, is the idealization of social deprivation. The narrator remarks of Clare Skymer:

> He was often cold and always hungry, but his life was anything but dull. The man who does not know where his next meal is to come from, is seldom afflicted with ennui. That is the monopoly of the enviable with nothing to do, and everything money can get them. A foolish west-end life has immeasurably more discomfort in it than that of a street Arab. The ordinary beggar, while in tolerable health, finds far more enjoyment than most fashionable ladies.[52]

The "ordinary beggar" here, I suggest, is not the fruit of MacDonald's divine imagination but of his human fancy.[53] MacDonald could not have been completely blind to the suffering and death of so many "street Arabs."[54] Neither, having worked in Bolton in England's northern industrial heartland in 1855, would he have been unaware that, having survived childbirth, numerous children only lived a few poverty-stricken and exploitative years. Few "street Arabs" would have been in "tolerable health," and although "seldom afflicted with ennui" were no doubt afflicted in worse ways. Yet MacDonald says of Clare: "Not once yet had he lost heart. In very virtue of unselfishness and lack of resentment, he was strong. Not once had he shed a tear for himself, not once had he pitied his own condition."[55] We must conclude that this child is not human or, more to the point, not symbolic of true humanity.

---

51. RS 289; cf. 162, 252, 376.
52. RS 291.
53. A mistake MacDonald warns against (*Orts* 41).
54. Plotz suggests that terms such as "street Arabs" were used as a coping mechanism to avoid having to face the suffering of real children. See Plotz, *Romanticism*, 35–38.
55. RS 291.

The Abused and Disturbed Child

Annie in *Alec Forbes of Howglen*

A more genuine image of child suffering is found in Annie, who plays opposite (and eventually marries) Alec in *Alec Forbes of Howglen*, one of MacDonald's most autobiographical Scottish novels.[56] Small-town education centers around the sadistic schoolmaster Murdoch Malison, a violent tawse-wielder who "had *nothing of the childlike in himself,* and consequently *never saw the mind of the child* whose person he was assailing"; a master with a "savage sense of duty" and the belief that "justice . . . consisted in vengeance."[57] He is the antithesis of the child: an unimaginative rationalist who "never saw beyond the symptoms [surface]."[58] When children come home covered in bruises (and one permanently disabled by a shattered kneecap), parents, it seems—like MacDonald—turn a blind eye to evil. Having suffered such education themselves, there is resigned parental acceptance of the status quo. Convention is not challenged. Malison is only once confronted by a brave parent (Alec's mother).

Similarly, there is tacit acceptance of Malison's divine counterpart who presides over small-town religion capriciously choosing some for favor and others for damnation. The picture is one of denial: the children suffer stoically and when released from school do their best to enjoy life. At weekends, adults are harangued by hellfire preachers in the "Missionar-kirk" or attempt to find solace in the "muckle kirk,"[59] but, likewise, when released, most do their best to forget God midweek. The spiritual and material worlds are strangely discontiguous, particularly, it appears, in the moral realm where two standards appear to operate. For example, when Alec meets Malison out of school—the former the victim of the latter's sadism—they have a disturbingly pleasant conversation concluding with Alec inviting his tormentor to dinner. The narrator paints an unlikely schizophrenic picture of the master:

> I shall not have to show much more than half of Mr. Malison's life—the school half, which, both inwardly and outwardly,

---

56. GMWR 187–90.

57. AF 1:127, 61, 62.

58. AF 1:133.

59. "Missionars" was a derogatory term for Independents from England. The "muckle kirk," the "big church," was the Church of Scotland parish church. See *AF* 1:226.

was very different from the other. The moment he was out of the school, the moment, that is, that he ceased for the day to be responsible for the moral and intellectual condition of his turbulent subjects, the whole character—certainly the whole deportment of the man changed. He was now as meek and gentle in speech and behaviour as any mother could have desired.[60]

Through the reader's disquiet at Alec's civility to his tormenter, MacDonald is challenging unthinking "civility" towards the God that Malison represents. He is asking: Would you invite this "God" back to your home? It is one of the novels that prompted Samuel Law Wilson to complain about MacDonald's caricaturing of Calvinism.[61] Here, Malison's divine counterpart presides over a religion of darkness whose worshippers are misguided and lack sense. In one scene, for example, recently orphaned Annie visits the honest but over-zealous dissenting stonemason, Thomas Cramm. The image is of drawing towards darkness:

> For Thomas had been sitting in the dark till he could see in it (which, however, is not an invariable result), while out of the little light Annie had come into none at all. But she obeyed the voice, and went straight forward into the dark . . .
>
> "Noo, my lass, ye'll ken what faith means. Whan God tells ye to gang into the mirk, gang!"
>
> "But I dinna like the mirk," said Annie.
>
> "No human sowl *can*," responded Thomas. "Jean, fess a can'le direckly."[62]

Cramm is sitting in the darkness of Calvinism trying to "see in the dark," but it is Annie, the "candle" entering from the world of nature, who carries light. "Mirk" could equally be "Kirk" since, through the blunt character of Cramm, MacDonald is just as critical of the Kirk whose aged and ineffective minister is in the pay of the local laird.[63]

Cramm is an honest, uneducated soul trapped within his religion, unable to converse without trying to convert, often speaking in religious

---

60. *AF* 1:215. Malison is based on Huntly teacher Colin Stewart, said to be even more violent than his fictional counterpart. See *GMWR* 189.

61. Page 28.

62. *AF* 1:256–57.

63. *AF* 1:226–27.

jargon.⁶⁴ His cynical friend the carpenter, for example, sighs "it's a weary warl'" as they pat down the earth on Annie's father's freshly-dug grave, to which Thomas responds:

> "Ye hae no richt to say sae, George . . . for ye hae never met it, an' foughten wi' 't. Ye hae never draan the soord o' the Lord and o' Gideon. Ye hae never broken the pitcher, to lat the lamp shine out, an' I doubt ye hae smo'red it [and you've probably smothered it] by this time. And sae, whan the bridegroom comes, ye'll be ill-aff for a licht."⁶⁵

But it is Thomas who is trapped in lightless religion. However, he is one whose "genuine religious feeling and *experience* . . . will now and then crack the prisoning pitcher, and let some brilliant ray of the indwelling glory out, to discomfit the beleaguering hosts of troublous thoughts."⁶⁶ He is, in other words, a faithful believer in spite of the "prisoning pitcher" of Calvinism, and those "troublous thoughts" primarily concern whether he and his friends are among the elect—a subject mentioned twenty-four times, often by Annie.

Annie is a vulnerable child who genuinely suffers. After the death of her father she is lodged with avaricious shopkeeper Robert Bruce, the snake in this dubious Eden, a man more concerned to bank her modest dowry than look after her. Bruce, in Thomas's opinion, "wadna fling a bane till a dog, afore he had ta'en a pyke at it himsel,"⁶⁷ and Annie finds herself little more than a slave, forced to sleep in a rat-infested attic, kept on a starvation diet, taunted by Bruce's sons, and has her luxurious hair cut off by Bruce's wife to sell to the barber to make a few more pennies for the till.

There is much scope here for—and indulgence in—Victorian sentimentality, however, the abuse is real. MacDonald is exploring the suffering of an innocent and God's response. Terrified of rats, she cries out: "O God, tak care o' me frae the rottans." The instant reply "from heaven

---

64. He is modelled on the Aberdeenshire evangelist, James Maitland (*GMWR* 190), and his gruff honesty makes him one of the most convincing, even endearing, characters; a genuinely caring man who becomes for Annie "an hiding place from the wind, and a covert from the tempest" (*AF* 2:244; Isa 32:2).

65. *AF* 1:13–14.

66. *AF* 2:111.

67. *AF* 1:31. Bruce's real-life counterpart had to leave Huntly, so damaged was his reputation after the publication of this novel. See *GMWR* 190.

in answer to this little one's prayer: the cat" sets the tone for the story.[68] God has all under control. Annie, however, unaware that she is "elect," is tormented by angst about her standing with God, compounded, rather than ameliorated, by hellfire sermons and Thomas's well-meaning attempts to get her "convertit." This scenario, where children are subjected to weekday abuse at school, weekend abuse by the church, and, in Annie's case, ongoing abuse at home, prompts a Dostoevskian question from MacDonald: "A *man* ought to be able to endure grief suffering wrongfully, and be none the worse; but who dares demand that of a child?"[69]

The answer in this narrative is: those who believe that God is like Murdoch Malison. In other words, humans with false notions of God are responsible for suffering, not God. But unlike Dostoevsky's indignation about childhood suffering, or Christ's anger at injustice, MacDonald here offers a very lame response. Noting the destructiveness of a northern winter on "the old and sickly, in poor homes, with scanty food and firing," he remarks: "Little children suffer too, though the gift of forgetfulness does for them what the gift of faith does for their parents."[70] MacDonald, then, focuses on God's ability to help God's children to endure and forget suffering rather than face the possibility that genuinely destructive evil exists that should be addressed. The message is that God *always* responds to innocents like Annie. She finally has an epiphany, realizing that:

> "He has been wi' me a' the time, my God! He gied me my father, and sent Broonie [her favorite cow] to tak' care o' me. . . . And he sent the cat when I gaed till him aboot the rottans. An he 's been wi' me I kenna hoo lang, and he's wi' me noo. . . . And I'll try sair to be a gude bairn. Eh me! It's jist wonnerfu! And God's jist . . . naething but God himsel."[71]

That Annie simply decides to be "a gude bairn" is a "conversion" that offends those such as Wilson as it bypasses the "moral appliances of Evangelical religion,"[72] instead suggesting that it is the Spirit working through nature that draws humanity towards divine relationship.

There is, in my view, a flaw in this work that reveals a weakness in MacDonald's anthropology; it concerns the relationship between

---

68. *AF* 1:52.
69. *AF* 1:127.
70. *AF* 1:130; cf. Pridmore, "Estimate of Childhood," 65.
71. *AF* 3:164.
72. Wilson, *Theology of Modern Literature*, 286.

Murdoch Malison ("murder, son of evil") and his pupils. So far, with large doses of temporary "willing suspension of disbelief," the idealized children we have met are believable, if only as recognizable symbols pointing towards an *aspect* of childhood or Christlikeness. Gibbie, as noted, is described as "a rarity": at minimum he is that; more plausibly he is an impossibility used to illustrate an idea. The problem in *Alec Forbes* is that—apart from Robert Bruce's fairly "normal" taunting sons—the other children appear too *nice*. Yes, they (especially the boys) get up to childhood pranks and are called "loons," but their collective reaction to Malison's abuse raises questions. It begins with the egregious account of Truffy (possibly modeled on MacDonald's own brother),[73] the boy "kneecapped" by Malison.

This emaciated child had been deposited at school by a grandfather whose parting words were: "Noo ye jist gie them their whups weel, Maister Mailison, for ye ken that he that spareth the rod, blaudeth the bairn."[74] Malison does not disappoint. The problem is that after a vicious assault and a long convalescence, the child returns to school, disabled, with "a smile on his worn face, which shone," only too ready to shake hands with his torturer and let bygones be bygones.[75] The smile and demeanor imply that suffering has done the child good: he is transformed. We *might* just accept this as somehow typological, but it gets worse.

Malison, a licensed minister, has designs on the living at the Kirk, and, in a quest to secure the position, preaches a sermon. It goes disastrously wrong. The congregation splutters with suppressed laughter and Malison leaves in disgrace. Truffy, however, mortified that his new-found father-figure has failed, stumps after him to see him safely home and the following morning "laid a splendid bunch of cottage flowers on [the master's] desk, and the next morning it was so crowded with offerings of the same sort that he had quite a screen behind which to conceal his emotion." MacDonald declares: "Wonderful . . . is the divine revenge!" The children "would wipe away the humiliation of their tyrant"; that despite years of suffering, they "loved the man beneath whose lashes they had writhed in torture."[76]

---

73. *GMAW* 60.

74. *AF* 1:240.

75. *AF* 1:270.

76. *AF* 2:232. John Pridmore notes: "It is almost impossible for the modern reader to be other than appalled" by this account (Pridmore, "Estimate of Childhood," 69).

However forgivingly one reads this, it seems—as F. R. Leavis once remarked of one of George Eliot's more inferior works—to be "the work of a very gifted mind, but of a mind misusing itself."[77] Here we have a conflation of the Romantic child icon with real children: a projection of inherent innocence and moral integrity onto children as a class resulting in absurdity. The intended message is that childhood suffering is never wasted, however, this account undermines any meaningful understanding of that proposal. It implies that the answer to MacDonald's question—"Who dares demand [suffering] of a child?"—must be "God," for in order to reform one sadistic man, God has allowed a class of children to suffer terribly. That children *as a class* are undamaged by evil and have the innate ability to make profound moral choices—in this case to unconditionally forgive and love a sadist—is more than simply a rejection of the doctrine of original sin. It is, again, the claim that the child is impervious to surrounding quotidian corruption and absorbs evil on behalf of humanity.

Charley Osbourne in *Wilfrid Cumbermede*

In an era when Marx, Engels, Dickens, and others were passionately addressing social ills and social philosophy, Ruskin was probably right to accuse MacDonald of unreality. He writes, for example, of the first volume of *Unspoken Sermons* that:

> They are the best sermons—beyond all compare—that I have ever read, and if ever sermons did good, these will. . . . If they were but true. . . . But I feel so strongly that it is only the image of your own mind that you see in the sky![78]

These words might well have given some impetus to the writing of *Wilfrid Cumbermede* which, four years later, explored the nature of such mental images "in the sky."

Significantly darker than narratives discussed so far, *Cumbermede* explores the life of a disturbed "child" which ends in suicide. The *Spectator* described the plot as "uncommonly good" notwithstanding the "tendency to religious or rather spiritual speculation and exposition."[79]

---

77. Leavis, *Great Tradition*, 50.
78. *GMAW* 337.
79. "Wilfrid Cumbermede."

Lengthy dialogues explore whether one can trust one's senses to "decode" correctly nature's cues and discern God. Nature, "the robe of Deity,"[80] is, in this novel, often distorted, muted, ignored, or misunderstood. This dark mental landscape, if taken in isolation, would firmly contradict Gabelman's and Lewis's insistence that MacDonald was a sunny and playful man,[81] a narrative testing MacDonald's own theses that all things work together for good (all the time) and that death itself is a good. Here, the abuse is psychological rather than physical, but still religiously motivated. It explores depression, repression, domination, madness, evil, death, and suicide, focused on the question: "Are not the forms of madness most frequently those of love and religion?"[82]

As a work "shadowing out ... my present condition of mind," as the "autobiographical" narrator, Cumbermede, puts it,[83] it expresses MacDonald's radical idealism; objective physicality becomes increasingly peripheral. After the suicide of his friend, Cumbermede remarks: "At this time I had no outer life at all. Whatever bore to me the look of existence was within me." And as he becomes more reflective than active, wonders what would happen "if thought, lording it alone, should assume a reality beyond its right?"[84] In this text, nature is veiled by convention; each character is self-focused, blind to the divine presence within and without as a result of self (and, by implication, rationalism) "lording it alone."

The novel portrays a web of mutually dependent yet, ultimately, self-centered, destructive relationships. Fathers are corrupt, domineering, inept, scheming, or—in the case of the main protagonist, Cumbermede—missing. Unlike those discussed above, this narrative comes closest to facing the reality of a corrupt world. Questioning his own proposal that those who seek good will always find it, MacDonald asks: Is it really possible for a child to find God when all the evidence points to the contrary? A striking passage, when the "true hearted" Cumbermede is reflecting on the suicide of his best friend (also portrayed as a true-hearted child), brings this question into focus:

> To say that the world had grown black to me is as nothing: I ceased—I will not say *to believe* in God ... but I ceased to hope

---

80. WC 507.
81. Gabelman, *George MacDonald*, 66–67; Lewis, *George MacDonald*, 14.
82. WC 448.
83. WC 2.
84. WC 487 (perhaps a dig at "*cogito, ergo sum*").

in God. The universe had grown a negation which yet forced its presence upon me—a death that bred worms. If there were a God anywhere, this universe could be nothing more than his forsaken moth-eaten garment. He was a God who did not care.[85]

Echoing Darwin, if nature is the "robe of God" then it is a discarded robe, perhaps picked up by a demon, or—as one contemporary sceptic put it—nature is a "fierce schoolmistress who circles the brow of her children with fire instead of filling their brains with light."[86]

The plot centers around Wilfrid Cumbermede's friendship with Charley. The former, unaware that he is heir to the estate on which he lives (the earth), is searching for the truth about his missing father (God). At the outset, MacDonald introduces doubt as to whether we can trust our senses. The child Cumbermede observes that the trees in the distance always move when the wind blows and concludes that they are the source of the wind: "I used my natural senses and this is what they told me."[87] Similarly, Charley continually misinterprets cues from nature, people, and God, concluding eventually that life is pointless and that suicide is the only reasonable response. The narrator concurs. Suicide is a rejection of worldly evil; an intuitive act of fleeing to the presence of God:

> Whenever the thought arose that God might have given him a fairer chance in this world, I was able to reflect that apparently God does not care for this world save as a part of the whole; and on that whole I had yet to discover that he could have given him a fairer chance.[88]

Here, as in *Alec Forbes*, the abuse is attributed to distorted religion. Charley's minister father is a dogmatic zealot, convinced his sensitive son is damned. However, there is a deeper, sinister aspect to the father's abusive behavior; an evil, repressive demeanor—a madness—that is the cause of the son's eventual death:

> I can hardly doubt, however, that [Charley] inherited a strain of madness from his father, a madness which that father had developed by forcing upon him the false forms of a true religion.[89]

---

85. WC 475.
86. Morency, "Religion and Education," 183.
87. WC 5–6.
88. WC 449.
89. WC 447.

Like honest stonemason Thomas Cramm, locked in the "pitcher" of Calvinism, MacDonald is suggesting that the father's religion is "true" but encased or expressed in "false forms." This somewhat disingenuous phrase implies that it is possible to distinguish between the content of religion and its "form"—its outward expression. But equally—as MacDonald often argues in his sermons (and narratives such as *Phantastes*)—false forms might simply be considered the visible expression of *false* religion. I suggest this reluctance to simply denounce this misguided Protestantism as false is indicative of the continued hold of childhood faith, as well as a failure to accept that "form" is always expressive of "content."

Mr. Osbourne, Charley's father, haunts the narrative like an evil spirit, coming between him and divine revelation. On the journey to start their schooling in Switzerland, Cumbermede notes that the father was "ever blocking up our horizon, whether he sat with his broad back in front of us on the coach-box, or paced the deck of a vessel, or perched with us under the hood on the top of a diligence."[90] The damage wrought on Charley's young mind through his father's psychological abuse is extensive—abuse which continues into adulthood as the son, now a lawyer, continues to suffer domination and criticism. He is not even allowed home without his father being there: "He does not wish me to be there without his presence to counteract my evil influences. He seems to regard my mere proximity as dangerous." Stressing once more that the root of madness is religion, Charley continues: "I sometimes wonder whether the severity of his religion may not have affected his mind."[91] The narrator later remarks: "It is a terrible thing when the father is the cloud, and not the sun, of his child's life."[92] It is Charley's father, not Charley himself, who is held responsible for the latter's suicide, a result of having corrupted Christianity—of having "brand[ed] the truth of the kingdom with the private mark of opinion."[93] If the father had truly loved his son:

> Doubtless, if in the mind so sadly unhinged, the sense of a holy presence could be developed—the sense of a love that loves through all vagaries—of a hiding-place from forms of evil the most fantastic—of a fatherly care that not only holds its insane child in its arms, but enters into the chaos of his imagination, and sees every wildest horror with which it swarms; if, I say, the

90. *WC* 133.
91. *WC* 292.
92. *WC* 139.
93. *WC* 456.

conviction of such a love dawned on the disordered mind, the man would live in spite of his imaginary foes.[94]

The message is that God, the perfect father, is the shelter for an otherwise insane humanity, the place of refuge, healing, and identity. Cumbermede finds this refuge by centering himself in the self that is "everlasting eternal giving."[95] His friend is denied the opportunity.

Doubt, in this convincing sketch of depression and suicide, rather than being a positive catalyst for faith, produces despair. Even Cumbermede confesses that he had contemplated suicide.[96] All characters have mental issues, particularly Charley whose dysfunctional mind is unable to access the healing power of nature, unable to see light beyond the darkness. When visiting a glacial ice cave, for example, whereas Cumbermede rejoices in the numinous aestheticism of the blue, seemingly infinite light analogous to an encounter with God, Charley cannot cope. For him it is an encounter with death:

> "O Charley!" I exclaimed, looking round in my transport for sympathy. It was now my turn to cry out, for Charley's face was that of a corpse....
>
> "It's an awful place, Wilfrid. I don't like it. Don't go in again. I should stand waiting to see you come out in a winding-sheet. I think there's something wrong with my brain. . . . I see everything horribly dead."[97]

This scene dramatizes MacDonald's insistence that for God to condemn the mentally disturbed, those unable to respond positively to God in this life, is morally reprehensible:

> The notion that a creature born imperfect, nay, born with impulses to evil not of his own generating, and which he could not help having, a creature to whom the true face of God was never presented, and by whom it never could have been seen, should be thus condemned, is as loathsome a lie against God as could

---

94. *WC* 447.

95. *WC* 483; cf. Matt 16:25.

96. *WC* 475. Reflecting, it seems, personal experience. Raeper notes that "MacDonald plummeted into depression during his university years from which it took an anxious time of searching and effort to emerge" (*GMWR* 237).

97. *WC* 142.

> find place in heart too undeveloped to understand what justice is, and too low to look up into the face of Jesus.⁹⁸

MacDonald concludes that post-mortem salvation must be a *possibility* if human free will is to make any sense. It is an *inevitability* if the loss of a soul amounts to defeat for God; that is, that for God to destroy the "streams of life" flowing from Godself—such as the incapacitated Charley—equates not to the defeat of evil, but the destruction of something of the essence of God, for, "Is he not defeated every time that one of those lost souls defies him?"⁹⁹

This narrative, therefore, questions the nature of reality. If what humans conceive as reality is a mental construct, what hope do humans have of finding truth when their minds distort and misinterpret received cues? Even when Cumbermede has a "spiritual" encounter, he questions its validity:

> I fear to build any definite conclusions upon it, from the dread of fanaticism and the danger of attributing a merely physical effect to a spiritual cause. But are matter and spirit so far asunder?¹⁰⁰

We will consider the latter ontological question in due course. Here, with certain parallels with Murdoch Malison, MacDonald questions the character of God through the character of Charley Osbourne. If Mr. Osbourne senior—a man who "puts the evil foremost in his creed and exhortations"—genuinely worships God, the implication is that God is either evil, or "very indifferent to what his creatures think of him."¹⁰¹

The theological principles offered here are that God "will not force himself on [people], but help them to grow into the true knowledge of him," and that those who claim to worship the true God may "have only a little of that knowledge."¹⁰² However, in MacDonald's view, God is continually orchestrating events to draw people to God:

> I do not believe we notice half of the coincidences that float past us on the stream of events. Things which would fill us with

---

98. *US3* 126.
99. *US3* 125.
100. *WC* 146–47.
101. *WC* 295.
102. *WC* 295.

astonishment, and probably with foreboding, look us in the face and pass us by, and we know nothing of them.[103]

Humanity is thus culpable, through negligence, of failing to discern truth. Charley, however, illustrates that this trite response is inadequate. In his case, the sins of the father are being visited on the child; however willing, he is mentally unable to decode the cues from either God or nature.

Having conceded—at least theoretically—that his father *might* possibly have some good in him, Wilfrid Cumbermede and Charley observe one of nature's divine artworks, a beautiful moonlit evening:

> "I wish I could let it into me, Wilfrid," said Charley....
>
> "Let what into you, Charley?"
>
> "The night and the blue and the stars."
>
> "Why don't you, then?"
>
> "*I hate being taken in. The more pleasant a self-deception, the less I choose to submit to it.*"[104]

The blue of the night, like the blue light in the ice cave of childhood, represents the infinite presence of God—a presence inaccessible to the mentally-disturbed Charley. While conceding that God *might* be behind the beauty of nature, his fear of deception rejects this possibility. Even in adulthood the father's hold is strong, a father who had told him "that the love of nature is not only a delusion, but a snare." Charley summarizes: "Of all miseries—to believe in a lovely thing and find it not true—that must be the worst."[105]

Charley's suicide is precipitated by an unfortunate coincidence (seeing his beloved innocently kiss his best friend, which he interprets as her rejection of him) which—since MacDonald insists that events are orchestrated by God—means that God, as well as the father, is culpable. The logic of this can only be reconciled by MacDonald's rejection of "the tree lies where it falls" theology:[106]

> That my Charley, whose suicide came of misery that the painful flutterings of his half-born wings would not bear him aloft into the empyrean, should appear to my Athanasia [his beloved] lost

---

103. WC 456.

104. WC 296 (emphasis mine).

105. WC 298–99.

106. Maurice had also declaimed: "This cannot be Protestantism. Cannot be Christianity" (Maurice, *Theological Essays*, 442).

in an abyss of irrecoverable woe; that she should think of God as sending forth his spirit to sustain endless wickedness for endless torture;—it was too frightful.[107]

Suicide has, instead, ushered the disturbed man into God's presence. Although buried in unconsecrated ground, Cumbermede observes that:

> I saw the body of Charley laid in the holy earth. For the earth *is* the Lord's—and none the less holy that the voice of the priest may have left it without his consecration. Surely if ever the Lord laughs in derision, as the Psalmist says, it must be when the voice of a man would in *his* name exclude his fellows from their birthright.[108]

And, speaking through the voice of Cumbermede, MacDonald has to conclude that, ultimately, one may rejoice over suicide:

> When the crystal shrine has grown dim, and the fair forms of nature . . . are contorted hideously by the tormented mind . . . when the body is no longer a mediator between the soul and the world, but the prison-house of a lying gaoler and torturer—how can I but rejoice to hear that the tormented captive has at length forced his way out into freedom?[109]

This narrative proposes that childlike obedience to perceived truth, however mistaken, is of more value to God than belief which does not lead to obedience. For the mentally ill, perception is necessarily skewed, but *all* are, to some extent, "lunatics" for, as Cumbermede's confession above shows, even he has been deluded about his worship, which now he realizes to be that of self. It leads to the question: "Who can tell how often this may be the fact—how often the lunatic also lives by faith?"[110] This is a question explored, for example, in the characters of the mad laird in *Malcolm* or the "fool" in *The Wow O' Rivven*,[111] individuals who exhibit more faith than most and find post-mortem rest in the arms of a loving God. As Hans Urs von Balthasar remarks:

> There is a gleam of unconscious, unintended sanctity about the real fool. He is the unprotected man, essentially transcendent,

---

107. *WC* 451.
108. *WC* 448.
109. *WC* 448.
110. *WC* 448.
111. A short story in *POS*.

open to what is above him. . . . Since he is never quite "in his right mind," never quite "all there," he lacks the ponderousness that would tie him down to earth. He stands nearest to the saint, often nearer than the morally successful man preoccupied with his perfection.[112]

It is a narrative that blurs the distinction between willfulness and weakness: is Mr. Osbourne senior, for example, culpable or simply deluded?

This narrative, therefore, rejects any simplistic notion of post-mortem judgement, relying instead on a purgatorial entrance to the afterlife. It is an extension of MacDonald's belief that all evil (or what seems evil) is ultimately used by God for good: like Truffy's horrific abuse at the hands of Malison, Charley's illness after the ice cave incident results in him being "more cheerful than . . . before" and him "[growing] a good deal."[113] Charley's sister, even, is portrayed as being refined by the suicide of her brother. On meeting her at a subsequent social event, Cumbermede cannot, at first, believe that it is her:

> It was indeed Mary Osbourne; but oh, how changed! The rather full face had grown delicate and thin, and the fine pure complexion if possible finer and purer, but certainly more ethereal and evanescent. It was as if suffering had removed some substance unapt, and rendered the body a better-fitting garment for the soul.[114]

Suffering is the rain of God that creates springs in the human heart.[115] It is the only way MacDonald can reconcile the evil he sees in the created order with the belief in God as "the causing goodness."[116]

Finally, the focus here is almost exclusively on nature as being God's vehicle for communication to humanity. The Bible, like nature, is primarily considered as a book for "the rousing of a man's conscience" rather than imparting any concrete information,[117] and nature itself is seen as the main influence in Cumbermede's awareness of God:

---

112. Von Balthasar, *Realm of Metaphysics*, 143. Von Balthasar quotes Erasmus: "It seems to me that the Christian religion taken all together has a certain affinity with some sort of folly" (Von Balthasar, *Realm of Metaphysics*, 168).

113. WC 143.

114. WC 460. Having myself subsequently met the sister of a friend who killed himself, in my view this account is particularly problematic.

115. CW 106–7.

116. WC 447.

117. WC 173.

> The fact is I was coming in for my share in the spiritual influences of Nature, so largely poured on the heart and mind of my generation.... I was under the same spell as [Wordsworth and Coleridge]. Nature was a power upon me. I was filled with the vague recognition of a present soul in Nature.[118]

A Realist Fairyland

An immediate judgement as to which of these narratives is the more realist might favor *Cumbermede*: it appears to offer a more "real" (and depressing) world. However, on reflection it is evident that whether innocent or disturbed, MacDonald's children inhabit the same world—a fantasy world. In my view, Lewis was right to suggest that the opening chapters of *Cumbermede* are especially "fantastic":[119] one feels that the tale is more like a dream (or a nightmare) than a picture of reality. But equally, Gibbie's pastoral Eden—where honest (male) peasants read poetry to each other and play pan-pipes while submissive females dutifully listen and are instructed[120]—is just as fantastic, and, like the art of the period, MacDonald's narratives are generally devoid of steam engines or industry.[121] This disconnect between lived reality and the MacDonaldian ideal led a frustrated Ruskin, who favored "stern facts," to complain:

> I suppose it is quite impossible for you dear good people, who think it your duty to believe whatever you like—and to expect always to get whatever is good for you, to enter into the minds of us poor wicked people, who sternly think it our duty to believe nothing but what we know to be fact, and to expect nothing but what we've been used to get.[122]

Perhaps he had failed to appreciate that even fantasy can shed light on the nature of reality.

I have suggested also that, unlike the traditional *Bildungsroman* where the protagonist is shaped by external forces, MacDonald's innocent children achieve the opposite—it is their world, not they, that changes. But this also would be a misreading: it is rather (as we will consider more

---

118. *WC* 131.
119. Note 14, page 100.
120. *SG* 183–84.
121. Barringer, *Pre-Raphaelites*, 106.
122. *GMAW* 334.

fully later) an issue of perception. As we look through the eyes of these children (and those playing opposite them) we see different perspectives on an essentially idealist "fairy" universe. Gibbie (and to a lesser extent Diamond), being the perfect *imago*, is almost unable to see or experience evil; his pure vision sees the numinous glow of nature; evil cannot touch his innocent soul. Annie, however, is less perfect, but once the "pitcher of Calvinism" is broken, she too is able to clearly perceive the divine glow. It is Charley's and Cumbermede's vision that is the most distorted, the former never able to see clearly, blinded as he is by, as it were, inoperable (at least in this life) religious cataracts.

All these, though, are children, or perhaps one should say firmly on the road to childhood. Even Charley is a child; he is simply a blind child, unable, for that reason, to be an obedient child, however willing. Murdoch Malison, likewise, is blind to the true nature of his abuse: it takes the ministrations of his charges to begin to open his eyes, just as Annie becomes a "candle" to Thomas Cramm. It is a theology that stresses orientation rather than position or status: that those who turn in God's direction are on the road to salvation, not those who claim to be "elect" or "convertit." It is "adults" such as shopkeeper Robert Bruce (who becomes an elder in the Missionar-kirk for business reasons), or the zealot Mr. Osbourne—those of whom Jesus said, "If you were blind, you would have no sin; but now you say, 'We see.' Therefore your sin remains" (John 9:41)—who will experience the full force of God's purgatorial fire.

In these fantasy worlds, evil is also considered primarily a matter of perception—an erroneous vision of God—and this aspect of MacDonald's theology has implications that will need to be explored more fully. We now turn to an outline of that theology.

5

An Overview of George MacDonald's Theology

WE ARE WORKING TOWARDS a detailed reading of *Lilith*—that most enigmatic of George MacDonald's works that names the vampire, the nemesis of the child—but before doing this, two steps are needed. It is helpful to look a little closer at the Evangelical climate in which the narrative was forged (the following chapter), but first, while certain theological proposals and strong themes have already emerged from our encounters with MacDonald's fictional children (and the supporting cast), it is helpful to have a more complete and systematic summary of his theology by paying closer attention to his direct voice in essays and letters, as well as additional narrative sources. We begin with some comments regarding MacDonald's view of cognition and epistemology.

MacDonald's Approach to Cognition and Epistemology

John Henry Newman wrote of MacDonald's age that it was a time when faith had become stereotyped:

> Its doctrines are not so much facts, as stereotyped aspects of facts; and it is afraid, so to say, of walking around them. It induces its followers to be content with this meagre view of revealed truth.[1]

---

1. Newman, *Essay in Aid*, 55.

MacDonald, however, clearly dissatisfied with "meagre views of received truth," made it his business to "walk around them." His is a Maurician emphasis on holistic truth (that is, "organic" truth perceived "symbolically")[2] on the basis that truth in Christianity is fundamentally related to a person, not to propositions; "to know" is not *savoir* but *connaître*: "*vous connaîtrez la vérité et la vérité vous rendra libres*" (John 8:32). Like Newman, he disdained what he perceived as the dry, sterile output of "logicians . . . more set upon concluding rightly, than on drawing right conclusions,"[3] instead arguing that imagination must *lead* its "plodding brother," reason.[4] Only imagination, he argues, can disinter faith from certain death, that is, from Carlyle's graveyard of conventional words, or, as he termed it, "mummies of prose." The poet has a duty to hold words up to the light so they once more glow with meaning,[5] or, as Coleridge had put it, "genius" rescues "the most admitted truths from the impotence caused by the very circumstances of their universal admission."[6] He is thus at some distance from Calvin who famously valued "solid enquiry" above "vain speculation"[7]—perhaps more so from Calvin's successors for whom, in his view, their master's thought had hardened into a "pitcher" opaque to the light of divine truth; a pitcher that, like Gideon's, had to be broken.[8]

There were, however, critics of imaginative thinkers such as MacDonald. In George Eliot's view, for example, Romantics were dreamers, poor poets whose grandiloquence stemmed from "the want of taking for a criterion the true qualities of the object described, or the emotion expressed," subsequently "float[ing] away into utter inanity without meeting any criterion to arrest [them]."[9] For John Ruskin, irrationality led such as MacDonald to believe that "the primrose is anything else than

---

2. Page 27.
3. Newman, *Essay in Aid*, 91.
4. *Orts* 14. See page 23.
5. *Orts* 9.
6. Coleridge, *Collected Works*, 7:82.
7. Calvin, *Institutes* 1.4.47.
8. A contemporary of MacDonald was less forgiving of Calvin: "We often hear it said that Calvinists went far beyond Calvin. My own study of the question leads to a diametrically opposite conclusion. I doubt whether any of Calvin's followers went as far as Calvin himself" (Moore, "Influence of Calvinism" 335).
9. Eliot, "Worldliness and Other Worldliness," 15.

a primrose: a star, or a sun, or a fairy's shield, or a forsaken maiden";[10] Romantics were "unhinged" from reality and "too weak to deal fully with what is before them"—they may "feel strongly" but have lost the ability to "think strongly."[11] How might one defend MacDonald against such charges?

One key issue is cognitive approach: the "logician" constructs reality based on deductive or inductive principles. MacDonald's approach fits a third category, abduction, which recognizes that many human theories about reality are posited on the basis of a more intuitive approach to presenting states of affairs that lead to conclusions that cannot (at least initially, often never) be formally verified, and are inevitably affected by the choice of "lens" through which one looks. Without infinite *a priori* knowledge, finite individuals, of necessity, must choose a model by which to view the world, a choice which then affects what is seen. Psychologist Iain McGilchrist puts it like this:

> How we think about our selves and our relationship with the world is already revealed in the metaphors we *unconsciously* choose to talk about it. That choice further entrenches our partial view of the subject. Paradoxically we seem to be obliged to understand something—including ourselves—well enough to choose the appropriate model before we can understand it. Our first leap determines where we land.[12]

It is a principle articulated at length by Newman for whom "real assent" to any proposition is inevitably based on a working model rather than objective facts:

> Let us not by our words imply that we are appealing to experience, when really we are only accounting, and that by hypothesis, for the *absence of experience*. The confusion is a fact, the reasoning processes are not facts.[13]

Using the term "abduction," Newman's "hypothesis" was formulated by C. S. Peirce (1839–1914) as "the process of forming explanatory hypotheses . . . the only logical operation which introduces any new idea," and

---

10. Ruskin, *Modern Painters*, 3:173. MacDonald is guilty as charged: "The faces of some flowers lead me back to the heart of God" (*US3* 251). "To know a primrose is a higher thing than to know all the botany of it" (*US2* 196).
11. Ruskin, *Modern Painters*, 3:170, 173–74.
12. McGilchrist, *Master and His Emissary*, 97 (emphasis mine).
13. Newman, *Essay in Aid*, 68 (emphasis mine).

that abduction encompasses "all the operations by which theories and conceptions are engendered."[14] As a cognitive process, it *precedes* deduction or induction. The problem for Ruskin is not that MacDonald and his "dreaming" friends are imaginative (in his view, imagination is "the source of all that is great in the poetic arts")[15] but that they are presenting hypotheses that are not subsequently open to deductive or inductive verification.

MacDonald's starting point is that God rewards the honest seeker,[16] and his "lens" is Christocentric. Inasmuch as divine revelation is necessarily beyond logical analysis and therefore limited (reflecting Ruskin's conclusion that to know anything must be to know it partially),[17] the human child has to abductively choose the "best fit" to explain the presenting phenomena and trust that this is either (a) valid on the basis that God does not intentionally deceive God's children or (b) if invalid, that this will become clear, since God is committed to leading God's children into truth. This, as noted, is MacDonald's "fiduciary hermeneutic," the choice to view the world from the perspective of faith.

The child is proposed as a model to account for the dynamics and content of the human–divine relationship; MacDonald's fiction then explores this hypothesis in "real" life. The unreality of his "realist" novels is not an inability to write, rather a sense that the hypothesis does not completely match or account for human experience—or relates to only one aspect of it. His imaginative fantasies, which have much looser moorings to perceived reality, are, for this reason, significantly more effective. (But, as David Reynolds discusses, they may be exemplary of the tendency among "liberal" authors, according to their Calvinist accusers, of disguising what they really mean so that they can slip heresy under the radar.)[18]

MacDonald follows Coleridge in positing that the Spirit's drawing of the human imagination is not the result of human effort, but of divine

---

14. Douven, "Abduction."

15. Ruskin, *Modern Painters*, 2:134.

16. A pervading biblical theme (e.g., Deut 4:29; Prov 8:17; Jer 29:13; Matt 7:7–8; Luke 11:9–19; Acts 17:27).

17. Ruskin, *Modern Painters*, 4:58–59.

18. In the American context, David Reynolds discusses Jeremiah Evarts's view that liberals "generally conceal their religious opinions [in their novels] with particular care" while Calvinists "generally avow their religious opinions with the utmost frankness" (Reynolds, *Faith in Fiction*, 96–97).

initiative,[19] perhaps absolving him of the charge of Pelagianism. Grace is needed. In other words, abduction (not that Coleridge or MacDonald used the word) is not just human cognition reaching out into the void and coming up with an imaginative "best fit," but is the active drawing by God of human consciousness towards Godself; it is the confidence that "the child sees things as the Father means him to see them."[20] God draws the divine "spark" in humans, the imagination, back to its source. Emphasizing that the concept is more than simply another form of reasoning but involves divine initiative, Daniel Hardy reflects that for Coleridge, it was "'the being drawn towards the true center' of all, the Logos and the Spirit."[21] MacDonald conceives of this as the "gravitational" pull of the Spirit urging union with God, the fire-core of existence around which the human being orbits:

> It is but that the deeper soul that willed and wills our souls, rises up, the infinite Life, into the self we call *I* and *me*, but which lives immediately from him, and is his very own property and nature—unspeakably more his than ours: this deeper creative soul, working on and with his creation upon higher levels, makes the *I* and *me* more and more his, and himself more and more ours; until at length the glory of our existence flashes upon us, we face full to the sun that enlightens what it sent forth, and know ourselves alive with an infinite life, even the life of the Father.[22]

Daniel Hardy's articulation of abduction seems to summarize MacDonald's view. In both the individual life and in human social history, the Spirit is drawing humanity from beyond the horizons of cognition towards eschatological consummation, demanding that faith reach out imaginatively beyond the *known* towards the *becoming*—"allowing our imaginations to be drawn forward by divine attraction: an ongoing process of envisioning and re-envisioning, so that we are stretched forward by the divine purposes."[23] It is an iterative process that reaches for truth but never possesses it, and explains MacDonald's suspicion of systems

---

19. "It is not uncommon... in Coleridgean scholarship," writes Robin Stockitt, "to overlook the profoundly religious nature of [Coleridge's] definition" of the primary imagination (Stockitt, *Imagination and the Playfulness of God*, 65).
20. *HG* 56.
21. Hardy et al., *Wording a Radiance*, 54n2.
22. *US3* 53–54.
23. Hardy et al., *Wording a Radiance*, 77.

claiming to fully contain truth, including his own aversion to producing or subscribing to one. He makes this very clear:

> We are far too anxious to be definite, & have finished, well-polished, sharp-edged systems—forgetting that the more perfect a theory about the infinite, the surer it is to be wrong, the more impossible it is to be right. I am neither Arminian nor Calvinist—to no system could I subscribe.[24]

He also notes: "Our Lord had no design of constructing a system of truth in intellectual forms."[25] Instead, he prefers to conceive of faith as a journey towards the infinite heart of God, reminiscent of Gregory of Nyssa's *epektasis*.

Finally, we note that MacDonald's theology is primarily pastoral; he aims to lead people "to the living Truth, to the Master himself."[26] He appears to have two audiences in view: those who fear and those who despise the "headmaster" God and, whether anxious believers or informed "cultured despisers," are familiar with Christianity. This is most evident in his narrow treatment of evil where the tacit assumption is made that his "congregation" would like to escape from hell and (re)connect with God, and that the problem of evil is sited in human rebellion (rather than, say, ignorance). As our narrative readings have revealed, his focus on moral evil is arguably at the expense of a broader and more adequate account. As a pastoral theologian, his main concern is to elicit personal response, not produce watertight theoretical frameworks—he wants to foster "children."

The emphasis on personal revelation leads to the focus on being an *obedient* child—obedient to truth perceived imaginatively through the abductive drawing of the Spirit towards Godself from beyond the horizons of consciousness. If that perception is flawed, he argues—reflecting the comments above regarding the iterative nature of revelation—God will soon, through obedience, lead his child back to the right path.[27] "Faith," he insists, "can have no existence except in obedience."[28] "Obedience is the soul of knowledge."[29] MacDonald appears to be prioritizing

---

24. Sadler, *Expression of Character*, 51.
25. *US1* 66.
26. *US3* 155–56.
27. *US1* 56; *US2* 212.
28. *US2* 247.
29. *HG* 18.

the Apostle John's words (also A. J. Scott's epitaph): "If anyone wills to do His will, he shall know concerning the doctrine" (John 7:17)[30]—a text he explicitly links to imaginative discipleship:

> As he that is willing to do the will of the Father, shall know of the doctrine, so, we doubt not, he that will do the will of THE POET, shall behold the Beautiful.[31]

This Johannine priority is a ubiquitous theme constantly reminding his readers to *act* on the truth as demonstrated by Christ, "the god of obedience among the children of disobedience":[32]

> He took on him the form of man: he was man already. And he was, is, and ever shall be divinely childlike. He could never have been a child if he would ever have ceased to be a child, for in him the transient found nothing. *Childhood belongs to the divine nature. Obedience, then, is as divine as Will, Service as divine as Rule.*[33]

The recurring demand for obedience represents a protest against the kind of contemporary expressions of church that were the target of Newman's criticism; churches content with theoretical, "stereotypical" faith:

> I can find no words strong enough to serve for the weight of this necessity—this obedience. It is the one terrible heresy of the church, that it has always been presenting something else than obedience as faith in Christ.[34]

And, perhaps with hierarchical church structures in mind, childlike obedience is set over against notions of power and control—"empire": "It was empire [Jesus] rejected when he ordered Satan behind him like a dog to his heel."[35] Finally, we note that obedience is not simply a temporal demand: since mutual submission is intrinsic to the Trinity, it is the eternal orientation of the child of God. "Obedience is the grandest thing in the world to begin with. Yes, and we shall end with it too."[36] We now turn to a summary MacDonald's theology.

30. Johnson, *George MacDonald*, 31. See also *RF* 19.
31. *Orts* 36.
32. *TWC* 228.
33. *US1* 19 (emphasis mine).
34. *US2* 243.
35. *US3* 99.
36. *Orts* 307.

Doctrine of God

The popular title of Jesus's discourse about the child, and that of MacDonald's first *Unspoken Sermon*, sums up MacDonald's doctrine of God: God is both "a child" and "in the midst." We begin with the latter.

The Fire of God—Creating and Consuming

God, for MacDonald, is absolute Being, the "fire-core of the universe"[37] that is both creative and destructive, heaven and hell. Like that of Jacob Boehme, it is a vision of creation *emanating* from God, but God is also the *"consuming* fire which is essential love,"[38] sustaining what is good and consuming evil. God is hell: "It is a fearful thing to fall [unworthily] into the hands of the living God" (Heb 10:31). David Bentley Hart, writing from an Eastern Orthodox perspective, notes that such views are by no means unique: "The kingdom is also an event of discrimination, a condemnation of all the falsehoods that enslave creation. The kingdom wears the aspect of damnation, as well as redemption, and the language of hell enters Christian discourse alongside the evangel of peace." Hart continues:

> Hell is with us at all times, a phantom kingdom perpetuating itself in the wastes of sinful hearts, but only becomes visible to us as hell because the true kingdom has shed its light upon history. In theological tradition, most particularly in the East, there is that school of thought that wisely makes no distinction, essentially, between the fire of hell and the light of God's glory, and that interprets damnation as the soul's resistance to the beauty of God's glory.[39]

From a Western perspective, Hans Urs von Balthasar concurs: for an unrepentant sinner, "the fiery torrent of eternal love that flows around and through him would remain a torrent of eternal wrath."[40] This is MacDonald's view. Thus evil "alone is consumable,"[41] and, in a phrase rejecting popular ideas of hell, remarks: "Death alone can die everlastingly." This

---

37. *US2* 166. MacDonald's focus here is Christ's glory (Mark 9:3; Rev 1:14–16).
38. *US1* 30 (emphasis mine).
39. Hart, *Beauty of the Infinite*, 399.
40. Von Balthasar, *Theo-Drama*, 4:350.
41. *US1* 31.

comment is made in *Alec Forbes* as spring begins to thaw winter's chill. When God shines fully in the spring of the eschaton, evil will finally end:

> The winter, old and weary, was halting away before the sweet approaches of the spring—a symbol of that eternal spring before whose slow footsteps Death itself, "the winter of our discontent," shall vanish. Death alone can die everlastingly.[42]

This divine emanation is not impersonal or involuntary; it is an aesthetic model that views creation as God's willed artwork, "an expression of the thought, the feeling, the heart of God himself,"[43] or, as he put it to his future wife: "The beautiful things round about you are the expression of God's face . . . the garment whereby we see the deity."[44] It represents a rejection of the Newtonian universe with its absentee God: "This world is not merely a thing which God hath made, subjecting it to laws."[45] Instead, God is intimately present in all God has made (which begs the question how we account for the things that are *not* beautiful, considered shortly).

Since God's creative thoughts are synonymous with creative acts, creation is the "boundless free giving of the original Thought."[46] It is a panentheistic cosmology; that is, creation emanates from, and is sustained by, God: God is fully invested and present in creation but creation does not equate to God (pantheism). Our reality is not, as it were, the sum of God's thoughts: there exists a realm *behind* the "back of the north wind" to which humans have no access at present; that realm is God's infinite being, the final consummate destiny of all creation. The glacial ice cave in *Wilfrid Cumbermede*, where "streams, ever creeping into the day of vision from the unlike and the unknown, unrolling themselves like the fronds of a fern out of the infinite of God," illustrates this.[47] The picture is of a fractal reality emerging from a profound, that is, unfathomable, divine source, the implication being that beyond the visible world with its door of death, the infinite and eternal being of God is—should God permit—inviting further encounter. It is "fractal" in that, in some sense, God is replicating or expressing Godself in lesser forms that unfold in ways that "embody" and reveal something of the essence of the divine nature.

42. *AF* 1:266.
43. *Orts* 246.
44. Sadler, *Expression of Character*, 27–28.
45. *Orts* 246.
46. *TWC* 494.
47. *WC* 142. See page 118.

Rather than speculate ontologically,⁴⁸ MacDonald emphasizes that practically, "in him we live and move and have our being":

> Do you not believe . . . that there is all about us, and in us, an infinite thought; that the atmosphere in which we live and breathe . . . is thought, and that thought is the thought of One, and that One is the thought whence we came—that is, the thinking God, thinking always?⁴⁹

It is an idealist, emanationist, theocentric model.⁵⁰ Human selfhood is entirely generated and sustained by God: "God thinks you out of himself, and you live because he lives; you have no independent existence at all,"⁵¹ a phrase which, at first sight, appears to deny the divine gift of autonomous selfhood.

MacDonald, however, insists that free will is genuine. Selfhood may existentially be fully dependent on God's sustenance but this does not imply determinism. Human being is conceived as God allowing God's "thoughts" to think for themselves: that from a remote orbit of gravitational weakness, human will has the power to choose to return to the heart of love, or, in rejecting that love, experience the hell of "outer darkness" where the fire of God is most destructive:

> The fire of God, which is his essential being, his love, his creative power, is a fire unlike its earthly symbol in this, that it is only at a distance it burns—that the farther from him, it burns the worse, and that when we turn and begin to approach him, the burning begins to change to comfort, which comfort will grow to such bliss that the heart at length cries out with a gladness no other gladness can reach.⁵²

---

48. It appears to be a Kantian idealism where "appearances are to be regarded as being, one and all, representations only, not things-in-themselves, and that time and space are therefore only sensible forms of our intuition, not determinations given as existing by themselves, not conditions of objects viewed as things-in-themselves" (Kant quoted in Honderich, *Oxford Companion to Philosophy*, 387).

49. *God's Words* 3; cf. Acts 17:28.

50. Noting that emanationism, most often associated with Plotinus, unlike MacDonald's scheme, posits that the creative energy of the One is spontaneous, unwilled.

51. *God's Words* 8.

52. *US2* 162.

"God has, as it were," he summarizes, "put us just so far away from Him that we can exercise *the divine thing in us, our own will*, in returning towards our source."[53]

That God's power is essentially love is a refusal of the sadistic schoolmaster God of the Reformers; their mistake was to "yield the idea of the Ancient of Days, 'the glad creator,' and put in its stead a miserable, puritanical martinet of a God." It is in this context that MacDonald turns with loathing "from all copies of Jonathan Edwards's portrait of God" (perhaps having read "Sinners in the Hands of an Angry God"),[54] a comment that particularly irks contemporary neo-Reformed critics John Piper and Timothy Keller who conclude that MacDonald is "not really a Christian."[55]

"To Us a God, to Himself a Child"

The image of God as loving power is contrasted with God's kenotic choice to be "lovingly powerless"; that is, in some sense God chooses to be a child, or, as Novalis had remarked, focusing on the inherent nature of God, the divinity is "to us a God, to himself a child."[56] Expounding "The Child in the Midst," MacDonald explores this by emphasizing that God is not "childish," but "childlike":

> One of the saddest and not least common sights in the world is the face of a child whose mind is so brimful of worldly wisdom that the human childishness has vanished from it, as well as the divine childlikeness. For the *childlike* is the divine, and the very word "marshals me the way that I was going."[57]

Jesus chose an ordinary child because he was drawing attention to something essential in childhood which we are to emulate, "not a blurred and half-obliterated childhood."[58] That essence is not innocence *in se*, but divine childlikeness, "spiritual childhood": the welcome of the child "in my name" does not merely mean "because I will it" but "means *as representing me*; and, therefore, *as being like me*." He continues:

53. *ML* 54 (emphasis mine).
54. *US3* 161–62.
55. Dart, "Would We Have Been Friends?"
56. Novalis quoted in *Rampolli* 34.
57. *US1* 3. The quote is from *Macbeth*.
58. *US1* 6.

> *In my name* . . . involves a revelation from resemblance, from fitness to represent and so reveal. He who receives a child, then, in the name of Jesus, does so, perceiving wherein Jesus and the child are one, what is common to them.[59]

The common denominator between child, Son, and Father is childlikeness.

A reasonable objection to this argument—one raised by Presbyterian Samuel Law Wilson—is that what is endearing in a child might not be so attractive in a God:[60] one may accept that a child carries the *imago Dei*, but this does not imply that all childhood characteristics (such as throwing tantrums) can be found in God. But MacDonald is not suggesting this; he is simply insisting that since Christ identified with a child, the latter must, in some fundamental sense, represent the deity in whose image it is made.

The point is that in the context of a discourse about power (which disciple would be the greatest in the kingdom) the use of a child is significant, for a child knows, deep down, that it does not rule in an adult world. God, likewise, is "powerless"—a child—which leads to a concise articulation of his doctrine of God:

> For it is his childlikeness that makes him our God and Father. The perfection of his relation to us swallows up all our imperfections, all our defects, all our evils; for *our childhood is born of his fatherhood.*[61]

That God is a powerless child, then, is not so much a divine choice as an expression of the morally perfect divine nature: perfect love "does not seek its own" (1 Cor 13:5), it never coerces. That "perfection of relation" that "swallows our imperfections" is love; the "fire-core" is "love . . . a radiant perfection. Love and not self-love is lord of the universe."[62] Here, the (divine) child is father to the man and the *imago Dei* is, above all else, the image of the childlike God.

This loving "relation of the Father and the Son contains the *idea of the universe*. . . . The child-relation is the one eternal, ever enduring, never changing relation."[63] This core concept in MacDonald's thought is the hallmark of a reality where individual identity can only be found in

---

59. *US1* 10–11.
60. Wilson, *Theology of Modern Literature*, 294.
61. *US1* 24–25 (emphasis mine).
62. *US3* 132.
63. *HG* 161 (emphasis mine).

relationship with the divine other, and where human identity is only real if it reflects the divine purpose—the divine *idea*. "The child" is, therefore, a metaphor which does not simply speak of submissiveness (or any other specific attribute) but one which is at the root of reality because it is intrinsic to the nature of the triune God.

MacDonald's view of the Trinity, however, reflects the nineteenth-century Western tendency to speak of the Spirit as the bond of love between Father and Son and this, as Hart observes, can "give the appearance that the Spirit is not as irreducibly 'personal' as Father and Son."[64] This is reflected in MacDonald's preference for the term "Spirit of Christ"[65] rather than Holy Spirit. He encourages openness to the Spirit, writing, for example, that "God gives the spirit of his son, the spirit of himself, to be in him [who is obedient], and lead him to the understanding of all truth"[66] and laments the lack of awareness of the Spirit in the church, but he is very much the sort of a philosophical idealist that regards reality as primarily a mental construction. In his view, the Spirit is God's "mind" or the "mind of Christ" that the child may share.[67]

Despite this period leaning towards dualist terminology when speaking of God, MacDonald, by placing this "idea of the universe" at the heart of his theology, is stressing the mutual love within the Trinity which Hart terms the "triune coinherence" of God, at the heart of which is perichoretic joy; a dance as each "person" of the Trinity rejoices in, and affirms, the "others." The implication, according to Hart, is that each "person" of the Trinity necessarily embraces the "others" such that, for example, "The Father's entire being, which he possesses in his paternal depth, is always also both filial . . . and spiritual." It is this insight which, I believe, MacDonald is expressing: that humans are made in the image of a deity who is essentially relational and *filial*.

---

64. Hart, *Beauty of the Infinite*, 175.
65. Rom 8:9; Phil 1:19; 1 Pet 1:11.
66. *US3* 155.
67. *US1* 54.

Christology

The childlikeness, Hart's "filiality," of the Father is reciprocated by the Son being the perfect *imago* (John 14:9), a perfect reflection of the childhood and the light of the Father.[68] MacDonald writes:

> He has never lost his childhood, the very essence of childhood being nearness to the Father and the outgoing of his creative love; whence, with that insight of his eternal childhood of which the insight of the little ones here is a fainter repetition, he must see everywhere as the Father means it.[69]

It is a mutuality that emphasizes the inherent unity of the triune God in contrast, for example, to the moral and existential separation implied by the Federal Calvinism of such as Samuel Rutherford for whom "the Lord the Creditor, and Christ the Cautioner did strike hands together,"[70] as if the former needed to take unilateral action to satisfy the latter. Father and Son are not morally divided: soteriological schemes that imply the Son must protect humans from the wrath of the Father are false.[71] And since humans are made in the image of God—the Son being the perfect expression of this[72]—they represent a "fainter repetition" of "his eternal childhood"; they are "little child Gods":

> For the finite that dwells in the infinite, and in which the infinite dwells, is finite no longer. Those who are thus children indeed, are little Gods, the divine brood of the infinite Father.[73]

The centrality of Christ as the perfect *imago Dei* in MacDonald's theology leads to particular sensitivity over the use of the term "Word of God." "The Word," he insists, "is that by which we live, namely, Jesus himself";[74] the Bible, therefore, is not "the Word of God" but *a* word of

---

68. John 1:4–5, 18; 1 John 1:5.
69. HG 55–56.
70. Samuel Rutherford quoted in Torrance, *Scottish Theology*, 98.
71. US3.
72. See, for example, Barth, *Doctrine of Creation*, 231–42.
73. HG 66. In a letter, he writes: "One moment's contact between his heart and his child's makes of that child a young God. 'I said ye are Gods'" (Sadler, *Expression of Character*, 305). The reference is to Ps 82:6; cf. "partakers of the divine nature" (2 Pet 1:4).
74. US1 118.

God[75]—a protest against "bibliolatry" which, as Iain McGilchrist wryly notes, stems from the fact that at the Reformation, "the Flesh [was] made Word" and dwelt among us.[76] MacDonald, therefore, underlines that "all reading of the Book is not reading of the Word."[77]

The "Morality" of God

MacDonald rejects Calvin's voluntarist position, that "everything which [God] wills must be held to be righteous by the mere fact of his willing it"[78]—such as choosing some for damnation. While this assertion *in se* cannot be refuted for God is "constrained" by God's own goodness, MacDonald is troubled by theology unconcerned about God's actions violating the human understanding of moral rectitude, begging the question as to whether God and humanity share the same moral "space"—a question that arose when we considered the apparent moral schizophrenia of schoolmaster Murdoch Malison.[79]

To give a recent example, John Piper believes (citing Matt 25:46; Rev 14:11) that "judgment is not remedial or temporary but punitive and everlasting" (views rejected by F. D. Maurice that led to his expulsion from his Chair at King's College London in 1854). In this "light" he considers the fate of his three sons, concluding in voluntarist tones:

> But I am not ignorant that God may not have chosen my sons for his sons. And—, though I think I would give my life for their salvation, if they should be lost to me, I would not rail against the Almighty. He is God. I am but a man. The potter has absolute rights over the clay. Mine is to bow before his unimpeachable character and believe that the Judge of all the earth has ever and always will do right.[80]

---

75. *US1* 142.
76. McGilchrist, *Master and His Emissary*, 323.
77. *AQN* 127.
78. Calvin, *Institutes* 3.23.2. Calvin denied being a voluntarist, but evidence points to the contrary. See Danielson, *Milton's Good God*, 69.
79. See pages 109–10.
80. Piper, "How Does a Sovereign God Love?" Such views tend to be expressed by those who are sure it does not apply to themselves.

MacDonald, agreeing with Herbert Spencer's polemic against similar glosses in his time on the "unimpeachable character" which tortures eternally,[81] describes it as "paganism":

> One of my earliest recollections is of beginning to be at strife with the false system here assailed. Such paganism I scorn as heartily in the name of Christ, as I scorn it in the name of righteousness.[82]

Such views are "an insult" to God and "a dishonour to his creature, to hold concerning him," and to believe that those like Charley in *Wilfrid Cumbermede*, who may have had little chance in this life to "accept Christ," are forever damned—

> is as loathsome a lie against God as could find place in heart too undeveloped to understand what justice is, and too low to look up into the face of Jesus. It never in truth found place in any heart, though in many a pettifogging brain. There is but one thing lower than deliberately to believe such a lie, and that is to worship the God of whom it is believed.[83]

The lines here are clearly drawn. MacDonald holds that—since all being, including hell, is sustained by God—all morality, that is, ethical norms, is "in" God; apparent anomalies must be down to the limitations of human perspective. But whereas Piper is prepared to accept a discontinuous morality, MacDonald is not. He argues that God and humanity must be morally alike—not in terms of scope or application, but certainly in terms practical ethics:

> To say that what our deepest conscience calls darkness may be light to God, is blasphemy; to say light in God and light in man are of differing kinds, is to speak against the spirit of light.[84]

This issue is exemplified by Piper's focus on the potter/clay duality, an analogy that stresses not only the otherness of God but could be read as absolute *un*likeness (reminiscent of Chesterton's remark regarding the futility of comparing a hare with an isosceles triangle).[85] MacDonald, in contrast, recognizing that at some level we are made in the image of God

---

81. See page 21.
82. *US2* 235.
83. *US3* 126.
84. *US3* 169.
85. Chesterton, *Heretics*, 76.

(that the materials the potter works with are not simply unlike and inert) argues that likeness includes moral values:

> To say on the authority of the Bible that God does a thing no honourable man would do, is to lie against God; to say that it is therefore right, is to lie against the very spirit of God. To uphold a lie for God's sake is to be against God, not for him. God cannot be lied for. He is the truth. The truth alone is on his side.[86]

Moral confusion stems from a lack of childlike vision. Discussing Jesus's contrast of the "wise and prudent" with "babes" (Matt 11:25–27) he argues that the former, with their myopic preoccupation with self-preservation, are unable to perceive the truth of the kingdom: "in proportion to our care about our own well-being, is our incapability of understanding and welcoming the care of the Father."[87] He observes, in a criticism that would certainly apply to the zealous father of Charley Osbourne, that:

> All those evil doctrines about God that work misery and madness, have their origin in the brains of the wise and prudent, not in the hearts of the children.[88]

It is not wisdom *per se* that is objected to, but the danger that it separates "babe" from Father, especially if wielded by those claiming the institutional authority of church or synagogue. "Terribly has his gospel suffered in the mouths of the wise and prudent."[89] In contrast, the "Romantic" child is uncorrupted by false culture:

> The Father, then, revealed his things to babes, because the babes were his own little ones, uncorrupted by the wisdom or the care of this world, and therefore able to receive them.[90]

Still trailing clouds of glory, the child intuitively understands "a little how things go in the presence of their father in heaven, and thereby to interpret the words of the Son."[91] In this innocent state, children understand the morality of heaven:

86. *US3* 116–17.
87. *HG* 154.
88. *HG* 155.
89. *HG* 156.
90. *HG* 158.
91. *HG* 159.

> The babes were the prophets in heaven, and the angels were glad to find it was to be so upon the earth also; they rejoiced to see that what was bound in heaven, was bound on earth; that the same principle held in each.[92]

It is the world's distorted morality that gives rise to "one dull miserable human system after another usurping [the gospel's] place."[93] God and humans share the same moral space; to punish eternally is as morally wrong in heaven as on earth. Only the child understands the moral implications of the pervading "ideal relation" of Father to Son at the heart of reality:

> No wisdom of the wise can find out God; no words of the God-loving can reveal him. The simplicity of the whole natural relation is too deep for the philosopher. The Son alone can reveal God; *the child alone understand him*.[94]

The Justice and Mercy of God

MacDonald's aim was to dismantle the "dull miserable human system" constructed by "the wise and prudent" based on the Westminster Confession which, in his view, with its juridical focus, had allowed sin to trump grace. Calvin, for example—having insisted that "guilt is from nature" and that having Christian parents was no antidote for "the primary and universal curse" affecting children's lives[95]—had inspired MacDonald's Scottish predecessor, Samuel Rutherford. His was a ruthlessly forensic approach to faith that viewed God as a harsh law-giver.[96] Infants, for example, would go to hell on the grounds that "being without the Covenant" (that is, too young to enter into a contract) they "cannot be chosen and predestinate in Christ to salvation."[97] As T. F. Torrance observes, Scottish voices such as Rutherford's played a significant role in drafting the Confession, a document with a "very legalistic and constitutional character in which theological statements were formalised at times with

---

92. *HG* 160.
93. *HG* 157.
94. *HG* 163 (emphasis mine).
95. Calvin, *Institutes* 2.1.7.
96. Torrance, *Scottish Theology*, 99.
97. Torrance, *Scottish Theology*, 101.

an almost 'frigidly logical definition'"[98] that would result in "persistent problems" for Scottish theology.[99] Torrance observes that Rutherford's nineteenth-century successors, such as George Hill, were equally forensic, labelling the latter's theology as "methodologically erroneous and inadequate [and] strictly not a fully *Christian* doctrine of God."[100]

Kirk intransigence—putting the Confession above the Bible[101]—led to John McLeod Campbell's dismissal,[102] an event that Thomas Erskine of Linlathen had described as:

> [The casting] out from the Church of his fathers one of the saintliest of her sons. . . . He never ceased to regard it as the stoning by the Church of Scotland of her best prophet, the deliberate rejection of the highest light vouchsafed to her in his time.[103]

Torrance identifies the main issue:

> The question had to be asked, therefore . . . *what kind of God does this imply?* That was the great question with which the General Assembly was faced in 1830, with McLeod Campbell's revolt against the idea of God that lay behind the doctrine of predestination and limited atonement in what George Hill regularly referred to as "the Calvinistic System" that prevailed in the Kirk.[104]

It was this question that motivated MacDonald's quest for his "true father" (the plot of many of his novels)—what was God *really* like? The problem was that this "strictly not fully *Christian* doctrine of God" implied a schizophrenic Miltonian deity who was one minute "just" and the next minute "merciful":

> He thundereth these words into their eares.
> You guilty souls where are you? Have you thus

---

98. Torrance, *Scottish Theology*, 129.
99. Torrance, *Scottish Theology*, 281.
100. Torrance, *Scottish Theology*, 133.
101. Newell, "Unworthy of the Dignity," 251–53.
102. See page 18. The vote in the General Assembly on May 24, 1831, went 119 to 6 against Campbell (Newell, "Unworthy of the Dignity," 252). Scott, a close friend of MacDonald, had been declared a heretic for preaching at Campbell's church. See *GMAW* 192–93.
103. Hanna, *Letters of Thomas Erskine*, 523. See also Goodloe, "John Mcleod Campbell."
104. Torrance, *Scottish Theology*, 262–63.

> Transgrest? See now how you are like to us!
> ... Thus spake God's Justice; then his Mercy brake
> A deeper silence and him thus bespake.
> Where art thou Adam?
> Is that Face of thine
> Muffled in Clouds that was so like to mine?
> Where art thou? lost! O sad!

As William Poole remarks: "Thus the thin end of the wedge of dualism is inserted into the Godhead."[105]

MacDonald objects strongly to this division. Following Erskine, who had written, "In God mercy and justice are one and the same thing,"[106] MacDonald states:

> There is *no* opposition, *no* strife whatever, between mercy and justice. Those who say justice means the punishing of sin, and mercy the not punishing of sin, and attribute both to God, would make a schism in the very idea of God. . . .
>
> In God shall we imagine a distinction of office and character [magistrate and father]? God is one; and the depth of foolishness is reached by that theology which talks of God as if he held different offices, and differed in each. It sets a contradiction in the very nature of God himself.[107]

In this sermon, "Justice," MacDonald declares that the doctrine of substitutionary atonement is "an evil thing, to be cast out of intellect and heart"; Christ's passion was not a "satisfaction" of God's justice, a sacrifice of appeasement.[108] Erskine had already stated unequivocally: "I am aware that the doctrine of expiation through the vicarious death of Christ is sacred and precious to the hearts of many, nevertheless I am compelled to regard it as a human invention opposed to the character of God."[109] MacDonald, in less measured tones, declares:

---

105. Poole, *Milton*, 110.
106. Thomas Erskine quoted in Torrance, *Scottish Theology*, 268.
107. *US3* 114–15.
108. *US3* 133–34.
109. Torrance, *Scottish Theology*, 272.

> From such and their false teaching I would gladly help to deliver the true-hearted. Let the dead bury their dead, but I would do what I may to keep them from burying the living.[110]

Christ deals with the power, not the penalty, of sin; sin was the cause of the abuse of Christ, not a requirement for satisfaction by the Father of lights. Rejecting the caricature of Christ submitting to the wrathful blows of the Father on behalf of the elect, he writes: "I declare my utter and absolute repudiation of the idea in any form whatever," concluding: "The whole device is a piece of spiritual charlatanry—fit only for a fraudulent jail-delivery."[111]

The polemic continues in the sermon "Righteousness," denouncing the "rubbish heap of legal fiction called vicarious sacrifice, or its shadow called imputed righteousness,"[112] describing it as "this most contemptible of false doctrines," "falsehood," "a mean, nauseous invention, false and productive of falsehood," and "an embodiment of untruth." "It is the meagre misshapen offspring of the legalism of a poverty-stricken mechanical *fancy*, unlighted by a gleam of divine *imagination*."[113] He repeats: "only the child with the child-heart, so far ahead of and *so different from the wise and prudent*"[114] will see through the deception. The issue is not the tension between divine justice and mercy, but that between divine justice and human justice.

The refusal to separate God's justice from God's mercy is driven by the conviction that love and light are divine moral attributes which cannot survive such separation. God the Father cannot co-exist with God the schoolmaster. This does not, however, imply a marginalization of the gravity of sin or its offense to a holy God. The "outer skirts" of God's presence will, to the unrepentant, be experienced as wrath, but this is not wrathful retribution; it *is* God's mercy which even in judgement loves the sinner and is working for that sinner's deliverance.

---

110. *US3* 136.
111. *US3* 137, 145.
112. *US3* 224.
113. *US3* 210–11 (emphasis mine).
114. *US3* 224 (emphasis mine).

Cosmology

In MacDonald's emanationist model, "The thought of God is the truth of everything."[115] Humans specifically are "but a thought of God."[116] As noted, he does not speculate on the ontic nature of the cosmos, simply that "matter is the result of mind, spirit, thought. The relation between them is . . . simply too close, too near for us to understand."[117] Rather, he focuses on perception, distinguishing between the "philosopher . . . who lives in the thought of things, [and] the Christian . . . who lives in the things themselves"[118]—those who merely observe and those who engage. Although one would imagine an idealist scheme favoring the philosopher, the distinction concerns failing to discern the true, divine meaning behind natural phenomena. We "circle" God at an "epistemic distance" where human moral choice is genuine.[119]

To explore these issues, we consider the short story *The Broken Swords* (1864) about a fatherless and sensitive young man who, on receiving an army commission, is sent to war. On showing signs of mental breakdown prior to a military assault, he has his sword broken over his head and is dismissed in disgrace from the army. Subsequently, his regiment is destroyed by a land mine. Returning to England, mortified by his failure, the *Bildungsroman* tracks his journey through the margins of society as he tries to avoid recognition and find absolution. After casual and industrial labor (in between which nature works her healing) he re-enlists with the army, dying a hero's death.

It is an *exitus-reditus* parable: like the "prodigal son," human existence involves being sent from the father's presence into a distant soul-forming world where destiny hinges on the decision to return. Equating this to the metanarrative of the Bible, he proposes:

> Every tragedy of higher order, constructed in Christian times, will correspond to the grand drama of the Bible; wherein the first act opens with a brilliant sunset vision of Paradise, in which childish sense and need are served with all the profusion of the indulgent nurse. But the glory fades off into grey and black,

---

115. *US3* 105.

116. Note 36, page 68.

117. *ML* 76. Ilia Delio argues that from the perspective of quantum phenomena, matter and mind are inseparable. See Delio, *Making All Things New*, 55–70.

118. *WMM* 3:95.

119. Discussed further below, see page 155.

and night settles down upon the heart which, *rightly uncontent with the childish, and not having yet learned the childlike,* seeks knowledge and manhood as a thing denied by the Maker, and yet to be gained by the creature; so sets forth alone to climb the heavens, and instead of climbing, falls into the abyss. Then follows the long dismal night of feverish efforts and delirious visions, or, it may be, helpless despair; till at length a deeper stratum of the soul is heaved to the surface; and amid the first dawn of morning, the youth says within him, "I have sinned against my *Maker*—I will arise and go to my *Father*."[120]

This succinct summary of MacDonald's soul-making theology (also a précis of this story) equates prelapsarian innocence with childishness and human destiny with childlikeness, sin being a misguided self-centered quest for "manhood." This present reality is the pigsty of the prodigal; childlikeness may be achieved by the decisive act of returning from the wasteland to the father.

The story opens with two sorrowing sisters sitting with their newly-uniformed brother the night before his departure from "paradise." The light of the moon pales the red army coat: "In her thoughtful light the whole group seemed more like a meeting in the land of shadows, than a parting in the substantial earth." The implication is that the earth is insubstantial, prompting a Kantian question:

> But which should be called the land of realities?—the region where appearance, and space, and time drive between, and stop the flowing currents of the soul's speech? or that region where heart meets heart, and appearance has become the slave to utterance, and space and time are forgotten?[121]

The implication is the latter, but the negative view of materiality here is revealing, a jaundiced view at odds with Gabelman's claim that MacDonald has a "wholly orthodox" view of the cosmos and celebrates materiality.[122] Here, space-time is an obstacle impeding the "flowing currents of the soul's speech"; it is divisive, preventing "heart from meeting heart."

The key is found in Jacob Boehme, a mystic who influenced MacDonald directly, and possibly indirectly through F. D. Maurice,[123] espe-

---

120. *POS* 214 (emphasis mine). Greville MacDonald personally reprinted this volume in 1924, indicating that in his view it was significant.

121. *POS* 211.

122. Gabelman, *George MacDonald*, 164.

123. According to the sleeve notes of Boehme, *Signature of All Things*, Maurice

cially in his proposal that God's presence is experienced as both light and dark fire. Boehme's use of Renaissance alchemical terms and creative metaphor to discuss what amounts to transcendental philosophy is, more often than not, baffling. Nevertheless, a picture emerges of quotidian reality as the fall-out (that is, in some sense the contaminated matter) from a primeval, divinely-inspired explosion now orbiting a divine "sun." Matter emerges out of "nothing":[124] "for the forms of nature are awakened [by an "ethereal blaze" analogous to a lightning-strike], and are as a turning wheel, and so they carry their spirit the wind."[125] For Boehme, also, God is "fire" at the center of this "turning wheel":

> The Father's fiery property makes itself in the divine essence of the eternal love in a mercury of joyfulness; for the Father's property is the fire-source.[126]

Both writers equate God's "fiery property" with "the eternal love" and emphasize that "outward nature"—since God is the hypostasis, the *ground*, of all being—glows with God's fire:

> For God is a spirit, and as subtle as a thought or will, and nature is his corporeal essence, understand the eternal nature; and the outward nature of this visible comprehensible [footnote, "palpable"] world is a manifestation or external birth of the inward spirit and essence of evil and good, that is, a representation, resemblance, and typical similitude of the dark fire and light world.[127]

Without claiming any nuanced understanding of Boehme's impenetrable philosophy, two things are evident: first, that the "sun-God" of love is central to created reality; second, that in "outward nature" (the cosmos), God is manifest as a "light world" which coexists with "dark fire," which in some sense is "the essence of evil and good." Created being is therefore a place where not all is light, where shadows fall, and where "dark fire" burns. It is an ambiguous ontological model ("the essence of evil and good") complexified by MacDonald proposing a dualist *perceptive* model. In other words, what one sees—whether good or evil—depends

called him a "generative thinker."

124. "Nothing," for Boehme, is the unformed raw material that God then shapes to form "creation"—Milton's "chaos."

125. Boehme, *Signature of All Things* 2.40.

126. Boehme, *Signature of All Things* 7.27.

127. Boehme, *Signature of All Things* 3.4.

not only on the "object" in view, but the nature of perception—particularly its *moral* nature: if one looks with the eyes of a child—or if one is transparent, like Diamond—the dark fire does not burn.

Robert Paslick, noting resonances between Boehme and Zen Buddhism, observes that both hold that "after the Fall . . . the material world is still a mirror of the paradise of the divine nature,"[128] revealing two important shared principles. The first concerns the sacrality of creation. "Reality"—the world that humans engage with—is the visible aspect of the interpenetration of two universes that coexist and intertwine: from a Buddhist perspective, "there is no complete separation of worlds, as if nature were all darkness and paradise were some transcendent," leading Paslick to an image that MacDonald uses in the novel *Lilith*: "The tree outside my window in my so-called real world is also the tree standing in paradise."[129] In *Lilith*, Mr. Vane ("Mr. Self-Centered") is taken outside of his normal self-focused reality into a parallel universe. Being disorientated and disturbed, not least because his guide also appears as both raven and man, his mentor consoles him with the words:

> "Perhaps it may comfort you," said the raven, "to be told that you have not yet left your house, neither has your house left you. At the same time it cannot contain you, or you inhabit it!"[130]

We explore this narrative in detail later, but the point here is that the "house" of personal consciousness is situated within a larger reality. He is, the raven tells him, "in the region of the seven dimensions," and pointing to a tree in the surrounding pine forest, remarks: "That tree stands on the hearth of your kitchen, and grows nearly straight up its chimney."[131]

This emphasis on the role, and limitations, of perception leads to a second principle: that the problem (sin, conceived as self-centeredness) and the solution (becoming God-centered) to the human condition are found in human consciousness. This is not to say the solution is located in individual human consciousness, simply that becoming a child ("salvation") is appropriated subjectively as a conscious moral choice. Evil equates to selfish moral choice. For such choice to be genuine, true vision is needed: the self-centered, such as Vane, must learn to see properly in order to make wise choices. Nature is radiant with God's light but human

---

128. Paslick, "From Nothingness to Nothingness," 22.
129. Paslick, "From Nothingness to Nothingness," 22.
130. *Lilith* 25.
131. *Lilith* 25–26.

consciousness may, in rebellion, be drawn towards the "dark fire," unaware that this is also an aspect of God—the hell of God's burning outer garments. However, those with a true childlike heart will be able to experience the light of God *and* the purging dark fire of God in the here and now without being burned.

The idea that moral choice influences how one views and experiences reality is found, for example, in Buddhism and Christianity. Paslick notes, negatively, that in Keiji Nishitani's understanding of Zen Buddhism, "the more fully self-reflective the subjectivity of the self becomes, the more it becomes aware of the presence of nihility at the ground of its existence," leading to despair.[132] Or, in Dietrich Bonhoeffer's language in *Act and Being*, the sinful "narcissism of the human will" leads to an awareness that "I myself am Adam,"[133] a self-awareness akin to Charley Osbourne's conclusion, "*I* am *a* devil."[134] In contrast, positively, Nishitani finds peace and identity in the "paradoxical realm of . . . serious play where nonaction is genuine action and where nonthinking is genuine thinking." It is the place of surrender, echoing Christ's words, "he who loses his life for My sake will find it" (Matt 10:39).[135] True self-identity is only found in a conscious, unselfish turning towards the Other, which Bonhoeffer suggests is "not a self-losing to oneself, but a self-finding in Christ";[136] true peace, the region where conscience is redundant,[137] is only to be found in the willing embrace of God's purgatorial fire—the return to the "primal Sun of life."[138]

MacDonald's positive view of materiality is, then, ambiguous. Moral ontological ambiguity (that the cosmos is "the essence of evil and good") and perceptive duality (that there are childlike and unchildlike ways of seeing) lead to a very ambivalent view of the perceived world. However satisfying the above model may be, it is clear that it falls into the category of an abductive hypothesis: it may be a good "fit" and account for subjective experience, but clearly there are thorny issues, the most intractable

---

132. Paslick, "From Nothingness to Nothingness," 24.
133. Bonhoeffer, *Act and Being*, 162, 165.
134. *WC* 330.
135. A repeating refrain (cf. Matt 16:25; Mark 8:35; Luke 9:24; 17:33; John 12:25).
136. Bonhoeffer, *Act and Being*, 179.
137. Bonhoeffer quotes Luther: "Whoever lacks conscience is Christ or the spirit of evil" (Bonhoeffer, *Act and Being*, 177), characterizing being "in Christ" as the perfect gaze towards Christ, the opposite of narcissism.
138. *US3* 54. See also note 22, page 129.

being the perennial problem of locating the source of evil in the divine nature. MacDonald's answer to this appears to be, after Boehme, to posit that much of what we call evil is not really evil but erroneous perception of God's dark fire.

In MacDonald's universe, there is no destructive evil that is contrary to God's will, no event that does not (eventually) mediate God's presence, nothing that does not short-circuit the inevitable decision to return to the Father. Evil is solely down to human moral failure, and right relationship with the world is reduced to a moral choice: to be a "philosopher" or a "Christian,"[139] a rebellious or a submissive child. To choose the latter is to begin the return journey to the place where "heart meets heart," but—in the light of the above comments—involves turning away from the "pigsty," or at minimum, turning a blind eye to aspects of reality as if it was unholy rather than numinous. MacDonald, in other words, ignores evil rather than accounting for it.

The Broken Swords makes it clear that honorable death is preferable to dishonorable life. On his return to England, "the youth" (who is never named and appears to represent "everyman") travels northwards. Sleeping rough, nature works her office, "For the face of nature is the face of God, and must bear expressions that can influence, though unconsciously to them, the most ignorant and hopeless of His children."[140] In contrast, the negative aspects of lived reality are marginalized. Unusually for a MacDonald story, the protagonist finds work in a cotton mill. Despite "windows so coated by dust that they looked like frosted glass; showing, as it passed through the air to fall on the dirty floor, how the breath of life was thick with dust of iron and wood, and films of cotton,"[141] one does not feel the grinding degradation of slave labor, and despite the plague being in the city, one does not sense danger. There is much sentimentality, and, just as unreal children seem impervious to evil in other narratives, so factories lack toxicity, neither are children's arms torn off by machines. Instead, the emphasis is on the factory being devoid of "'divine air' and the open heavens, whose sunlight only reached him in an afternoon, as he stood at his loom."[142] The factory, as a human construct, blocks divine light: evil is privation rather than depravation. The

---

139. Page 146.
140. *POS* 218.
141. *POS* 224.
142. *POS* 224.

implication is that factories—and, in this narrative, war—represent human rebellion, but that God uses both to save his child from eternal death, earthly death being virtually inconsequential.

In this narrative, the "deep infinite skies" of God's immutable presence "contain" quotidian reality:

> For above every cloud, above every storm, rise up, calm, clear, divine, the deep infinite skies; they embrace the tempest even as the sunshine; by their permission it exists within their boundless peace: therefore it cannot hurt, and must pass away, while there they stand as ever, domed up eternally, lasting, strong, and pure.[143]

On this view, "the deep infinite skies" give permission for both good and evil to co-exist within "their boundless peace." That evil "cannot hurt, and must pass away" reflects MacDonald's pastoral focus on believers who will benefit from eschatological resolution, but also implies that evil, ultimately, like death, is of no consequence.

However one views reality (we should perhaps heed his advice that it is "too near for us to understand"), of most concern to MacDonald is the function of human will: the environment in which humans are placed with its light and dark fire demands that a choice be made, but whatever the choice, humans remain the progeny of the Father.[144] We now consider the human occupants of this universe.

Anthropology

The Human Creature

MacDonald's cosmological focus on morality rather than mechanics prioritizes original blessing (the *imago Dei*) over original sin. For example, he finds meaning in Wordsworth's proposition that humans come into the world "trailing clouds of glory," and that the *exitus-reditus* trajectory (paradise–vale of soul-making–heaven) is recapitulated in the life of each individual. As Christ, the perfect child, was continually aware of his divine prenatal existence (a questionable thesis),[145] all humans are

---

143. *POS* 220; cf. Shelley's *Adonais*, discussed by MacDonald: "Life, like a dome of many coloured glass / Stains the white radiance of eternity" (*Orts* 6).

144. *US2* 115–37.

145. See, for example, International Theological Commission, "Consciousness of Christ."

aware, at least to some extent, of their divine origin. Thus after quoting with approbation Wordsworth's "Intimations of Immortality" and Henry Vaughan's reminiscences of "those early dayes, when I / Shin'd in my angell-infancy!" he writes:

> Whoever has thus gazed on flower or cloud; whoever can recall poorest memory of the trail of glory that hung about his childhood, must have some faint idea how his father's house and the things in it always looked, and must still look to the Lord. With him there is no fading into the light of common day.[146]

Likewise, he is open to the "mechanics" of evolution, but only inasmuch as this can be co-opted to serve his core thesis that God's sole aim is to create children:

> For this vision of truth God has been working for ages of ages. For this simple condition, this apex of life, upon which a man wonders like a child that he cannot make other men see as he sees, the whole labour of God's science, history, poetry—from the time when the earth gathered itself into a lonely drop of fire from the red rim of the driving sun-wheel to the time when Alexander John Scott worshipped him from its face—was evolving truth upon truth in lovely vision, in torturing law, never lying, never repenting; and for this will the patience of God labour while there is yet a human soul whose eyes have not been opened, whose child-heart has not yet been born in him.[147]

That this evolutionary vision contradicts the idea that the child has some kind of prenatal heavenly existence is immaterial; rather, he is replacing negative views of childhood with positive ones. Simian savagery and original sin are replaced by evolutionary truth ("evolving truth upon truth in lovely vision") and the *imago Dei*. Whatever the mechanics, the goal of God's creation is that "child hearts" might be brought to birth.

MacDonald's idealism leads to a focus on the mind, notably the roles of imagination and will. Regarding the former, this is simply a world where "science" alone is inadequate to account for reality:

> We are here in a region far above that commonly claimed for science, open only to the heart of the child and the childlike

---

146. *HG* 54–55.
147. *US1* 29.

man and woman.... For things as they are, not as science deals with them, are the revelation of God to his children.[148]

Whatever the nuances of MacDonald's ontology, practically speaking "nature" mediates God. It offers "Posterns... to the supernal; ... Loopholes to the Infinite."[149] Nature's true meaning is transcendent and must be perceived imaginatively:

> The truth *of a thing*, then, is the blossom of it, the thing it is made for, the topmost stone set on with rejoicing; truth in a man's imagination is the power to recognize this truth of a thing; and wherever, in anything that God has made, in the glory of it, be it sky or flower or human face, we see the glory of God, there a true imagination is beholding a truth of God.[150]

We find corresponding ideas in Boehme. The secrets of the universe are only open to the imaginative child. In his terminology, God will only give the pearl of the philosopher's stone to a true magus—one who will "walk in the person of Christ... that he may have magical sight."[151] God does not give wisdom to the unchildlike (he who is "not in this birth of restoration, and walks not himself in the way wherein Christ walked upon the earth"), but—with echoes of Wisdom playing at God's side during the creative act (Prov 8:22–31)—gives it to his children: "for the pearl of which I write is paradisical, which God does not cast before swine, but gives it to his children for their play and delight."[152] Both writers emphasize that the imaginative child is loved by, not alienated from, God, but there remains a moral imperative to choose wisely.

Selfhood and Identity

If a true child is one that, having imaginatively discerned, chooses wisely, an evil child is unimaginative (or willful) and chooses unwisely. This essential dichotomy drives MacDonald's doctrine of evil: the choice concerns whether to accept or reject one's God-given, and therefore only

---

148. *US3* 62.
149. *Poems* 2:18.
150. *US3* 69.
151. Boehme, *Signature of All Things* 7.73.
152. Boehme, *Signature of All Things* 7.74.

true, identity. The *cor curvum in se* ("ontic narcissism")[153] leads to false identity, is the essence of sin, and—if we are to believe "The Lost Soul"—results in destruction.[154] In contrast, "The man who does not house self, has room to be his real self—God's eternal idea of him."[155]

Three implications are apparent. First, that "self" and "identity" primarily have meaning with reference to the divine "other" who not only gives life but as Father remains intrinsically connected to, invested in, and sustaining of that life which shares the divine nature. Second, that each person is *uniquely* made in the image of God; that is, each person is, to use David Kelsey's terminology, an "unsubstitutable" self whose true identity is a very specific "eternal idea." Third, since true selfhood is the opposite of destructive self-reflexivity, there is an implicit social dimension. A man's "consciousness of himself," he writes, "is the reflex from those about him, not the result of his own turning in of his regard upon himself."[156] At first sight, this appears recognition that selfhood is not monadic but socially forged, however this is not the case: a person's correct *evaluation* of their consciousness or identity is found through interaction with others, not that it is so forged. True identity, he insists, inheres in "God's eternal idea."

Humans orbit the divine sun at an "epistemic distance," that is, the place where choice is genuine and determines trajectory—towards or away from God.[157] While acknowledging God's sovereignty, MacDonald stresses that "the whole labour of God is that the will of man should be free as his will is free," and that this would make no sense if it could

---

153. *Cor curvum in se* ("the heart turned in on itself") is the phrase used by Luther (after Augustine) to express the essence of sin. For Bonhoeffer, it was "the ontic inversion into the self," or, as Bernard Noble's translation put it, "ontic narcissism" (Bonhoeffer, *Act and Being*, 46).

154. A poem implying annihilation. See pages 167–68.

155. HG 87.

156. US3 224.

157. "A term used by John Hick [1922–2012] implying that humans are generally unaware of God's presence in the world. Hick locates the origin of evil in his notion of epistemic distance . . . that an individual's cognitive distance from God will entail a self-centredness. . . . This stance gives rise to moral evil" (Stoeber, *Evil and the Mystics' God*, 70–72). Hick, like MacDonald, argues that in the end there will be "no personal life that is unperfected and no suffering that has not eventually become a phase in the fulfilment of God's good purpose" (Stoeber, *Evil and the Mystics' God*, 376).

somehow be overridden. "That," he argues, "would be to make a will in order that it might be no will."[158]

While human choice is genuine (a conclusion I will challenge), God is, nevertheless, sovereign despite those in God's image being described as "little gods," a phrase underlining the dangerous human potential to become self-centered. Without this being a real danger, the notion of self-sacrifice would have no meaning. "God gives his children *selves*, with wishes and choices, that they might have the true offering to lay upon the altar; for on that altar nothing will burn but *selves*."[159] If such offering is not made voluntarily, self is, paradoxically, self-destructive: it is "the one all-potent annihilator of individuality."[160] Reflecting on Jesus's discourse about denying self (Luke 9:23–24), he emphasizes that the child must choose the path of obedience, of total submission:

> We must become as little children, and Christ must be born in us; we must learn of him, and the one lesson he has to give is himself: he does first all he wants us to do; he is first all he wants us to be. . . . *we must take the will of God as the very life of our being.*[161]

All persons, being made in God's image, are, and never cease to be, children of their divine Father. Original sin is not the issue—he seems to concur with Novalis that this is an "ancient, heavy guilt-*illusion*" that breeds "death and misery";[162] the issue, rather, is *present* sin. The *reditus* leg of the journey often begins with a person's awareness of "what in himself is despicable, disappointing, unworthy . . . what sometimes he calls *the old Adam*, sometimes *the flesh*, sometimes *his lower nature*, sometimes *his evil self*," defined in the negative as "that part of his being where God is not."[163] Recognition of this is the beginning of truly sharing the divine nature:

> When a man wills that his being be conformed to the being of his origin . . . *thus receiving God, he becomes, in the act, a partaker of the divine nature*, a true son of the living God, and an

---

158. *ML* 55–56.
159. *CW* 234.
160. *CW* 311.
161. *US2* 210 (emphasis mine).
162. *Rampolli* 18 (translation MacDonald's, emphasis mine).
163. *US3* 77.

heir of all he possesses: by the obedience of a son, he receives into himself the very life of the Father.[164]

This seems to reflect the early Church Fathers' distinction between "image" and "likeness" in Genesis 1:26. The latter equates to being a "true (obedient) son"; the former—since the person is aware of the need to be conformed—equates to an "untrue" (disobedient) child. Being made in God's image, therefore, has to do with potentiality rather than status, a potential realizable through Christ's death—not that Christ made humans acceptable in God's sight, but that Christ defeated the forces of evil preventing a response. Christ dealt with the power, not the penalty, of sin, re-gifting humans with free will such that the choice to return to the Father is genuine.

In MacDonald's soteriology, however, that power is not—as Wilson laments—mere human effort aided by a vague all-pervading natural force:[165] it is the presence of Christ in his child. Although MacDonald seems allergic to the term "grace" because of its "atonement" overtones,[166] essentially he describes grace working in individuals to draw them towards childhood. In fact, he writes, "grace and truth [are,] in a word, childlikeness."[167] There must be divine–human cooperation, however: "He has made us, but we have to be":

> "As many as received him, to them gave he power to become the sons of God." He does not *make* them the sons of God, but he gives them power to become the sons of God: in choosing and obeying the truth, man becomes the true son of the Father of lights.[168]

This soteriology reflects the Protestant emphasis on the need for a personal response to God's grace but is based on the premise that the individual must avail itself of Christ's universal provision rather than salvation inhering in the sovereign God's election to save by the imputation of righteousness to an otherwise guilty soul. We discuss MacDonald's soteriology further below.

---

164. *US2* 153–54 (emphasis mine).

165. See pages 27–28.

166. The word "grace" is used only twenty times in the three volumes of *Unspoken Sermons*.

167. *US1* 13.

168. *US2* 126–27 (emphasis mine).

The Problem of Evil

The Nature of Evil

In this emanationist universe, evil exists where God is prevented from "shining" by wills that, in their opposition to God, cast shadows. Although both human and "demonic" (as we will explore in our reading of *Lilith*), the focus is on the human: sin lives in "that part of [a person's] being where God is not."[169] Sin as "culpable privation" (as self-caused opaqueness) is articulated in the novel *Castle Warlock*. Cosmo, an archetypal child, the devoted son of the waning laird, is on the roof of a coach, "his heart swelling at the thought of being so soon in his father's arms," when he observes shadows cast by the sun and becomes philosophical:

> How dark were the shadows the sun was casting!
> Absurd! the sun casts no shadows—only light.
> How so? Were the sun not shining, would there be one single shadow?
> Yes; there would be just one single shadow; all would be shadow.
> There would be none of those things we call shadows.
> True; all would be shade; there would be no shadows.

Evil would not be visible if God did not "shine." Cosmo then understands why

> the Jews came to assign evil to the hand of God as well as good, and what St. Paul meant when he said that the law gave life to sin; for by the sun is the shadow; where no light is, there is no darkness, where no life, no death.

He concludes that if God were to shine unimpeded, no "object" (will) would be able to prevent God's shining; all would be transparent. In which case, he wonders, "where there is no longer anything covered or hid, shall sin be able to live?"[170] The image implies that God temporally (that is, in this present life) allows sin to exist, but will shine fully, and "destructively," in the eschaton—that is, God's light will destroy the shadows in individuals (not the individuals themselves) and renew creation. As Novalis had put it:

---

169. Note 163, page 156.
170. *CW* 241.

> The external world is a world of shadows, which casts its shadows onto the realm of light. At present, it is true, that the inner world seems to us so dark, lonely and without form, but how different will it appear when this darkness has gone, and those shadowy forms have been removed. We will be able to enjoy the world more than ever, for our spirit has become ethereal.[171]

This central theological question, that of the relationship between the "realm of light" and the "external world of shadows," preoccupied MacDonald. Is God responsible for the shadows? Here, MacDonald suggests that the Jews *assigned* evil to the hand of God; in other words, that God was apparently the source of evil, but that the appearance was deceptive. God allowing Godself to be thus implicated is, instead, evidence of divine forbearance regarding temporal rebellion, but also hints at the more radical view that all evil not only works for good, but *is* a good.[172] The world is a "vale of probation" (Novalis),[173] or, as John Keats put it, a "system of Soul-making," a "School instituted for the purpose of teaching little children to read," an unpleasant but necessary experience:

> Do you not see how necessary a World of Pains and troubles is to school an Intelligence and make it a soul? A place where the heart must feel and suffer in a thousand diverse ways?[174]

Or as MacDonald put it:

> What is the whole system of things for, but our education? Does God care for suns and planets and satellites, for divine mathematics and ordered harmonies, more than for his children?[175]

This "World of Pains" always brings positive results and is controlled by God. Scenes of widespread, apparently meaningless, suffering, such as animals "evermore issuing from the fountain of life, daily born into evil things," inevitably focus on eschatological resolution; in this case, the view that animals, too, will be resurrected.[176] Without this perspective,

---

171. Novalis quoted in Travers, *European Literature*, 28.

172. In 1710, Leibniz had also argued that evil was a catalyst for good. See Leibniz, *Theodicy*, 130.

173. Novalis, *Henry of Ofterdingen*, 118.

174. Colvin, *Letters of John Keats*, 256.

175. *US2* 77.

176. *HG* 210.

MacDonald is forced to concur with Darwin that God would have to be considered a demon:

> To believe that God made many of the lower creatures merely for prey, or to be the slaves of a slave, and writhe under the tyrannies of a cruel master who will not serve his own master; that he created an endless succession of them to reap little or no good of life but its cessation . . . is to believe in a God who, so far as one portion of his creation is concerned, is a demon.[177]

In this life, then, God is ensuring that all things work together towards the fundamental goal of creating children.

Evil Sheepdogs and Wicked Fairies

"Sorrow herself will reveal one day that she was only the beneficent shadow of Joy," writes MacDonald, but then ponders: "Will Evil ever show herself the beneficent shadow of Good?"[178] That evil, like Milton's Satan, is the (albeit unwitting) servant of good is a perennial refrain, expressed thus, for example, in *Little Daylight*: "But I never knew of any interference on the part of a wicked fairy that did not turn out a good thing in the end."[179] Or, in a letter to the wife of A. J. Scott: "But you must not be too much disappointed if he should not get [the position], for you know *nothing can go wrong, or be really a misfortune.*"[180]

Evil, however, is not only the servant of good, but *is* a good, as illustrated by Gibbie's view that the Good Shepherd has "evil sheepdogs" at his command.[181] These dogs are not merely "around and about" the shepherd: these "strong, sharp-toothed sheep-dogs" are specifically there because the great shepherd *sent* them to worry the recalcitrant rebel until s/he repents;[182] but are these "sacred creatures"—"pain, fear, anxiety, and shame"—necessarily evil?[183] All are human *responses* to some external stimulus rather than "evil" in themselves, and are in the same category as doubts:

177. HG 206.
178. AF 2:242.
179. NW 269.
180. Sadler, *Expression of Character*, 112 (emphasis mine).
181. Page 160.
182. US2 194.
183. See note 39, page 104.

> Doubts are the messengers of the Living One to rouse the honest. They are the first knock at our door of things that are not yet, but have to be, understood; and theirs in general is the inhospitable reception of angels that do not come in their own likeness.[184]

That what we name "evil" may not be so is evident. David Kelsey, for example, remarks that the food chain is part of God's creation that was called "good."[185] MacDonald, however, needs to go further: since *all* humans are God's children, whether currently rebellious or submissive, all evil must be God's tool for reform, "For whom the LORD loves He chastens, And scourges every son whom He receives" (Heb 12:6; Prov 3:12). So the "dogs of the great shepherd" are targeted at the "unchildlike soul" characterized by "arrogance and ignorance" who feels it has "rights *against* God"; despite operating in "the will of the flesh," it is still a child—one in whom God's "candle still burns," albeit dimly.[186] The dogs, then, are not evil but angels in disguise sent by the Good Shepherd who leaves the ninety-nine to search for the lost one (Matt 18:12; Luke 15:4).

So what about the wicked fairies? We find more information about them in *Little Daylight*.

> Now wicked fairies will not be bound by the laws which the good fairies obey. . . . But it is all of no consequence, for they never succeed [in gaining their ends]; nay, in the end it brings about the very thing they are trying to prevent. So you see . . . wicked fairies are dreadfully stupid, although from the beginning of the world they have really helped instead of thwarted the good fairies, not one of them is a bit wiser for it.[187]

This echoes Milton's view of Satan:

> That with reiterated crimes he might
> Heap on himself damnation, while he sought
> Evil to others, and enrag'd might see
> How all his malice serv'd but to bring forth
> Infinite goodness, grace and mercy shewn
> On Man by him seduc't[188]

---

184. *US2* 201; cf. Heb 13:2.
185. Kelsey, *Eccentric Existence*, 208.
186. *US2* 193–94.
187. *NW* 287.
188. Milton, *Paradise Lost*, 1:214–19.

Unlike the angelic dogs, "wicked fairies," it appears—who have been trying to undermine things "from the beginning of the world"—*are* morally evil. That moral evil is essentially willful is admissible; that "wicked fairies" have always "really helped . . . the good fairies" is more problematic. It implies that willful moral evil is part of God's design. Since God cannot be held responsible for moral evil, we must conclude that the "wicked fairies" do not really have free will (that God is the puppet-master behind the scenes) and this moral evil is really a good. This appears to be the message of the narratives we have explored.

The Ministry of Pain

Thus pain, and suffering, is a good. In the novel *What's Mine's Mine*, where an honest Scots clan is pitched against a whisky-brewing English interloper, MacDonald speaks of the "ministry of pain." Alister, the young (honest peasant) laird is ploughing with two bulls in harness. When the animals start an altercation, he "took the reins, and administering a blow each to the animals, made them stand still."[189] In the following monologue, aimed at enlightening one of the Englishman's daughters horrified by the gratuitous violence, he explains:

> There are tender-hearted people who virtually object to the whole scheme of creation; they would neither have force used nor pain suffered. . . . Millions of human beings but for suffering would never develop an atom of affection. The man who would spare *due* suffering is not wise. It is folly to conclude a thing ought not to be done because it hurts. There are powers to be born, creations to be perfected, sinners to be redeemed, through the ministry of pain, that could be born, perfected, redeemed, in no other way.[190]

This may be a fictive voice, but MacDonald is clearly exploring the Keatsian view that suffering is a necessary "evil" intrinsic to "the whole scheme of creation" without which "millions" would never be born, perfected, or—significantly—*redeemed*. The phrase "*due* suffering" implies "you asked for it": that willful behavior has negative consequences. In *Mary Marston*, for example, after the death of their baby, both parents

---

189. WMM 1:169.
190. WMM 1:169.

(the father responsible for the death through neglect) become ill. It is the beginning of the father's reformation:

> Whatever the effect of illness may be upon the temper of some, it is most certainly an ally of the conscience. All pains, indeed, and all sorrows, all demons, yea, and all sins themselves, under the suffering care of the highest minister, are but the ministers of truth and righteousness.[191]

But are *"all demons"* and *"all sins themselves"*—even if under "the care of the highest minister"—really "ministers of truth and righteousness"? This is a strong claim.[192] One might justifiably conclude: "It is by the prince of demons that he drives out demons" (Matt 9:34).[193] MacDonald appears unable to accept that undeserved, destructive evil exists. Here, for example, he suggests that such affliction must be caused by "exceptional faultiness of character" rather than that, as Jesus once observed, "neither this man nor his parents sinned" (John 9:3), or, if this is not the case, that it is given "for the greatness of good" it would bring. In short, symptoms such as "pain, fear, anxiety, and shame" are always evidence of sin (or the Good Shepherd's remedial response to it), ignoring the fact that many sinners live very happy and healthy lives, and many saints are tormented to faithlessness.

The problem is that "millions of human beings" suffer the consequences of evil whose "ministry" results in the exact opposite of "developing affection." MacDonald seems to have backed himself into a corner: his universalism implies that God is morally bound to make "all things work together for good" for *all*.[194] This contributes to the inadequacy and unbelievability of many of his fictive portrayals, especially of children exposed to evil.

---

191. *MM* 232.

192. Dramatized in *Castle Warlock*. The laird regards his drunken English guest "with something of the pity an angel must feel for the wretch to whom he is set to give his last chance—ere sorer measures be taken in which angels are not the ministers" (*CW* 127).

193. Cf. Matt 12:24; Mark 3:22; Luke 11:15.

194. In the discourse about "babes" and the "wise and prudent" (and elsewhere) the implication is that *all* humans are already "children" and that the good father will therefore bring them home. Other passages, however, imply a decision is needed to become a child, and only then does real childhood begin (as briefly discussed on page 156).

In mitigation, one must note that MacDonald was not writing in a vacuum. Like many Victorians, life was not easy. He was predeceased by five of his eleven children and throughout his life battled with tuberculosis, often coming near to death and experiencing chronic pain. He expresses a personal view of suffering and the possibility of death in *The Diary of an Old Soul*:

> Yestereve, Death came, and knocked at my thin door,
> I from the window looked: the thing I saw,
> The shape uncouth, I had not seen before.
> I was disturbed—with fear, in sooth, not awe;
> Whereof ashamed, I instantly did rouse
> My will to seek thee—only to fear the more;
> Alas! I could not find thee in the house.
>
> I was like Peter when he began to sink.
> To thee a new prayer therefore I have got—
> That, when death comes in earnest to my door,
> Thou wouldst thyself go, when the latch doth clink,
> And lead him to my room, up to my cot;
> Then hold thy child's hand, hold and leave him not,
> Till Death has done with him for evermore.[195]

These stanzas are, perhaps, more realistic than much of his fiction: approaching death "disturbs," engenders fear, and then shame about being afraid. However, the reference to the "cot" and the prayer to "hold thy child's hand" indicate that even at this point of personal doubt he is confident of being a child. But he is writing as a believer: our question here concerns those who are *not* "children." A believer may be able accept MacDonald's assertion:

> It is worth all suffering—yes that suffering that springs from vacancy, abortiveness & futility—to be at length one with God.[196]

However, evidence regarding the impact of evil on unbelievers does not support this claim unless one accepts the tenuous claim that the suffering of those such as the suicidal Charley Osbourne, or the sensitive soldier in *The Broken Swords* who dies a futile premature death, is of benefit.

195. *Rampolli* 190.
196. Sadler, *Expression of Character*, 65.

Soteriology

MacDonald's soteriology is driven by a profound suspicion of "schemes of salvation" that exclude large swathes of humanity such as the "good Brahmin,"[197] savages,[198] or the suicide. Instead, he focuses on the universal human encounter with God. Since hell is the impenitent soul's destructive encounter with God's righteous being, "salvation" involves repentance and the restoration of correct vision. This is an iterative process: true sight of God precipitates repentance which, in turn, enhances and expands vision. Put differently, "evil" comes down to *how* one sees and experiences rather than *what* one is seeing and experiencing. Since salvation is a process, not an event, daily obedience is of more value than (theoretical) belief; the latter, he argues, is immaterial,[199] "for to hold a thing with the intellect, is not to believe it. A man's real belief is that which he lives by."[200] We begin to explore MacDonald's soteriology, therefore, by considering further how both "hell" and "salvation" are aspects of God's being before considering in what sense Christ has effected salvation.

Hell and Salvation

The abiding post-Reformation question—"How do I know I am one of the elect?"—led to the more practical concern—"How do I escape from hell?"—a concern also to MacDonald, for despite equating hell with God's being, he does not minimize its severity or imply its non-existence. Writing in the preface to a contemporary dramatization, *Letters from Hell*, he warns against assuming that moral objections to caricatures of hell or questions about its eternal duration imply its non-existence:

> In these days has arisen another falsehood—less, yet very perilous: thousands of half-thinkers imagine that, since it is declared with such authority that hell is not everlasting, there is then no hell at all.[201]

---

197. *RF* 2:97.

198. *US3* 34.

199. For example: "Opinion, right or wrong, will do nothing to save him. . . . With his opinions, true or false, I have nothing to do" (*US3* 139).

200. *US2* 239; cf. "Do you put faith in *him* . . . or in the doctrines and commandments of men?" (*US2* 247).

201. Thisted, *Letters from Hell*, viii, a book which may have inspired Lewis's *Screwtape Letters*.

MacDonald does object, though, to medieval images of the "hell of Exhausted Mercy"—"a hell the smoke of whose torments would arise and choke the elect themselves about the throne of God"[202] (he suggests that Dante's mind was "lowered" by his narrative)[203]—that God's creative power must sustain life in a state of eternal destruction such that "the breath still breathed into the soul of man by his Maker is no longer the breath of life, but the breath of infinite death."[204]

We need to be clear here about MacDonald's cosmology. At the center of his universe is the "burning" love of God, at the other extreme is "outer darkness." The latter is the realm of "The Lost Soul" (see below) where, as it asymptotically approaches nihility (MacDonald implies that sentience is never quite extinguished), God's presence nevertheless sustains life. This place of outer darkness is MacDonald's hell. It is *not* the place where the fire of God as a purgatorial force is felt most keenly (which he often refers to as "hell");[205] that moment of purgatorial mercy has already been rejected. It is an "outer darkness" reserved for those who have "hate[d] the fire of God." A time when:

> God withdraws from a man as far as that can be without the man's ceasing to be; when the man feels himself abandoned, hanging in a ceaseless vertigo of existence upon the verge of the gulf of his being, without support, without refuge, without aim, without end—for the soul has no weapons wherewith to destroy herself—with no inbreathing of joy, with nothing to make life good.[206]

It is the place where the fire of God burns, where human perception is dulled, and divine manifestation is more ominous:

> The outer darkness is but the most dreadful form of the consuming fire—the fire without light—the darkness visible, the black flame. God hath withdrawn himself, but not lost his hold. His face is turned away, but his hand is laid upon him still. His heart has ceased to beat into the man's heart, but he keeps him alive by his fire.[207]

---

202. *AF* 2:195.
203. "George MacDonald on Dante," 37.
204. *AF* 3:266.
205. For example: "I believe that no hell will be lacking which would help the just mercy of God to redeem his children" (*US3* 155).
206. *US1* 47.
207. *US1* 48.

The fire of God's presence, therefore, all-pervasive and sustaining of life, is equally present at heart and skirt of the universe. The continuum of God's presence is perceived "morally": the child perceives God as love and its location as being at the heart of this loving universe in the embrace of God; the rebel perceives God as a dark fire of hate and its location as being in exile at the periphery of existence.

While this leads to a broadly universalist position on the basis that it is unlikely that those experiencing the hellfire of God will resist God's love for ever (he suggests Judas and Satan will find refuge in God),[208] it does not equate to the naive view that God simply hugs everyone, no matter what:[209] suffering is sometimes necessary to deliver humans from sin. If a sinner does not respond to this therapy, with perhaps a nod to Jonathan Edwards he concludes: "There would, I presume, be nothing left for God but to set his foot upon him and crush him, as we would crush a noxious insect."[210] It *will* result in the "destruction of the sinner," but this assertion is qualified: "That, however, would, it appears to me, be for God to suffer defeat, blameless indeed, but defeat."[211] The somewhat macabre poem "The Lost Soul," for example, implies annihilation. A shriveled soul, once a self-wise philosopher, lies in "insensate gloom." Another, watching this "death," empathetically senses destruction:

> As if I lay in thy grave,
> I feel the Infinite sucking back
> The individual life it gave.
> Thy spring died to a pool, deep, black,
> Which the sun from its pit did lave.[212]

---

208. *US1* 94–95. See also *US3* 241–43, and note 215 below.

209. George McCrie objects to the image of God with his arms wide open to accept sinners "without the need for any interposed Mediator," describing it as "effeminate, silly sentimentalism" (McCrie, *Religion of Our Literature*, 303).

210. *SF* 325.

211. *US3* 129. This idea is not new. Leibniz, for example, writes, "[Yet] objections multiply . . . when one considers salvation and damnation: for it appears strange that, even in the great future of eternity, evil should have the advantage over good, under the supreme authority of him who is the sovereign good, since there will be many that are called and few that are chosen or are saved. . . . Sundry pious persons, learned also, but daring, have revived the opinion of Origen, who maintains that good will predominate in due time, in all and everywhere, and that all rational creatures, even the bad angels, will become at last holy and blessed" (Leibniz, *Theodicy*, 132).

212. *HL* 163.

The "Infinite sucking back [of] individual life" is a strong metaphor for annihilation, and the poem includes the lines:

> It lies alone in its lifeless world,
> As a frozen bud on the earth lies curled
> Sightless and soundless, without a cry,
> On the flat of its own vacuity.

Lines which are rendered in the 1893 version as:

> Like a frost-killed bud on a tombstone curled,
> Crumbling it lies on its crumbling world,
> Sightless and deaf, with never a cry,
> In the hell of its own vacuity![213]

The words "insensate," "tombstone," "frost-killed bud," and "vacuity" strongly imply annihilation, so despite a strong consensus regarding MacDonald's universalism, these words do indicate an element of doubt.[214] His views chime with those of Maurice, summarized by Geoffrey Rowell thus:

> It would be wrong to describe Maurice as a universalist, for universalism states as a dogmatic certainty that all men will be eventually saved, and Maurice suspected the certainty of system. There is no doubt, however, that his understanding of God led him to hope that all men would eventually be saved.[215]

Maurice, emphasizing God's love, summarized his view thus:

> We do not want theories of Universalism; they are as cold, hard, unsatisfactory, as all other theories. But we want that clear, broad assertion of the Divine Charity which the Bible makes, and which carries us immeasurably beyond all that we can ask or think.[216]

---

213. *Poems* 2:36–37.

214. One early commentator draws attention to "his universalism—his belief in the ultimate restoration to goodness and to God of every human soul even of that first and greatest of prodigals, the Devil" ("Interesting Discourse," 25). In 1910, John Hunter had a lecture entitled: "George MacDonald: novelist, poet, preacher, prophet of Universalism" (Amell, "Man of Beatitudes," 22). Raeper notes that MacDonald had "suffered over the Universalist issue" (*GMWR*, 242). See also Hein, *George MacDonald*, 81–82.

215. Rowell, *Hell and the Victorians*, 88.

216. Maurice, *Theological Essays*, 442.

Such "larger hope" had been expressed by Erskine in 1827—"that loving support to all who dared preach universal redemption"[217]—and his words sum up the prevailing mood among subscribers:

> I have a hope (which I would not willingly think contrary to the revelation of mercy) of the ultimate salvation of all. I trust that He who came to bruise the serpent's head will not cease His work of compassion until He has expelled the fatal poison from every individual of our race. I humbly think that the promise bears this wide interpretation.[218]

MacDonald expressed this hope thus:

> But at length, O God, wilt thou not cast Death and Hell into the lake of Fire—even into thine own consuming self? Death shall then die everlastingly,
>
> > And Hell itself will pass away,
> > And leave her dolorous mansions to the peering day.[219]

Elsewhere, using an image from Burns, he observes: "All the snow that fell on [the river] vanished, as death and hell shall one day vanish in the fire of God."[220] He summarizes thus:

> Hell is God's and not the devil's. Hell is on the side of God and man, to free the child of God from the corruption of death. Not one soul will ever be redeemed from hell but by being saved from his sins, from the evil in him. If hell be needful to save him, hell will blaze ... until he takes refuge in the will of the Father.[221]

In an important respect, he argues, the biblical "messengers of the good tidings" have been misunderstood. We are not threatened punishment for the sins we have committed; the message "is of forgiveness, not of vengeance; of deliverance, not of evil to come," continuing:

> Not for anything he has committed do they threaten a man with the outer darkness. Not for any or all of his sins that are past shall a man be condemned; not for the worst of them needs he

---

217. *GMAW* 194.
218. Hanna, *Letters of Thomas Erskine*, 71.
219. *US1* 48. The quote is from Milton's "Hymn on the Morning of Christ's Nativity."
220. *AF* 1:131. See Coleridge, *Collected Works*, 1:80.
221. *HG* 8–9.

> dread remaining unforgiven. *The sin he dwells in, the sin he will not come out of, is the sole ruin of a man.*[222]

Since many die not having renounced sin, in MacDonald's view, the *epektasis* of the soul is a trajectory that intersects with, and punctures, death. (Tolkien rightly observed that MacDonald was obsessed with death, but this does not necessarily imply a morbidity, rather a celebration of death as the doorway to the divine embrace.)[223] Post-mortem salvation is a possibility, as is the need for a purgatorial "clearing up" operation on those who call themselves Christians but are addicted to "*things*"—"fetters of gold."[224] Righteousness, therefore, is an ongoing, obedient response (in this life and the next) to divine forgiveness and "salvation" involves turning to God with a childlike heart. But how is this achieved?

The Christ Event

Two fundamental concerns drive his articulation of the Christ event which he expresses thus: "the worst heresy, next to that of dividing religion and righteousness, is to divide the Father from the Son."[225] The first division leads to a religion of belief (theory) rather than faith (obedience); the second creates the conditions for the false notion that Jesus shields us from the angry Father. Both are summarized in his objection to the idea of imputed righteousness:

> That is, that, by a sort of legal fiction, Jesus was treated as what he was not, in order that we might be treated as what we are not. This is the best device, according to the prevailing theology, that the God of truth, the God of mercy, whose glory is that he is just to men by forgiving their sins, could fall upon for saving his creatures![226]

As John McLeod Campbell had noted in 1848 (also using the term "legal fiction"), it implied "a demand in the divine nature for a certain amount of suffering as the punishment of a certain amount of sin," and that Christ

---

222. *HG* 9 (emphasis mine).
223. Tolkien, "Tree and Leaf," 67.
224. *US2* 38–39.
225. *US2* 143.
226. *US3* 210; cf. *US2* 103–4; 1 John 3:7.

was "actually in His Father's eyes as a criminal through imputation of man's sin"—an idea "that men have revolted from."[227] MacDonald's objection is that the imputation of righteousness of which Paul speaks concerns Abraham being considered righteous because of *his own* faith, not because of the faith of another: "To impute the righteousness of one to another, is simply an act of falsehood; to call the faith of a man his righteousness is simply to speak the truth."[228] The alternative he offers is that God forgives sins (past sinful deeds), but must destroy the inclination to sinfulness: "Let me be regarded as the sinner I am; for nothing will serve my need but to be made a righteous man, one that will no more sin."[229] In his view:

> Christ died to save us, not from suffering, but from ourselves; not from injustice, far less from justice, but from being unjust. He died that we might live—but live as he lives, by dying as he died who died to himself that he might live unto God.[230]

So rather than being somehow infused with righteousness, the Christian journey involves "growing in and toward righteousness,"[231] a journey during which God "swallows up all our imperfections, all our defects, all our evils,"[232] which, as Presbyterian George McCrie fumes, entails "small need of the blood, or for anything more than an exercise of magnanimity."[233]

This tension highlights a problem that had been identified by MacDonald's predecessor, Thomas Erskine, who was "alarmed at the state of religious teaching in Scotland." "Everywhere," he wrote, "salvation from punishment was substituted for salvation from sin, and sin itself was conceived as a series of particular offences, rather than as the whole state of man's alienation from God."[234] Developing this theme, MacDonald argues that Christ's mission was to deal with this alienation by giving humans the power to overcome sinfulness:

---

227. Campbell, *Nature of the Atonement*, 67.
228. *US3* 213.
229. *US3* 212.
230. *US3* 96.
231. *US3* 218.
232. *US1* 24–25. See page 136.
233. McCrie, *Religion of Our Literature*, 302.
234. Rowell, *Hell and the Victorians*, 72–73.

> Repentance, restitution, confession, prayer for forgiveness, righteous dealing thereafter, is the sole possible, the only true make-up for sin. For nothing less than this did Christ die. . . .
>
> The work of Jesus Christ on earth was the creative atonement, because it works atonement in every heart. He brings and is bringing God and man, and man and man, into perfect unity: "I in them and thou in me, that they may be perfect in one."[235]

This polemical sermon, "Justice," building on Erskine's views, is the clearest statement of MacDonald's soteriology. He argues that God forgives, rather than punishes, past sin on the basis that punishment "is not the thing required of God, but the absolute destruction of sin."[236] Answering those such as McCrie who ask, "How could he be a just God and not punish sin?" MacDonald argues—quoting Psalm 62:12, which in his KJV reads: "Also unto thee, O Lord, belongeth mercy: for thou renderest to every man according to his work"—that mercy only exists, or is necessary, because sin exists; if there was no sin there would be no need for God to exercise mercy. In which case, are not mercy and justice in God equivalents?

> If God punish sin, it must be merciful to punish sin; and if God forgive sin, it must be just to forgive sin. We are required to forgive, with the argument that our father forgives. It must, I say, be right to forgive. Every attribute of God must be infinite as himself. He cannot be sometimes merciful, and not always merciful. He cannot be just, and not always just. Mercy belongs to him, and needs no contrivance of theologic chicanery to justify it.[237]

In short, since the problem of evil is couched primarily in terms of enslaved human will, Christ creates the conditions for that will to make a genuinely free choice to return to the Father. It is a prioritizing of declarations that Christ came to neutralize the power of evil (such as Hebrews 2:14–15) and a rejection of what are considered misinterpretations of passages that imply that righteousness is a "substance" that can be somehow imputed to a sinner (such as 2 Corinthians 5:21). It reflects the Maurician emphasis on the deepest place in the universe being the love of God, relegating sin to a temporary state that ends with the repentance,

---

235. *US3* 128–29; John 17:23.
236. *US3* 122–23.
237. *US3* 119–20.

not the destruction, of the sinner. It is a cosmology—and therefore a soteriology—based on the premise that:

> There is nothing eternal but that which loves and can be loved, and love is ever climbing towards the consummation when such shall be the universe, imperishable, divine.
>
> Therefore all that is not beautiful in the beloved, all that comes between and is not of love's kind, must be destroyed.[238]

To summarize: speech about "growing into childhood" reflects two priorities that characterize an acceptable response: first, that "childhood" is the essence and goal of human nature since this is the divine "idea of the universe," and second, that it is not a one-off salvation event, but an ongoing choice to be obedient. Humans *grow* into childhood: like Swedenborg's angels, they become progressively younger, and, like Gregory of Nyssa's soul, "expand" and become more divine as the journey towards God progresses. As MacDonald put it, writing towards the end of his life: "If we are not little ones of a perfect love, I can see no sense in things."[239]

It is, however, evident that MacDonald fails to account for the negative and destructive forces embedded in this "system of Soul-making" that genuinely damage creaturely wellbeing by acting *on* a person, rather than being the result of individual sin, particularly the thorny issue of destructive natural events, disease, or suffering that, if attributed to God, would imply suspect divine morality. Neither does he consider consequential evil: that, since we are located in a finite world, even with "the best (childlike) will in the world," human decisions may have destructive implications for others. The refrains "all will be well" and "a great good is coming"[240] are comforting, but they look to eschatological resolution without addressing "earthly" issues which, as David Kelsey insists, should really be on the table if theology is to do its job.[241] These are issues to be borne in mind as we read further.

---

238. *US1* 28.

239. Sadler, *Expression of Character*, 357.

240. The family motto was "Corage! God mend al!" an anagram of MacDonald's name. As *Phantastes* draws to a close, the protagonist hears nature whisper: "'A great good is coming—is coming—is coming to thee, Anodos'; and so over and over again" (*PH* 322).

241. Kelsey, *Eccentric Existence*, 212.

6

The View of Evangelicalism from Fairyland

George MacDonald's *Via Media*

THE INCREASINGLY VOCAL DEFENSE of *"The Truth!"*[1] by parties within Evangelicalism forms the backdrop to George MacDonald's thought. As explored in chapter 1, the picture is one of a church divided by contrasting responses to external pressures. While located in a wider ecclesial battle for survival, the skirmish between Evangelical conservatives and liberals exercises MacDonald because his personal journey was a migration from the former to the latter. However, although broadly "liberal"—and certainly anti-conservative—he offers another perspective which challenges both by questioning the validity of truth-claims. Truth, he argues, must be appropriated "aesthetically" by imaginatively discerning its symbolic and metaphorical nature. Although ostensibly making him vulnerable to the charge of subjectivism, he is suggesting that so-called external "facts" relating to religion are just as illusory and that—since phenomenally perceived by human consciousness—claims to validity are not as strong as supposed.

In this chapter we explore MacDonald's *via media*, his alternative to rationalist methodologies which, in his view, had lost connection with reality, "reality" for MacDonald being a cosmos redolent with God's immanent presence in nature and in human consciousness providing a

---

1. From a scene in *Lilith* explored in chapter 7. See page 220.

wider context in which to evaluate the fruits of logic. One way of exploring that wider context is MacDonald's use of fairy children. Being less earth-bound, they offer a more objective, incisive critique than their "realist" counterparts.

MacDonald's questionable account of evil is, I shall argue, a reaction to even more questionable accounts. We begin by exploring the conservative and liberal Evangelical perspectives against which he is reacting, noting that the polarities described here represent the extremes of a spectrum of views. Negative criticism should not distract from the fact that Evangelicalism as a whole was making a positive impact on British society. Evangelicals were generally associated with "the cultivation of vital Christianity."[2]

Evangelical Views of Evil

The Conservative View

The antagonism between conservative and liberal Evangelicals arguably led to a sense of unreality in the theology of both, that is, a disconnect between theological claims and lived experience; that propositions, although "logical," did not "ring true." For example, the conservative insistence on a young earth and a literal fire of eternal hell was undermined by scientific (in the former case) or moral (in the latter case) objections. Critics touched a raw nerve when challenging the veracity of conservative truth-claims, often provoking a vehement response since the foundations of faith were at stake. As Nicholas Lash observes:

> Perhaps only a faith that has lost its nerve feels obliged continually to insist that it is quite sure of itself, and knows quite clearly what is to be said concerning the mystery of God.[3]

Retreat, resulting in increasing polarization, ensued, the most notable example being Spurgeon who declared his inability to fellowship with those in the Baptist Union who denied the "real gospel." As Hopkins notes, his refusal to engage personally in the debates surrounding the "down grade" controversy—what he saw as the erosion of Baptist truth by

---

2. Bebbington, *Dominance of Evangelicalism*, 235.
3. Lash, *Theology on Dover Beach*, 31. Charley Osbourne remarks that his father's abusive and defensive behavior is because, "He's afraid [his religion] mayn't be true after all" (*WC* 173).

liberal influences—added to its acidity,[4] and "Spurgeon's views on holiness and sin sufficed unaided to set up a barrier between himself and the entire spectrum of contemporary liberal theological revision."[5]

The conservative inability to accept the liberal position that truth was "relational"—that is, contingent upon cultural context and conscious, personal engagement with it—led to the vehement defense of traditional Evangelical orthodoxy. Criticism of such received orthodoxy centered around the problem of evil: the perception that God was not so much addressing the issue of evil as responsible for it; that the "plan of salvation" on offer was subtly artificial; that eternal torment implied a morally corrupt deity; and that the proposition that humans were entirely depraved was untenable. Words like "darkness," "inflexibility," and "hardness" were frequently used to describe the extreme forms of Calvinism, said to foster a severe, negative view of life, even madness. Christopher White's review of American Christianity in the years 1830–1880, for example, notes that incidences of anxiety tending towards madness were not uncommon:

> Liberals across the spectrum—from free-preaching frontier Universalists and Congregationalists to urbane Unitarians—thought Calvinism promoted an unhealthy piety that made believers hopeless and mentally unstable. Different symptoms resulted—an infirm body, poor mental development, depression, insomnia, insanity.[6]

The case of Elizabeth Cady Stanton—who later became a "disenchanted Evangelical"[7]—illustrates the practical effects of the doctrine of election which so troubled Annie in *Alec Forbes*, amplified by Thomas Cramm's efforts to get her "convertit":

> The young . . . Stanton was terrified about salvation and was caught in a paralyzing conviction of her inability. Though she somehow mustered a moment of joyful conversion, her relief was cut short by Charles G. Finney's incessant harpings on "the depravity and deceitfulness of the human heart." Had her heart fooled her into thinking she had been saved? What could she do? How could she know?[8]

---

4. Hopkins, *Nonconformity's Romantic Generation*, 230.
5. Hopkins, *Nonconformity's Romantic Generation*, 144.
6. White, "Minds Intensely Unsettled," 231.
7. Hempton, *Evangelical Disenchantment*, 92–113.
8. White, "Minds Intensely Unsettled," 235.

White notes that such heart-searching was not a by-product of Calvinism but, like Manning's sermon from a Tractarian perspective,[9] one of its goals: "Calvinist doctrines were intended to produce an anxious alertness, an unsettling conviction of total sinfulness" from which there was no escape. MacDonald, likewise, was troubled by a gospel that led to people

> wasting themselves in soul-sickening self-examination as to whether they are believers, whether they are really trusting in the atonement, whether they are truly sorry for their sins—the way to madness of the brain, and despair of the heart.[10]

The picture is confirmed by a recent study of the effects of strict Calvinism in one of the last areas in Scotland where it survives in its most Federal form—the island of Lewis. Here, the church divides people into the elect and the reprobate, denying the latter access not just to communion but to the communion service. Like MacDonald's sketch of the disturbed Charley whose repressive religious father dominates the skyline of his son's life, the result here is "a profound sense of guilt" leading to increased incidences of depression and suicide that have been linked directly to Calvinist preaching.[11]

Those doing the preaching were not immune. R. W. Dale, for example, as assistant minister pressured to teach the "old theology" under the watchful eye of his predecessor at Carrs Lane Congregational Church in Birmingham, John Angell James, turned down a speaking engagement because he was battling with "seasons of depression, heavy, terrible, overwhelming."[12] Spurgeon also, having earlier in his career relished the preaching of damnation, later said the doctrine gave him "the bitterest anguish of spirit."[13] Echoing Iain McGilchrist's observation that at the

---

9. Pages 61–63.

10. *US2* 244.

11. Macritchie, "Celtic Culture," 274–75. Greville MacDonald notes: "In the Island of Lewis the ministers of the Secession Church had compelled the destruction of pipes and fiddles. 'If there was a foolish man . . . who demurred, the good ministers and the good elders themselves broke and burned their instruments, saying: Better is the small fire that warms on the little day of peace / Than the big fire that burns on the great day of wrath'" (*GMAW* 29n2). The quotation is from Carmichael, *Carmina Gadelica*, 1900; cf. note 15, page 63.

12. Dale, *Life*, 79. See also Johnson, *Dissolution of Dissent*, 45.

13. Hopkins, *Nonconformity's Romantic Generation*, 150–51.

Reformation "the Flesh is made Word,"[14] the author of the Isle of Lewis report concludes:

> What we have is a religion of words instead of an encounter with the living Word, words that have been made into an idolatry and substitute for what they represent. From a psychoanalytic perspective, what we have here is a schizoid faith, split away from incarnation, from the flesh and guts of the world, withdrawn from involvement in the world's suffering, from its history, its politics, its economics.[15]

That this represents extreme conservative Calvinism (Samuel Law Wilson's accusation)[16] is admitted; the issue, however, is that such "hard" views were always in the background in the nineteenth century, bleeding into the softer forms of Evangelicalism. As Mark Johnson observes, the forced marriage of the "moderate Calvinism" of the early part of the century (election) to Evangelicalism (Christ died for all) resulted in "a confused mixture,"[17] one that in the eyes of MacDonald had never exorcised the demons of the past. Rather than account for evil, many critics considered conservative theology a source of evil. In short, the conservative theological account of evil, and its practical consequences, did not "ring true."

The Liberal View

The same, however, could be said of the liberal position. Conservatives accused liberals of being "effeminate" and "sentimental," particularly those of a more Romantic persuasion such as the Congregational minister Thomas Toke Lynch (for MacDonald, "a man of true insight and large heart").[18] The issue came into focus in 1855 when Lynch published an inoffensive book of devotional poems called *The Rivulet: a Contribution to Sacred Song*, a work having an "obvious debt to the romantic spirit" illustrating the rise of a subjectivism that was seen as the polar opposite to the objectivity of the old school giving rise to what was termed "The New

---

14. McGilchrist, *Master and His Emissary*, 323. See page 139.
15. Macritchie, "Celtic Culture," 276.
16. Page 19.
17. Johnson, *Dissolution of Dissent*, 13.
18. *Orts* 220.

Theology."[19] Like William Hale White, who attributed his escape from Congregationalism to the ministrations of Wordsworth,[20] Lynch too—though a poor poet—was clearly influenced by his hero. Nature imagery abounds, and we are treated to stanzas such as:

> Flowers will not cease to speak
> And tell the praise of God
> Even to the careless man
> Who has upon them trod. . . .
>
> Pure juices sweetened by the skies
> Are in the grass; and, look!
> There feeds the lamb for sacrifice
> In meadows by the brook.[21]

These lines would, perhaps, have benefitted from the oblivion of history had it not been for John Campbell's heated objections. Campbell, who had been the Congregational minister at Moorfields Tabernacle in London in the 1830s to 1840s and then the self-appointed spokesman for Evangelical conservatism through his platform as the editor of Congregational publications, "had become increasingly obsessed [in the late 1840s] with what he correctly saw to be an erosion of the orthodox evangelicalism, or the moderate Calvinism of the Congregational churches . . . he singled out 'an increase in German error.'"[22] Campbell saw *The Rivulet* as anything but inoffensive, rather the first trickle of a liberal inundation in danger of swamping true Christianity. Lynch was, according to another critic (one James Grant), "pervaded throughout by the Rationalist Theology of Germany."[23] Such Romantic "rationalism" was, ironically,

---

19. Johnson, *Changing Shape of English Nonconformity*, 106. R. W. Dale wrote *The Old Evangelicalism and the New* in 1889. Old Evangelicalism was the conversionist theology of the Evangelical Revival, however with a focus that Christ died for all (unlike the "Old Dissent" of Calvinist Puritanism); the New Evangelicalism suggested that old dissenters had lived a "cloistered existence in their preoccupation with personal salvation . . . withdrawn from wider responsibilities of citizenship" (Johnson, *Dissolution of Dissent*, 6).

20. Hale White, *Autobiography*, 19.

21. Lynch, *Rivulet*, 7, 154.

22. Johnson, *Dissolution of Dissent*, 16.

23. Bebbington, *Dominance of Evangelicalism*, 156.

seen as producing an excess of speculation and imagination. MacDonald, for example, stood accused of:

> the enthronement of the individual consciousness over any objective rule of faith....
>
> [A theory] which discredits the authority of Scripture, and leaves every man free to shape his own theology according to his own tastes, feelings, and even prejudices, [and] is Rationalism, pure and simple.[24]

Neither Darwin's tentative conclusion that nature might be demon-designed or Tennyson's view that it was "red in tooth and claw," nor the conservative view that both humanity and nature were intrinsically corrupt were compatible with Goethe's view of nature as God's robe. As Spurgeon had pessimistically put it: "the best we can do with this world is to get through it as quickly as we can, for we dwell in an enemy's country,"[25] and, as Campbell pointed out, Lynch's own words betrayed him: nature was not as benign or numinous as those such as he claimed:

> O, *the bright and vast creation*
> *Can be terrible and stern,*
> From its stroke be no salvation,
> Though on every side we turn:
> Lord of nature, Lord of nature,
> Then to Thee our spirits yearn.[26]

Such an optimistic view of human nature was also criticized for ignoring "the awful controversy caused by sin,"[27] a phrase summative of the conservative view that Romantic liberalism was deficient in its account of reality, particularly relating to sin. Not only did the Romantic view of reality undermine conservative Evangelical orthodoxy, it also did not "ring true."

---

24. Wilson, *Theology of Modern Literature*, 316–17.
25. Hopkins, *Nonconformity's Romantic Generation*, 150.
26. Lynch, *Rivulet*, 109 (emphasis mine). See Watts, *Dissenters*, 3:9.
27. Wilson, *Theology of Modern Literature*. Note 80, page 28.

"A Little World of His Own"—The View from Fairyland

MacDonald would, I believe, have applauded Chesterton's views on madness:

> Imagination does not breed insanity. Exactly what does breed insanity is reason. Poets do not go mad; but chess-players do. . . . I am not, as will be seen, in any sense attacking logic: I only say that this danger does lie in logic, not in imagination.[28]

However, if extreme "logical" conservatism caused madness, then Romantic liberalism, one might say—reflecting Ruskin's and Eliot's verdicts on Romanticism—tended towards blindness. Both "views" of reality arguably resulted in an inability to see truly, to account for the world experienced by human consciousness. MacDonald offers an alternative perspective by using his "fairy vision,"[29] by viewing the world through the eyes of a fairy child—a fantasy creation of mid-nineteenth-century Romanticism and therefore prone to a somewhat over-optimistic view of the world, but one attempting, nevertheless, to see clearly and through whose eyes we survey a sometimes bleak, often idealized, landscape. Unlike the children of Calvinism, this Coleridgean child prioritizes imaginative vision on the understanding that imagination is a "repetition in the finite mind of the I AM"; it is also, therefore, a divine agent. From fairyland, from the other side of Chesterton's hedge,[30] it gives us a fresh perspective on the world of humans. The confusion comes when this child, one such as Gibbie, visits the real world. Before exploring this approach in MacDonald's fantasy text *Lilith*, we critically consider MacDonald's thought experiment.

At the outset, it is important to make the distinction between the ideal and the fantastic. The former is a state of affairs that might be possible in a world of perfection. As evil exists, the ideal is always unattainable in the present quotidian context but nevertheless may dictate a legitimate course of action which is a moral good. The fantastic only exists in fairyland and represents a state of affairs unattainable in the quotidian world but which may nevertheless throw the nature of that world into relief.

---

28. Chesterton, *Orthodoxy*, 10–11. In Chesterton's opinion, "only one great English poet went mad, Cowper. And he was definitely driven mad by logic, by the ugly and alien logic of predestination" (Chesterton, *Orthodoxy*, 5).

29. Greville MacDonald's phrase. See page 39.

30. Chesterton, *Orthodoxy*, 47.

One problem we face in MacDonald is the blurring of the boundaries between the real (the human proximate context), the ideal, the fantastic, and the transcendent—the latter being, in MacDonald's scheme, that which exists in God's imagination beyond present human knowledge, elements of which might be abductively revealed by the Spirit.

To give an example: F. D. Maurice's "brotherhood of man" theology led to a belief that the prime need was not for evangelism aimed at transferring people into the kingdom of God, but waking people to knowledge of their present status as members of it. Thus the task of the evangelist was to:

> [call forth] the heart and conscience of men, so that being first able to see their Father in heaven truly, and themselves in their true relation to Him, they may afterwards manfully investigate, as I am sure they will long to do, the conditions under which they themselves, His children, exist.[31]

This optimism underpinning Maurice's Christian Socialism, that "men"—especially poor men—would "manfully investigate the conditions under which they exist," is dramatized in *Robert Falconer*. Falconer, a superhero who appears to know most Londoners by name and can fell recalcitrant policemen with a single blow without charges being pressed,[32] offers some advice to a destitute Spitalfields weaver. The narrator notes:

> This man had lost his wife and three children, his whole family except a daughter now sick, by a slow-consuming hunger; and he did not believe there was a God that ruled in the earth. But he supported his unbelief by no other argument than a hopeless bitter glance at his empty loom.[33]

Unbelief rather than unemployment is the main issue. To wake his "higher nature" he is admonished to snap out of it and serve his even more impoverished neighbors on the basis that—

> *the nature of the Son of Man was in him*, and that to get him to do as the Son of Man did, in ever so small a degree, was the readiest means of bringing his higher nature to the birth.[34]

---

31. Maurice, *Theological Essays*, 29.
32. *RF* 3:113–14.
33. *RF* 3:91.
34. *RF* 3:101 (emphasis mine).

Being already a child, indwelt by the Spirit, all is needed is obedience to the initial spark of revelation to fan the fire of faith.

In such ways MacDonald was mediating his understanding of Maurice's academic prose to a wider audience, and I suggest that the process, the creative process of dramatizing that theology, reveals its shortcomings—not necessarily shortcomings in Maurice's theology, but, perhaps, in MacDonald's interpretation of Maurice. There is often a naivety, sentimentality, and unreality prompting one critic of the novel *Guild Court*, for example, to observe that "he might as well have located his characters in Eden or in the planet Mars."[35] So how should we read it?

It is clear from the above narrative that Falconer is a Christ figure[36]—the policeman incident reinforces this in that he is somehow above earthly law—but having arrived via fairyland (with Christ-like attributes but nevertheless a product of MacDonald's imagination) has clearly misread the social situation and assumed that either God has ordained poverty or that inequality is inconsequential compared to the more fundamental issue of unbelief. The tableau illustrates the admissible proposition that Christ is active in society and humans have a responsibility to acknowledge this, but sets this within a fantastic setting. Purporting to be a picture of nineteenth-century London, its idealist caricature is so far from lived experience that the message—the poor must be woken up and work towards their own salvation—is perceived to be a foreign import from fairyland. It is the story of a naive fairy visitor to an ideal world.

Similar comments might be made regarding characters such as Gibbie. Also a Christ-inspired being from fairyland (or "Eden or the planet Mars") Gibbie's muteness, like Diamond's incoherence, reinforces his fairy status: his inability to converse with humans (except imperfectly through his wife's intuitive relaying of his wishes or through the cumbersome efforts of writing on a slate)[37] indicates a fundamental otherness. He does not speak human language. He cannot relate to, neither does he

---

35. *"Guild Court."*

36. We encounter passages such as: "While Falconer spoke, his face grew grander and grander, till at last it absolutely shone. I felt that I walked with a man whose faith was his genius" (*RF* 3:120). In the previous novel that had introduced the character of Falconer there is authorial worship: "His [another 'merely human' character's] love was not a high one—not such as thine, my Falconer. Thine was love indeed" (*DE* 3:6).

37. Gibbie does speak three words in the novel. During the flood incident (see page 104), thinking the old shepherd and his wife have been swept away, he cries out, "O Jesus Christ!" (*SG* 196). Gibbie's muteness, it seems, is a divine prohibition rather than a disability.

belong in, the quotidian world, for the world he inhabits, on closer inspection, is on the borders of fairyland where a good fairy is making sure nothing terrible happens. Furthermore, he brings with him a perspective from fairyland that remains unforged in the crucible of human interaction. His belief, in other words, has no need to be refined or challenged in the furnace of conversation, of abrasive social interaction; it has no need to evolve. He is essentially a fairy fundamentalist, firmly convinced his dogma is the truth. The proposition that Christ deals with the problem of evil and in some sense absorbs it on behalf of humanity is blunted by the fairy context in that the evil of "the grey city" bears little resemblance to its real-world corrosive counterpart.

The reason for this is simply that MacDonald has projected onto the nineteenth-century landscape a Romantic naivety about human nature combined with the prevailing view that social hierarchy is ordained by God, that Church and State are guardians of this hierarchical flock, and it is the divine will that some were born to serve others. There was hitherto little will to change the status quo: literature exploring the education of the poor during the first half of the century, for example, is less concerned about bettering their lot than enabling them to fulfil their divinely-ordained station, and Evangelical children's literature likewise assumed that this was the norm. In *The Fairchild Family*, for example, John Trueman, the servant of a household that lives in an idyllic leafy suburbia, is described thus:

> He was a poor working man, and had a wife and six children. But I should not call him poor: I should rather call him rich; for he had cause to hope that his wife and all his children (that is, all who were old enough to inspire such hopes) had been brought to the knowledge of God; and as for John himself, there was reason to think that he was one of the most faithful servants of God in all the country round.[38]

MacDonald does not, in the main, challenge such social roles: his ideal peasants are content with their lot and are the salt of the earth; it is social climbers, such as Rev. Clement Sclater in *Sir Gibbie*, who want to "improve" themselves that endanger social equilibrium. The main sin of the arch-villain in *David Elginbrod*—the Count from Bohemia who uses a ring and powers of mesmerization to entrap weak women—is not, it

---

38. Sherwood, *History of the Fairchild Family*, 9.

seems, his immoral behavior but the fact that he is a fallen servant with pretensions beyond his station.[39]

MacDonald, then, is a man of his time with a Romantic perspective. That he tends to turn a blind eye to evil must be acknowledged. That in many ways he accepts the social views of his age must also be acknowledged, but, as we have explored, this does not prevent him making an incisive challenge to male middle-class views of women through texts such as *North Wind*, neither is his contribution to the theology of childhood inconsequential. What is of particular interest is MacDonald's use of fantasy to explore and articulate this theology.

The Nature of Fairyland

In *The Fantastic Imagination,* MacDonald focuses on "fairy stories" and underlines the legitimacy and purpose of an author "inventing a little world of his own":

> The natural world has its laws . . . but they themselves may suggest laws of other kinds, and man may, if he pleases, invent a little world of his own, with its own laws; for there is that in him which delights in calling up new forms. . . . When such forms are new embodiments of old truths, we call them products of the Imagination; when they are mere inventions, however lovely, I should call them the work of the Fancy: in either case, Law has been diligently at work.[40]

The Coleridgean language reinforces the divine source of human imagination, unlike that of fancy which is "mere invention." Both are worthy human endeavors that must conform to "law"—the nineteenth century was preoccupied with the need to conform to the fundamental divine principles undergirding reality[41]—but only the former embodies "truth" understood as something already conceived by God. "New *forms*" and "new *embodiments* of old truths" may be new expressions of truth, that is, of divine ideas, but do not add to it.[42] Unlike Chesterton and Tolkien,

---

39. He was private secretary to an English knight of the realm, not a Bohemian Count. See *DE* 2:146.

40. *Orts* 314.

41. A view which gained wider acceptance after Robert Chambers's anonymous publication of *Vestiges of the Natural History of Creation* (1844). See Reardon, *Victorian Age,* 289–90.

42. *Orts* 4.

for example, for whom an artwork was, in the scholastic sense, a "thing in itself" radiating its own truth, MacDonald focuses on the human imagination's ability to reflect and embody God's thoughts. Alison Milbank summarizes thus:

> The distinction between truth and its embodiment ... is quite foreign to Chesterton and Tolkien's [strongly realist] view of a work of art as a thing in itself. ... MacDonald strives to the same end as they [to stress the divine origin of art], but has a less positive conception of the value of the material as against the spiritual and disembodied.[43]

Instead of "spiritual and disembodied," the words "mental and conscious" might equally be used in recognition of MacDonald's radical idealism. This is particularly evident in the earlier essay *The Imagination: Its Function and Its Culture* where the subjective nature of reality is underlined:

> For the world is ... the human being turned inside out. All that moves in the mind is symbolized in Nature. Or, to use another more philosophical, and certainly not less poetic figure, the world is a sensuous analysis of humanity, and hence an inexhaustible wardrobe for the clothing of human thought.[44]

In fairyland, then, as in the real world, "Law is diligently at work," that is, it is a jurisdiction where divinely-ordained moral principles apply. Because they are divine, "no man must interfere with them"; the author "must not meddle with the [moral] relations of live souls." "In physical things a man may invent; in moral things he must obey—and take their laws into his invented world as well."[45] MacDonald's vision of human creativity thus parallels his vision of human being: just as human being equates to God's thoughts, so fairy being equates to human thoughts. Imagination is not only the connection between them but the ever-present flux of reality—temporal and transcendent. Fairyland, therefore—if the genuine product of imagination rather than the "mere inventions" of fancy—is, being divinely inspired, part of the kingdom of God. Furthermore, if aspects of fairyland *are* fanciful, since fancy must also conform to "Law" this too can shed light on the nature of reality. The child of fairyland is therefore a child of God. Being a citizen of both fairyland and the kingdom of God it has the right to critique the world of humans.

43. Milbank, *Chesterton and Tolkien*, 143.
44. *Orts* 9.
45. *Orts* 316.

However, as the knight remarks to Anados in *Phantastes*, "Somehow or other . . . notwithstanding the beauty of this country of Faerie, in which we are, there is much that is wrong with it":[46] sin and evil also exist in fairyland (dragons need to be slain) and fairy vision is not necessarily correct vision. Fairies, too, have their preconceptions and biases.

MacDonald views Evangelical liberalism and conservatism (among other things) through the eyes of this fairy child, offering not just an alternative view but a new way of seeing. While it is true that liberals were broadly "imaginative" and conservatives more "logical," it would be wrong to simply categorize them as such. While liberals did indeed lean towards a more imaginative view, both were essentially wedded to "scientific" methodology. The antagonism stemmed less from methodology as from different starting points leading to logically irreconcilable positions: God could not be a benign Father as well as a torturer; humanity could not be both sinless and depraved; the Bible could not be both inerrant and historically contingent; the earth could not be both 4,004 years old (Ussher's date confidently inscribed in family Bibles) and have evolved, and so on. MacDonald's fairy child provides a wider perspective, not opposed to intellection, but offering fresh vision to guide its "plodding brother, reason" towards a more contextual understanding.

Learning to See Again—Fairy Vision

MacDonald is challenging what he saw as naive, sadistic, and juridical caricatures of God. Concrete alternative theological proposals have emerged, but, as MacDonald explicitly states, his goal is not to impart information but to waken imagination. In a positivist age prone to what might be termed cataphatic literalist fundamentalism, MacDonald offers a mystical apophatic theological approach which *apparently* moves truth away from "objective" fact and locates it in human consciousness. However, it has more to do with rejecting the *illusion* of objective fact and locating truth in a wider concept of shared human–divine consciousness.

Making the Familiar Strange

By leading us into fairyland, MacDonald is giving us new categories with which to view reality by means of two processes. First, there is *making the*

---

46. PH 296.

familiar strange. With fairy vision we take a fresh and more objective look at the idols that have taken up residence among us. They are familiar, part of the religious landscape, but should they be there? This is dramatized in *Phantastes* where there is a thinly-veiled critique of Reformed religion and the "terrible idol" at its center.[47] The fantasy tale concerns the quest of Anados ("on the way up")[48] to find his true identity. False identity results from self-centeredness which gives rise to the presence of an evil shadow from which Anados longs to be free (a metaphor for the rebellious self becoming opaque to the light of God's radiance).[49]

Anados's emancipation is rendered more likely by his volunteering to serve a knight, a fellow traveler in Faerie whose own redemption is also imminent having slain a dreaded dragon. Knight and squire are travelling through a forest at sundown when they happen upon a religious service taking place in a woodland "cathedral" formed by a rectangle of yew trees. Religious and military architecture is evoked (as is death, as yews are associated with graveyards): gothic "trees grew to a very great height" forming "conical battlements all around the walls." The trees "contained . . . a parallelogram of great length" filled with worshippers, "men and women and children, in holiday attire" (that is, Sabbath dress) flanked on each side by three rows of priests: these men are armed with swords, "although the rest of [their] costume and bearing was more priestly than soldierly." The contrast between the devotional sincerity of the worshippers and the menacing presence of military priest-guardians gives an air of deception, compounded by the fact that the altar with the object of worship is so distant that the congregation, in the twilight, are unable to see it clearly. Anados, however, with fairy vision enhanced by his sacrificial decision to serve the good knight, "was able to perceive more clearly what took place . . . at the other end": "I knew that my sight was so much more keen than that of most people, that I had good reason to suppose I should see more than the rest could."[50] It is a disturbing picture. As night falls the sense of menace grows: young robed acolytes are led to the altar surrounded by priestly guardians that prevent the congregation

---

47. *US3* 142.

48. Possibly "pathless" (αν-οδός), but more probably (in my view) "way up" (that is, "path to God"), the literal meaning of ανοδός, "anode" (OED). MacDonald was, after all, a physicist.

49. See page 167.

50. *PH* 304–5. MacDonald saw himself as a prophet to his age, one gifted with "fairy vision" that surpassed that of those trapped in "lightless religion."

from seeing what is going on. As the congregation sings in worship and robed figures kneel at the altar—

> The knight whispered to me [Anados], "How solemn it is! Surely they wait to hear the voice of a prophet. There is something good near!"

> But I, though somewhat shaken by the feeling expressed by my master, yet had an unaccountable conviction that here was something bad. So I resolved to be keenly on the watch for what should follow.[51]

What follows is human sacrifice as the trusting acolytes are pushed through a hidden trapdoor in the idolatrous altar as the congregation sings.[52]

The scene ends with Anados unmasking the deception in an act which results in his own death. After gaining the platform, he wrests the throne from its pedestal exposing a pit: "up out of it rushed a great brute, like a wolf, but twice the size." The struggle that ensues results in the death of both, but for Anados this is the sweet death of self-sacrifice through which he is finally separated from his evil alter-ego, the shadow.[53] The narrative illustrates Milton's view that God uses evil to serve the good:

> O goodness infinite, goodness immense!
> That all this good of evil shall produce,
> And evil turn to good; more wonderful
> Than that which by creation first brought forth
> Light out of darkness![54]

Reflecting this, the story ends with an equally optimistic summary of MacDonald's doctrine of evil: "What we call evil, is the only and best shape, which, for the person and his condition at the time, could be assumed by the best good."[55] Conversely, the knight's evaluation that "there is something good near!" indicates that what is perceived as good is often evil.

51. *PH* 305–6.

52. *PH* 307–8.

53. As always in MacDonald, physical death is inconsequential. Anados enjoys a brief, disembodied, blissful, and shadow-free existence before waking from his "dream."

54. Milton, *Paradise Lost* 12.469–73.

55. *PH* 323.

This scene clearly presents a jaundiced view of popular religion as that presided over by a demon who is served by complicit priests intent on deception. *Phantastes* represents MacDonald's manifesto for all his future work. From this point on, "we find the child's simple faith dominating all his writings as surely as in his youth it first took control of his theology."[56] This vision from fairyland may or may not represent reality, but it does force a closer inspection of it. To frame the issue from an alternative perspective, since culture essentially inheres in the aggregate of symbols that result from a society's worship—what that society valorizes and "cultivates"—fairy vision helps to counteract the blindness of convention.

Making Strange the Familiar

The second function of fairy vision, if you will forgive the slightly pedantic distinction, is to *make strange the familiar*. This has less to do with exposing falsehood as revealing truth—the problem that familiarity, if not breeding contempt, has a tendency to breed indifference and complacency. "Are you," MacDonald asks, "so familiar with the artefacts of faith that they no longer provoke a response?" Fairy vision startles with its revealing perspectives, challenging the conclusions (social or individual) of prior experience, particularly those relating to the nature of God. If God is not a "wolf," what is God like? Repeatedly the reader is presented with a child who either claims to be, or represents, divinity, such as the Old Man of the Earth—a child who appears as the "oldest man of all" in *The Golden Key*[57]—or Gibbie with a cross cut into his back, or a child whose implicit trust in God as the perfect father, like Clare Skymer, is never misplaced. Furthermore, many of MacDonald's divine agents and theophanies are female, challenging the stereotypical view of God as male.

MacDonald's quest, then, as we noted in chapter 5, is to disinter the mummified verbal artefacts of faith and hold them up to the light so that either their true meaning might be revealed in all its glory, or they might be exposed as false. The fairy story is one of his main vehicles for this. Not that words simply had value according to their original symbolic meaning, rather it was the opposite: a quest to rediscover layered metaphor in a world increasingly focused on the conventional "surface"

---

56. *GMAW* 299.
57. *Fairy Tales* 137–38.

of words. Symbol had replaced the symbolized; theologically, *les mots* had dethroned *la Parole*. In this, MacDonald anticipated the later *fin de siècle* frustration of those such as Chesterton, which led to the latter's quest to "find new ways to restore language as a signifying medium of the real world: namely, the fantastic."[58] Likewise in Russia in 1914, Victor Shklovsky lamented that "words are now dead, and language is like a graveyard" leading to a call for the defamiliarization of both words and art.[59] Arguing that we can become so habituated to art (and, by implication, the world around us) that we fail to see it, Shklovsky suggested a three-fold strategy of defamiliarization: to refuse to name art, thereby making it strange; to offer an unusual viewpoint; and to engage in "the childlike description of something familiar as if it were seen for the first time."[60] In the next chapter we consider how MacDonald uses all three of these techniques in his most enigmatic work, *Lilith*.

58. Milbank, *Chesterton and Tolkien*, 29.
59. Milbank, *Chesterton and Tolkien*, 31.
60. Milbank, *Chesterton and Tolkien*, 31–34.

7

The Child Against the Vampire
—A Reading of Lilith

Lilith—Making Strange Theology

LILITH—ACCORDING TO GREVILLE MACDONALD "the majestic thought of his [father's] old age"—is illustrative and summative of MacDonald's life's work. Published when he was seventy-one (1895), it is opaque and enigmatic and he was nervous about publishing it.[1] His assurance that "there is nothing very obscure in it that is worth finding out"[2] is controverted by the subsequent kaleidoscope of interpretations and by the fact that the manuscript was repeatedly amended indicating a quest to communicate *something* with precision. As autobiographical fiction, its importance is underlined by MacDonald's comments about biography and fiction:

> Deep is the relation between the life shadowed forth in a biography, and the life in a man's brain which he shadows forth in a fiction—when that fiction is of the highest order, and written in love, is beheld even by the writer himself with reverence.[3]

---

1. "I often doubt if I shall write another book. There is one in the printers' hands now, which, however, I fear you may not quite like" (Sadler, *Expression of Character*, 364).

2. Sadler, *Expression of Character*, 366–67.

3. *Orts* 222.

Lilith, as we will see, concerns "the life in a man's brain."

Lilith is a mystical work. Just as "only a Kabbalist, one who ascends to a particular spiritual degree, attains what [the *Zohar*] conveys,"[4] or only a "true magus" can access the wisdom of Boehme,[5] "we are here in a region ... open only to the heart of the child."[6] Imaginative engagement (and patience) is needed, and rewarded. *The Times*, perhaps lacking such, observed that, compared to the dream of *Phantastes*, *Lilith* was more of a nightmare:

> To an intellect in which the Celtic is mixed with "the German paste" all this may seem very agreeable, and even subtly edifying, but this wilderness is tedious to the ordinary student.[7]

A close reading of this text is necessary since two of its central themes are evil and childhood.

Lilith is primarily set in a cabbalistic "region of the seven dimensions" presided over by archetypal figures, mostly female.[8] These are both an attraction and a threat to the protagonist—the aptly-named Mr. Vane—more the latter in the case of the central and ambiguous character of the vampire, Lilith. The region of the seven dimensions appears to exist primarily in the consciousness of Vane: a realm of bewildering hallucinatory dream-sequences where shape-shifting characters and set

---

4. "What is *The Zohar*?" We meet Lilith in the *Zohar* shortly.

5. Page 154.

6. Note 148, page 154. It would be wrong, however, to conclude that MacDonald is proposing an occult or gnostic scheme accessible only to the initiated. His central point is that all are children; all have access to God.

7. "Recent Novels."

8. In Kabbalah, seven—the number indicating divine perfection in Judaism (Brown, *Dictionary of NT Theology*, 2:690–92)—frequently occurs in relation to God's creative acts. Both the *Zohar* and *Lilith* also feature three mothers whom we will meet in due course. See Waite, *Doctrine and Literature of Kabalah*, 52, 61–62, 233. According to Waite, only two books on Kabbalah were published in the nineteenth century in English, the first, in 1865, somewhat critical; the second (Mathers, *Kabbalah Unveiled*) includes translations and commentaries on three books of the *Zohar* and conceivably influenced MacDonald (Waite, *Doctrine and Literature of Kabalah*, xi). Although Lilith does not appear in Mathers, mutual themes include an emphasis on God being both male and female (Mathers, *Kabbalah Unveiled*, viii, 21, 22, 25), that God has been dethroned from Christianity and "in his stead [you] have placed [a] demon" (2), that heaven and earth are intertwined (21), and that life is a dream followed by waking in eternity (31, 37). It is more likely, however, that MacDonald was more generally influenced by the growing late Victorian interest in the mind, psychic phenomena, and theosophy.

are constantly mutating and where boundaries are blurred. This impression is confirmed by specific references to mental states; at one point, for example, Vane remarks: "I realized I was inside the brain of the princess."[9]

Labyrinthine mansions, in MacDonald's work, are metaphors for the mind.[10] Here, Vane, having come of age, has inherited the ancestral mansion—the divine gift of human body and consciousness—which he has little motivation to explore. Like its human counterpart, the house has doorways to fairyland, a fantasy realm not so much beyond "reality" as entwined with it.[11] He is content to spend his time in the library, a repository of conventional wisdom collected by ancestors, hermetically isolated from the wider reality of which he is a part. One day, wandering into the attic, he discovers the mirror which is the gateway to a hitherto unexperienced region:

> "If I know nothing of my own garret," I thought, "what is there to secure me against my own brain? Can I tell what it is even now generating?—what thought it may present me the next moment, the next month, or a year away? What is at the heart of my brain? What is behind my THINK? Am I there at all?—Who, what am I?"[12]

This text centers on this existential question of true identity. The library at the center of—and dominating—the house represents the mind (particularly a "scientific" mind that has become anaesthetized by convention) whose "garrets" (imagination) are unknown territory and whose portals (the doors and mirrors of imagination) may lead to danger or, conversely, give dangerous forces entry. In the same way that *North Wind* challenges the conventional understanding of "inside" and "outside," Vane realizes that the inside of his "house," far from being a refuge, is dangerously sited at the edge of a greater reality of which he is ignorant.

It is a dream where Vane is aware, or suspects, that he is dreaming, a dramatization of MacDonald's conviction that mind is the stuff of the universe and that Novalis was right when he said, "Our life is no dream, but it should and perhaps will become one" (a quotation that opened his manifesto, *Phantastes*, and closes this one).[13] It is exemplary of what

---

9. *Lilith* 191.
10. Cusick, "MacDonald and Jung," 63.
11. Page 149.
12. *Lilith* 17–18.
13. *Lilith* 351.

W. H. Auden (and C. S. Lewis) called "his greatest gift,"[14] that of "dream realism," a gift used here to destabilize and defamiliarize, to make strange the familiar, and to explore a thesis set out in *The Portent* thirty years previously:

> A man who dreams, and knows that he is dreaming, thinks he knows what waking is; but knows it so little, that he mistakes, one after another, many a vague and dim change in his dream for an awakening. When the true waking comes at last, he is filled and overflowed with the power of his reality.[15]

Vane "wakes" often, only to conclude he is probably still dreaming. For example, fleeing from his dream reality to wake once more in his library, he ponders:

> Had I come to myself out of a vision?—or lost myself by going back to one? Which was the real—what I now saw, or what I had just ceased to see? Could both be real, interpenetrating yet unmingling?[16]

The narrative dramatizes the conviction that death is the final sleep from which *all* will wake into true consciousness; prior to that, life is a dream:

> For we *are* dreaming, fast asleep,
> This dream of ache and strife.[17]

All includes Lilith—the demonic and vampiric "queen of Hell,"—Satan, and all humanity. MacDonald is dramatizing (to extremes) the "larger hope" so despised by those such as Spurgeon. Thus a feature of the supernatural world beyond Vane's house is a vast cemetery/dormitory whose sexton is Adam. Only those who submit to the sleep of death in the world of the seven dimensions may truly wake in the next—truly real—transcendent world.

Adam is assisted by Eve, their role being to "watch the flock of the great shepherd"[18] until they wake, which, since Lilith also consents to sleep there, implies that she also is one of the great shepherd's sheep. The "second death," that unlike its Johannine counterpart always leads to life

14. Auden, *Forewords and Afterwords*, 270; Lewis, *George MacDonald*, 14.
15. POS 23.
16. *Lilith* 46.
17. DOP 186. These lines are missing from the later published version in *Poems* 1:420–21.
18. *Lilith* 46.

(Rev 21:8), is the final exit door from purgatorial reality leading to union with the Great Consciousness. In the meantime, the world of human consciousness (both pre- and post-mortem) is a purgatorial experience preparatory to that end. Adam and Eve's jurisdiction over the fantasy world indicates that it represents the postlapsarian nightmare realm of rebellious humanity, escape from which can only be achieved through the acceptance of "bread and wine" (a meal that Adam and Eve frequently offer their guests)[19] and repentance, prerequisites for submitting to the final sleep that leads to the eschaton (John 6:44, 54).

Reflecting Shklovsky's tactic of defamiliarization, the story opens with Vane seeing something with imaginative childlike vision "as if for the first time." It is "childlike" as it concerns the realization that he is the child of a dynasty to which he owes both existence and allegiance. Vane reads his "science" books—exploring the "history of the human mind in relation to supposed knowledge"[20]—unaware that this second-hand, historical knowledge is about to become present reality. It is the picture of a mind—MacDonald is perhaps thinking of a conservative Evangelical mind—content to accept without question the received wisdom of ancestors. However, one day a shaft of sunlight enters the library and illuminates a picture:

> I knew it as the likeness of one of my ancestors, but had never even wondered why it hung there alone.... The direct sunlight brought out the painting wonderfully; *for the first time I seemed to see it, and for the first time it seemed to respond to my look.* With my eyes full of the light reflected from it, something ... made me turn and cast a glance to the farther end of the room, when I saw, or seemed to see, a tall figure reaching up a hand to a bookshelf. The next instant ... I saw no one, and concluded that my optic nerves had been momentarily affected from within.[21]

The library, one might say, represents the "left hemisphere" of Vane's consciousness, a repository of conventional truth, classified and filed by ancestors. It might also represent conservative views of the Bible—τὰ βιβλία (*tà biblía*), "the (little) books"—as a complete and final literal-factual revelation of divine truth. However, the shaft of sunlight from *outside* the library changes everything: Vane is suddenly aware of a

---

19. *Lilith* 38, 295, 316–17.
20. *Lilith* 2.
21. *Lilith* 3.

transcendent context, the world behind or beyond the "text" of his life, a world inhabited by ancestors. As he puts it: "The house"—his mind and body—"had grown strange to me."[22]

This epiphany is Vane's first glimpse of a world beyond convention, the beginning of his search for his true identity. His ghostly visitor, the old butler informs him, was probably Mr. Raven, a one-time librarian that had been known to haunt the house. But when he later follows the ghostly librarian through the magic mirror into fairyland, he not only transforms into a raven, but also—we find out in due course—is really Adam, both sexton and librarian of bodies waiting for resurrection.[23] Books, like people, are doorways to fairyland.

Many characters appear in multiple guises. Lilith, for example, is both a beautiful woman and a leopardess, and in one scene—as if powerless to hide her true nature—her body disintegrates, but not before limbs have become snakes and "something . . . like a bat" has flown from her[24]—gothic images associated with evil and vampires. Consonant with MacDonald's view that "the world is . . . the human being turned inside out,"[25] he suggests, "you can tell what sort a man is by his creature that comes oftenest to the front."[26] Materiality is a manifestation of mind, and identity a schizoid hydra until such time as true God-given identity is accepted. Identity based on the false premise that one is "inside" one's house is merely illusory. Identity, MacDonald is arguing, is not defined by naming something or someone. The name simply represents the conventional understanding of what an entity appears to be in a certain context and can mask its true nature. Dramatizing Shklovsky's second defamiliarization tactic of refusing to name art, Vane, on being asked his name by Mr. Raven, finds himself unable to recall it. He has become strange to the art that is himself:

> I became at once aware that I could give him no notion of who I was. Indeed, who was I? . . . Then I understood that I did not know myself, did not know what I was, had no grounds on which to determine that I was one and not another.[27]

22. *Lilith* 17.
23. *Lilith* 37.
24. *Lilith* 66; cf. 190.
25. *Orts* 9.
26. *Lilith* 37.
27. *Lilith* 14.

He, like Carlyle's words, finds himself disinterred from the grave of convention and is suddenly aware of the groundlessness of his own self-understanding. His amnesiac namelessness forces him to question the nature of his reality. He cannot, for example, understand how one half of a book (human being) which he can see in his library—a *trompe l'œil* which "some inventive workman" (God) has fixed so that half of it appears to be sticking out of a cupboard door fronted with false book spines[28] (the visible world)—can appear in his world when the other half, according to Adam/Mr. Raven/the librarian, appears in *his* library in "fairyland." Adam's response summarizes the methodology in *Lilith*, underlining its purpose to force a re-evaluation of reality through making strange the familiar:

> You are constantly experiencing things which you not only do not, but cannot understand. You think you understand them, but your understanding of them is only your being used to them, and therefore not surprised at them. You accept them, not because you understand them, but because you must accept them: they are there, and have unavoidable relations with you! The fact is, no man understands anything; when he knows he does not understand, that is his first tottering step—not toward understanding, but toward the capability of one day understanding. To such things as these you are not used, therefore you do not fancy you understand them. Neither I nor any man can here help you to understand; but I may, perhaps, help you a little to believe![29]

This is MacDonald's response to naive cataphatic theology with its conventions: "your understanding of them is only your being used to them." His aim is to help the reader "a little to believe" by distancing faith from its nineteenth-century scaffolding. The attraction to MacDonald of casting Lilith as the main antagonist becomes clear as we consider her pedigree and nineteenth-century incarnation.

Lilith—Anti-Child and Antichrist

Lilith carries a terse epigraph, a rebuke from the Kabbalah: "Off, Lilith!" as if the Good Shepherd is calling off his most evil sheepdog. In that text, Lilith is the wife of Samael, or Satan:

28. *Lilith* 4.
29. *Lilith* 210–11.

> Their ultimate destruction is hinted, but meanwhile Lilith is the devastation of the world and the lash in the hands of the Holy Blessed One to strike the guilty. She is God's maidservant.[30]

Having made a brief appearance in Isaiah 34:14 as a hairy Babylonian demon of the desert,[31] Lilith, in Jewish tradition, is infamous for her sexual and infanticidal proclivities, and in this tale her passion is to drink the blood of "the Little Ones." In the cabbalistic text *The Zohar* (and in *Lilith*) she is the first wife of Adam who, refusing to submit and have children by him, becomes instead the mother of hordes of demons. Her pedophilic attraction to the cherubim, with their "little faces of tender children," turns to a jealous loathing that God uses as a tool to "lash" the children of Eve (after all, God scourges those God loves):[32]

> From the moment she came forth, she went up and down to the cherubim who have the "little faces of tender children" and desired to cleave unto them and be one of them and was loathe to depart from them (*Zohar* 1.18b). . . .
>
> But the Holy One, blessed be He, removed her from them and made her go below . . . He chid her and cast her into the depths of the sea, where she abode until the time that Adam and his wife sinned. Then the Holy One, blessed be He, brought her out from the depths of the sea and gave her power over all those children, the "little faces" of the sons of men, who are liable for punishment for the sins of their fathers (*Zohar* 1.19b).[33]

Lilith's punishment of the children of Eve is reflected in Jewish folklore, such as the tale of a couple who buy a house in Tunis, reputed to be haunted. Before its demolition, the wife insists on salvaging valuables, including a mirror. Their daughter "glanced at herself in the mirror all the time, and in this way she was drawn into Lilith's web":

> For that mirror had hung in the den of demons, and a daughter of Lilith had made her home there. And when the mirror was taken from the haunted house, the demoness came with it. For every mirror is a gateway to the Other World and leads directly to Lilith's cave.[34]

30. Waite, *Doctrine and Literature of Kabalah*, 255.
31. Russell and Briggs, "Legends of Lilith," 132.
32. See page 161.
33. Black Koltuv, *Book of Lilith*, 78, 81.
34. Schwartz, *Lilith's Cave*, 120–21.

In *Lilith*, the garret mirror in Vane's "mansion"—his little-used imagination—leads also to "Lilith's cave."

This essential antagonism of Lilith towards children, fueled by her jealousy that they carry the divine image, provides MacDonald with the ideal antitype: an antichrist and an "anti-child." Furthermore, because Eve gave birth to Cain as a result of the "filth of the serpent," Lilith, like Satan in the book of Job, was given the right *as God's maidservant* to punish Eve by stealing and killing her children.[35] Either, therefore, God is vindictively punitive and holds children "liable for . . . the sins of their fathers," or Lilith, like Milton's Satan, is the unwitting servant of good. This text strongly affirms the latter, but unlike Milton's Satan who with "reiterated crimes [heaps] on himself damnation," Lilith's crimes contribute to her salvation.

In the late nineteenth century, Lilith was a *femme fatale* with "a place in vampire lore either as the first and most powerful of the vampires, or at least as their queen,"[36] a dreaded dominatrix embodying the male fear that Victorian females might not be as submissive as imagined, as illustrated by Dante Gabriel Rossetti's seductive women, "part priestess, part temptress"—including *Lady Lilith*—who are more a picture of his state of mind than real women.[37] Women such as Lilith and Salome became symbols of female threat in an age when Romanticism was becoming more symbolic; psychological overtones and dream-like, evocative prose reflected a "surrealist perception of half-articulated or unexpressed mental phenomena," a phrase that sums up *Lilith*.[38]

The Landscape and Action in *Lilith*

The mirage-like "realm of seven dimensions" in *Lilith* conceals a simple yet highly ambiguous landscape. The daylight world of forests, rocky hills, and deserts populated by exotic or benign flora and fauna becomes a world of nightmare after sundown. As Vane journeys by night, monsters erupt from the ground beneath his feet, skeletons perform a macabre dance in a woodland cathedral like that in *Phantastes*, and while

---

35. *Zohar* 1.76b; 2.96 a–b in Black Koltuv, *Book of Lilith*, 81.
36. Humm, "Lilith."
37. Wilton, *Age of Rossetti*, 18–19.
38. Wilton, *Age of Rossetti*, 18–19. For a review of Lilith in nineteenth-century vampire narratives, see Wingrove, "La Belle Dame," 175–97.

he sleeps Lilith drinks his blood. She is the source of every nightmare scene and is frequently glimpsed on the edges of vision. She "possesses" a large part of his psyche. Reflecting MacDonald's preoccupation with the polarities of good and evil, day and night,[39] the fantasy world is the ambiguous meeting point of these two opposites whose boundary is blurred. An enigmatic moon presides over the night of Vane's nightmares: if not the direct radiance of God's light then at least indicative of indirect divine protection. The moon slays the monsters of the deep, and shines when most needed. But equally, this feminine light is associated with vampires, and Vane frequently encounters Lilith in cold moonlight. Is the moon benign or demonic? Similarly, Lilith, the queen of Hell who has enslaved "the great Shadow,"[40] is also the ruler of a city that, unlike the phantom night-visions that dissolve with the dawn, also exists in the realm of daylight. This realm of intersection and conflict preoccupies MacDonald— the liminal realm where humans have to choose between good and evil; a place at an epistemic distance from the divine sun where wrong choice leads to outer darkness.[41]

Two settlements are located in this landscape, placing "evil" opposite "childlikeness," but they also are fraught with ambiguity and paradox. The city represents an overt criticism of nineteenth-century materialism, a place whose inhabitants have allowed walls to separate them from divinity and whose primary aim in life is to exploit others. "They were rich, and had everything made for them in other towns," and considered it "a disgrace to work." The princess (Lilith) has taught them to mine jewels from the foundations of their houses; these they use to buy what they need from others who labor. They are an indolent and dull people, content to watch their city slowly crumble into ruin, inconsiderate of the plight of the poor.[42]

---

39. Such as in the disturbing tale, *The History of Photogen and Nycteris: A Day and Night Mährchen*, where a witch, Watho (perhaps derived from "waith," a term for illegal hunting), steals children in order to experiment on them. Stolen at birth, Photogen ("light's offering") is raised in "the full splendour of the sun" in whose light the witch "stript him and laid him in it, that he might ripen as a peach," whereas the girl, Nycteris ("night creature" or "night unrest"), a "little bat," is forbidden access to the outside world and kept in a room lit by the "feeble rays of a lamp in an alabaster globe." See *Fairy Tales* 304–41, notes on 354.

40. *Lilith* 204.

41. See note 157, page 155.

42. *Lilith* 165.

A counterfeit New Jerusalem, the city is centered on a temple where the princess resides. Unlike the former city of light that has no need of temple, sun, or moon (Rev 21:22–23), it has a heart of darkness—a black chamber at the heart of Lilith's temple. When Vane enters this, he experiences a procession of grotesque images, all of which he has encountered in the world beyond the city walls, bringing the realization that he is "in the brain" of the princess.[43] Lilith, radiating evil into this mental universe (or rather, absorbing light), is the antithesis of the God that emanates goodness. Furthermore, for Lilith to survive she must drink the blood of the city's newborn. Hers is a counterfeit and deceptive Eucharist. Like Adam and Eve, Lilith, in the silver robes of a vampire,[44] also offers Vane bread and wine, seductively saying, "Here we do not kill to eat . . . but I think you will like what I can give you,"[45] however her "wine" is the diluted blood of children. Unlike the true Eucharist that is preparation for the submissive sleep in Adam's cemetery, her false Eucharist aims to prolong a rebellious life: "Old age is to you a horror," she remarks, "to me it is a dear desire: the older we grow, the nearer we are to our perfection. Your perfection is a poor thing, comes soon, and lasts but a little while; ours is a ceaseless ripening."[46] The perfection that Lilith seeks, in other words, is the opposite of childhood and a chimera.

The "city" of human rebellion, MacDonald is proposing, being founded on evil, is inherently and doubly self-destructing. Since Lilith can only survive by killing newborn infants, the population is destined to decline. In addition—like the city whose ruin is described in Babylonian terms at the end of *The Princess and Curdie*—greedy mining for gems in the foundations will necessarily lead to collapse. In that narrative:

> One day at noon, when life was at its highest, the whole city fell with a roaring crash. The cries of men and the shrieks of women went up with its dust, and then there was a great silence.[47]

The plot centers on the need to spirit away newborn babies from the city before they become vampire prey. These are carried to a forest

---

43. *Lilith* 191.

44. Silver apparel, evocative of moonlight, was standard gothic vampire dress. Tieck's Brunhilda, for example, only wears silver and "pearls alone lent their pale lustre to adorn her bosom" (Wingrove, "La Belle Dame," 185).

45. *Lilith* 178–79.

46. *Lilith* 179

47. *PC* 255; cf. Rev 14:8; 16:9; 18:2.

where they form a tribe of "Little Ones" whose existing inhabitants care for the new arrivals, innocent of knowledge of either their own origins or those of their charges. The Little Ones are "innocent" and naive in the extreme. Like Peter Pan, they are eternally prepubescent and (apparently) prelapsarian. They are led by a girl, Lona—who "was become almost a woman, but not one beauty of childhood had she outgrown"—who reminds Vane of his beautiful, half-remembered mother and with whom he becomes disturbingly infatuated: "My every imagination flew to her; she was my heart's wife!"[48] She, and other female characters, cry out for Jungian or Freudian interpretations,[49] however, the issue in focus here is the children's naivety. Like Gibbie, they are not human: Vane has fallen in love with what appears to be an illusion, the product of his own fantasy, which is nevertheless considered real by both him and his fantasy-world guide, Adam.

Extreme versions of the children in Murdoch Malison's class, the innocence of these Little Ones has no real-world counterpart; they have become caricatures of childhood. They chatter happily, never argue, and revere Lona as their mother. Unlike Peter Pan, they have the dangerous potential to mutate into dull "giants" like their parents (and a few do). What is lacking is any positive view of adulthood. In Tolkien's words:

> If we use *child* in the good sense (it has also legitimately a bad one) we must not allow that to push us into sentimentality of only using *adult* or *grown-up* in a bad sense (it has also a legitimately good one). The process of growing older is not necessarily allied to growing wickeder, although the two do often happen together. Children are meant to grow up, and not to become Peter Pans. Not to lose innocence and wonder, but to proceed on the appointed journey.[50]

These children, however, are not allowed to grow up and MacDonald *has* been "pushed into sentimentality." They embody innocence until they make the choice to eat the bitter apples that grow in this Eden, at which point they mutate into sinful and dull "adults." The theological issue, however, is not so much natal innocence as that these Little Ones are invited by Adam to sleep in his cemetery, apparently bypassing the

---

48. *Lilith* 240. One imagines this was one of the reasons why Louisa MacDonald "was troubled by the book's strange imagery" (*GMAW* 548).

49. See, for example, Cusick, "MacDonald and Jung," 56–86; Dunne, "Friends of God," 338.

50. Tolkien, "Tree and Leaf," 47. See also Milbank, *Chesterton and Tolkien*, 147.

temporal "system of soul-making" where genuine issues relating to good and evil must be faced. Their origin is not the world of three dimensions; they have not tasted Dostoevsky's apple.[51] This reflects the duality that Rousseau and Blake set up between innocence and experience, nature and culture,[52] a duality that fails to account for the fact that true humanity involves distinguishing good from evil and making moral choices—possibly the primary message of Genesis 1–3. In Alison Milbank's words, the Romanticism of those such as MacDonald's has "served to strand children across a hermeneutic chasm."[53] The Little Ones appear to be stranded on the wrong side.

Vane, as noted, falls in love with one of these phantoms who, it transpires, is the daughter of Lilith (by Adam),[54] one who has inherited none of the traits of her vampire mother except extraordinary beauty; despite being the offspring of the "queen of Hell," the daughter is without sin. He is, therefore, far from the ideal human. His Ruskinian obsession with this prepubescent child-woman is disturbing. Vane's weakness is his attraction to all the beautiful women he meets which often spills over into unwise action, such as his abortive attempt to storm the city with an army of children and capture Lilith despite having been specifically warned by Adam against this. Nevertheless, God makes sure "all things work for good" (since this is the beginning of Lilith's reformation). When Vane asks what the consequences will be of him making a wrong choice, Adam's answer further clarifies MacDonald's philosophy of evil:

> "Then some evil that is good for you will follow."
> "And if I remember [to heed your advice]?"
> "Some evil that is not good for you, will not follow."[55]

In other words, when it comes to evil it is always a win-win situation.

Wrong choice is evident when Vane initially encounters Lilith. He finds her emaciated body, naked and cold, lying inert in a forest. Unaware that she is the arch-enemy of the Little Ones, and convincing himself that his main motive is to prevent "irreverent eyes [looking] on it,"[56] he

---

51. Note 46, page 106.
52. Milbank, *Chesterton and Tolkien*, 144.
53. Milbank, *Chesterton and Tolkien*, 144.
54. *Lilith* 204.
55. *Lilith* 129.
56. *Lilith* 131.

decides to give the body a decent burial, but, unsure whether she is really dead, he reports: "I . . . got as close to her as I could, and took her in my arms. I had not much heat left in me, but what I had I would share with her!"[57] The erotic overtones are evident. He remains with her for many days unaware that as he cradles her each night she is drinking his blood, regaining life while feigning death. Vane is, therefore, responsible for reviving the worst danger possible for the Little Ones. He, as a human being from the world of three dimensions, is needed to provide the blood which the parasite of evil needs for life; in other words, it is the evil in him (which he convinces himself is good) that nourishes this existential evil. Each descendent of Adam and Eve, MacDonald is saying, is responsible for the threat to childhood. The irony is that it is a descendant of Lilith (Lona) who protects the children.

The Tactic of Defamiliarization

Through these destabilizing and defamiliarizing tactics, MacDonald is demanding the reader consider the nature of evil. Evil may appear good, as in the case of seductive Lilith, but equally, good may appear evil, as in the character of Mara. Regarding the former, having insisted that "beauty is the only stuff in which Truth can be clothed,"[58] he muses: "Could such beauty as I saw, and such wickedness as I suspected, exist in the same person?"[59] The latter, who seems evil at first sight, is the guardian of the Little Ones, and also she who—in the form of a pure white leopardess—steals newborns from the city and deposits them in the forest for the Little Ones to find. Of course, mothers consider her evil unaware that she is protecting their offspring from the vampire princess who, in a further destabilizing tactic, also appears as a white leopardess but with black spots prowling the city searching for newborn blood. Furthermore, although her name is biblical—a reference to Naomi's self-designation as Mara, "bitterness" (Ruth 1:20)—in Buddhist theology, Mara is the equivalent of Satan who has three daughters, also known as Maras, whose job it is to seduce and destroy humans. It is possible that MacDonald was aware of this. Like her Buddhist counterparts, Mara in this tale is a shape-shifter (woman and leopardess) and may be a product of his reading of an

57. *Lilith* 133.
58. *Orts* 315.
59. *Lilith* 177.

1871 text on Buddhism which describes the Maras as demons who can "assume the most hideous forms."[60] In a final twist, we learn that Mara is the daughter of Eve.

To summarize this confusing scenario: the Little Ones are in mortal danger from Lilith, a fallen being created by God to be the original mother of the race but who is now the "anti-mother," and are protected by two step-sisters, one the daughter of Eve and one the daughter of Lilith herself through whom—it has been prophesied—Lilith's downfall will come. This is the final piece of the jigsaw. Lilith is aware that "there is an old prophecy that a child will be the death of her"[61] and therefore lives in fear of its fulfilment. However, in MacDonald's language, death equates to salvation and access to the eschaton: Lilith, the personification of evil, will also be saved. Nevertheless, it is essentially the story of the child against the vampire.

The Battle in (and for) the Mind

That all is foreseen, if not pre-scripted, by God is dramatized in a scene where Lilith, in the guise of a Persian cat (witchcraft), has managed to follow Adam and Vane back to the latter's library. In the library—Vane's mind—there is a battle between good and evil; Adam versus his insubmissive ex-wife, the mother of evil. The all-powerful Adam, who seems to equate more to Paul's new Adam than his old namesake,[62] casts spells that prevent the cat's escape before casually taking the ancient volume, hitherto an immovable feature of Vane's faux bookcase:

> He opened the vellum cover, and turned a leaf or two. The parchment was discoloured with age, and one leaf showed a

---

60. Alabaster, *Wheel of Law*, 151. Further parallels may indicate familiarity. The abortive attempt of the army of children to storm the city, some mounted on miniature elephants, appears a parody of the Buddhist narrative of the Mara attacking the Buddha. The Mara, "assuming an immense size, and with a thousand arms brandishing all kinds of martial weapons, riding on his elephant Girimaga, a thousand miles in height, led the way. The van stretched two hundred and fifty miles before him. . . . 'Advance my soldiers,' he shouted, 'seize and bind the Prince'" (Alabaster, *Wheel of Law*, 150).

61. *Lilith* 151, 233; cf. Gen 3:15.

62. Vane observes: "Then at last I understood that Mr. Raven was indeed Adam, the old and the new man; and that his wife, ministering in the house of the dead, was Eve, the mother of us all, the lady of the New Jerusalem" (*Lilith* 206).

dark stain over two-thirds of it.[63] He slowly turned this also, and seemed looking for a certain passage in what appeared a continuous poem. Somewhere about the middle of the book he began to read.[64]

The "continuous poem"—God's creative thoughts—reveals foreknowledge of Lilith's existence and actions. A reader might be tempted to skip the stanzas, however they reveal much about Lilith. First, she is indeed given life and substance by male fantasy. Articulating Lilith's thoughts, the poem begins:

> But if I found a man that could believe
> > In what he saw not, felt not, and yet knew,
> From him I should take substance, and receive
> > Firmness and form relate to touch and view;
> > Then should I clothe me in the likeness true
> Of that idea where his soul did cleave![65]

Just as God's thoughts become human reality, so human ideas create "substance." Confirming Calvin's worst fears,[66] male imagination gives birth to evil. Imaginative Romantic liberalism is not a panacea against the perceived evils of dogmatic conservatism. It gives birth to the distorted feminine and demonic "idea where his soul did cleave" and is given "firmness and form" through "Vane's" ("self-centered") male fantasies. This is not God's idea of who Lilith should be, but neither is it Vane's: she, like Vane, has lost her true identity having sold her soul to the great Shadow, Satan; Vane has given birth to something beyond his control. Both are slaves to the evil will of the Shadow.

Although in some sense the product of a human mind, she should not, however, be considered "immaterial": in MacDonald's idealism, such

---

63. In MacDonald's KJV, the only reference to two thirds or "two parts [of three]" occurs when God, after "smiting the shepherd," kills two-thirds of the "little ones" (Zech 13:7–9). The remaining third will eventually say: "The Lord is my God," but only after trial by fire. Perhaps this "dark stain" is a troubling reminder that many babies become "vampire prey." How does this fit in with the "larger hope"? Adam's page-turn illustrates MacDonald's view that apparently evil biblical statements should not be accepted at face value, but should be set to one side until qualified by a deeper truth. See US1 70. See pages 221–22.

64. *Lilith* 200.

65. *Lilith* 201.

66. Calvin, *Institutes* 1.4.1; 1.13.1; 1.15.6.

reality equates to the stuff of everyday life. She has erotic power and is the personification of those troubling male Victorian fears:[67]

> In me was every woman. I had power
>> Over the soul of every living man
>
> A power indiscernible by the five senses, but able to—
>
>> ... trammel brain and spine
>>> With rooted bonds which Death could not untwine—
>> Or life, though hope were evermore deferred.[68]

The phrase "which Death could not untwine—Or life" reiterates the conviction that freedom from evil—"untwining" oneself from evil—is not the *result* of death (that is, the "second death" that leads to eternal life) but a *prerequisite* of it: one cannot lie down in Adam's cemetery and await the great awakening without first having renounced evil. Neither is it a natural consequence of life, however long such "hope is deferred."[69] Rather, freedom from evil involves a renunciation of it, either in this world or the purgatorial afterlife.

The poem continues with Lilith rejoicing in her power to seduce the person through whom she is "clothed human," a seduction focused on antagonism to the divine presence. Claiming her right to human worship, to be the "candle" at the center of human consciousness,[70] she declares:

> Ah, who was ever conquering Love but I!
>> Who else did ever throne in heart of man![71]

Thus throned, and deluded that she has conquered Love, she is an antichrist. Furthermore, in her body she has a wounded side—a dark spot of evil that she tries to hide—and a wounded hand clenched in defiant possession, holding back the water of grace that will heal the land, counterfeit stigmata to match her counterfeit Eucharist.

---

67. Although revealing Victorian male fears of the feminine, this should be treated with caution. Just as "man"—male and female—is being "thought by God" in MacDonald's scheme, so Lilith, being thought by "man" has more to do with the polarities of good and evil than masculine and feminine.

68. *Lilith* 201.

69. "Deferred hope" appears a reference to Proverbs, refusing the "hope" of final death which "when the desire cometh, it is a tree of life" (Prov 13:12, KJV).

70. *Orts* 25.

71. *Lilith* 202.

She is, according to Adam, essentially parasitic: "Vilest of God's creatures, she lives by the blood and lives and souls of men. She consumes and slays, but is powerless to destroy as to create."[72] She may "slay" those who have existence in this life or the next, but eventually these lie down in Adam's cemetery to wake in a realm over which Lilith has no jurisdiction (the implication being that her evil designs work for the reformation of others). She is, then, ultimately impotent, even when it comes to the making or destroying of her own life. In her quest for autonomy she is described as having enslaved the "great Shadow," but in this she is deceived. Adam describes how, after rejecting his authority, she "fled to the army of the aliens, and soon had so ensnared the heart of the great Shadow, that he became her slave, wrought her will, and made her queen of Hell."[73] There is, however, paradox here for only one greater than her can bestow queenhood. It is but an illusion: in reality she is "slave of sin."[74] So what is MacDonald's understanding of the great Shadow?

Satan—The Great Shadow

Shadows are code for evil. Thus Mara, the guardian of the Little Ones, appears as a pure white leopardess whereas Lilith, their enemy, hunts as a white leopardess covered with black spots. As she metamorphoses into a woman, these coalesce into one permanent shadow on her side indicative of the evil eating at her heart. One night, however, Vane observes a dark shadow haunting the streets, apparently an informant bringing news of new birth back to the princess. One reading is that this is the "soul" of the princess—her essential shadow-nature—locating newborns but incapable of seizing them unless returning incarnate as the predator. But another, more plausible, reading is that this is the great Shadow, the devil, who "walks about like a roaring lion, seeking whom he may devour" (1 Pet 5:8). It may be a case of mistaken identity, but Vane does use the pronoun "he" in his account:

> he cast no shadow, and was himself but a flat superficial shadow, of two dimensions. He was, nevertheless, an opaque shadow, for he not merely darkened any object on the other side of him, but rendered it, in fact, invisible. In the shadow he was blacker than

72. *Lilith* 205.
73. *Lilith* 204.
74. *Lilith* 206.

> the shadow; in the moonlight he looked like one who had drawn his shadow up about him, for not a suspicion of it moved beside or under him . . . the shadow seemed once to look at me, for I lost his profile, and saw for a second only a sharp upright line.[75]

Lilith, it seems, is powerless unless "possessed" by the Shadow; she has to wait for its return before she can emerge in the form of a leopardess or a woman. Just as humans have no independent existence and are entirely dependent on God,[76] Lilith is entirely dependent on Satan. Deluding herself that she has enslaved the will of the great Shadow (as Adam suggests)[77] it is she who is the slave.

Reflecting Cosmo's thoughts on the nature of evil in *What's Mine's Mine*,[78] the essence of evil is, by this account, perfect shadow, a "black body" (a perfect absorber of electromagnetic energy) that absorbs all divine light but which itself has no substance. MacDonald offers no explanation for its origin apart from noting that the darkness in Lilith is something that "God could not have created."[79] If God is light, it is the ultimate antithesis—a will set perfectly against God's. In Lilith's case, her refusal to submit to Adam equates to opposition to God: "For her first thought was *power*," says Adam, "she counted it slavery to be one with me, and bear children for Him who gave her being."[80] MacDonald, however, does not believe in "pure" evil, but that the universe is essentially good, that, in words reminiscent of Maurice, "love, not hate, is deepest in what Love 'loved into being'";[81] a sentiment reflected in one of Vane's epiphanies: "evil was only through good! selfishness but a parasite on the tree of life!"[82] Lilith, therefore, is also not pure evil, just a distorted good creature whose will, as queen of Hell, is the ultimate Shadow.

Lilith's powerlessness apart from the Shadow accounts for the ease of her capture by the Little Ones, which, for an all-powerful queen of Hell, appears absurd. After a chaotic assault on Lilith's temple, during which Lilith kills her daughter (Vane's beloved and child of prophecy,

---

75. *Lilith* 163.
76. *God's Words* 8.
77. *Lilith* 204.
78. Page 158.
79. *Lilith* 286.
80. *Lilith* 204.
81. *Lilith* 127.
82. *Lilith* 113.

"Christ" in this episode who is later resurrected), a procession of Little Ones emerges from the temple with Lilith bound hand and foot, tied to an elephant. Through Lona's death there is a transfer of power: the Little Ones have become powerful, whereas Lilith has become powerless—the Shadow has left her knowing that her time has come. The account of its flight as a dark two-dimensional being that tries, and fails, to "possess" the children in its path implies that there *is* a pure will that is evil, distinguishable from the will of any host,[83] a paradox explored below.

The procession, after some days, arrives at Mara's House of Bitterness where the daughter of Eve sets out to reform her step-sister. The account of her final submission to Adam is revealing. "Bitterness" and ministry from Mara—whom the children know as "the cat-woman"—is needed to precipitate reform. As Vane explains to the accompanying children, Lilith needs the "ministry of pain":[84] "A friend is one who gives us what we need, and the princess is sorely in need of a terrible scratching."[85] The process involves Lilith experiencing the spectrum of God's being, from burning core of love to outer darkness, where she stares into, and then enters, the abyss of non-being. It is based on the conviction that, like Vane in search of *his* true identity, Lilith is not her "true self"—God's idea of her. It is MacDonald's dramatization of his conviction that none, even "Satan," can resist God's inexorable love.

As a "silver worm ... white-hot, vivid as incandescent silver, the live heart of essential fire" crawls across her prostrate body "until it reached her bosom, where it disappeared among the folds" and enters her "secret chamber,"[86] Mara urges her to embrace her true identity: "Alas, you are another now, not yourself! Will you not be your real self?" As the silver fire burns inside Lilith, Mara explains:

> The central fire of the universe is radiating into her the knowledge of good and evil, the knowledge of what she is. She sees

---

83. *Lilith* 259–62.

84. See page 162.

85. *Lilith* 270.

86. Phallic and erotic overtones are unavoidable, but MacDonald insists the "worm" or "serpent" "was piercing through the joints and marrow to the thoughts and intents of the heart" (*Lilith* 279; Heb 4:12). There are, nevertheless, parallels to the standard late nineteenth-century methods of ritually dispatching a vampire involving a spear through the heart. As Wingrove observes (to whom I am indebted for his insight into vampires): "By the time the Victorian age was at its height, only a fully-fledged ritual slaying would do to expunge the female vampire from the text" (Wingrove, "La Belle Dame," 192). Lilith gets off lightly in comparison.

> at last the good she is not, the evil she is. She knows that *she is herself the fire in which she is burning*, but she does not know that the Light of Life is the heart of that fire. Her torment is that she is what she is.[87]

As the knowledge of good and evil dawns, Lilith burns in the hell of her own making, unaware, or refusing to admit, that "the Light of Life is the heart of that fire." She refuses to repent, blaming God for making her: "He alone is to blame for what I am! . . . He meant me such that I might know it and be miserable!"[88] She is then forced to stare into the void of non-being. Vane is empathetically aware of "an invisible darkness":

> A horrible Nothingness, a Negation positive infolded her; the border of its being that was yet no being, touched me, and for one ghastly instant I seemed alone with Death Absolute! It was not the absence of everything I felt, but the presence of Nothing. The princess dashed herself from the settle to the floor with an exceeding great and bitter cry. It was the recoil of Being from Annihilation.[89]

Even this, however, results in defiance. Only when a "heavenly mirror" shows her two images—"the one what God had intended her to be, the other what she had made herself"[90]—does she finally, but reluctantly, submit ("her submission was not feigned, neither was it real").[91] At this point, Mara draws her patient's attention to her clenched fist, the fingers enclosed on something she refuses to release. Lilith replies defiantly: "I will yet be mistress of myself! I am still what I have always known myself—queen of Hell, and mistress of the worlds!" resulting in her being pushed over the threshold into "non-being." Like "the lost soul," in the "outer darkness" she is aware that the "source of life had withdrawn itself; all that was left her of conscious being was the dregs of her dead and corrupted life."[92]

---

87. *Lilith* 280.
88. *Lilith* 281.
89. *Lilith* 283.
90. *Lilith* 283.
91. *Lilith* 284.
92. *Lilith* 285–86.

Lilith finally submits. "'I yield,' said the princess. 'I cannot hold out. I am defeated.—Not the less, I cannot open my hand'"[93]—a symbol of her yet being a slave to something beyond herself, which Mara puts thus:

> "A slave thou art *that shall one day be a child!*" answered Mara.— "Verily, thou shalt die, but not as thou thinkest. Thou shalt die out of death into life. Now is the Life for, that never was against thee!"[94]

Despite her repentance, Lilith is still enslaved by sin.[95] Reflecting MacDonald's view of atonement as involving reconciliation with, and forgiveness from, those sinned against, as well as reparations for wrongs committed, the final step involves a confrontation with Adam.

The journey to Adam's cemetery, though, is significant, in that on the way the entourage has to traverse the "bad burrow" where earlier monsters of nightmare had erupted from the ground beneath Vane's feet. Despite Lilith's repentant state (she is now weeping copiously) the monsters once more heave from the ground with Lilith as their main target. The children are oblivious to their presence. There are paradoxes in this image. First, that children are immune to evil. Second, that despite implying that the evil in the land emanates from Lilith's mind, these monsters appear to have their genesis elsewhere: Lilith has renounced evil, so where do they come from? The repentance of the queen of Hell appears not to imply that existential evil has ceased, but that the great Shadow still holds sway in other "hosts"—Vane, perhaps, chief among them. Evil, in MacDonald's scheme, will only be defeated when all created beings—including the great Shadow itself—have chosen to turn towards the light (although this conclusion will be examined more closely below). Eve's response to Mara's optimism when they finally arrive at the house of death reinforces this:

> "Your children are no longer in her danger," said Mara; "she has turned from evil."
>
> "Trust her not hastily, Mara," answered her mother; "she has deceived a multitude!"[96]

---

93. *Lilith* 287.
94. *Lilith* 287 (emphasis mine).
95. *Lilith* 206.
96. *Lilith* 296.

But there is paradox here too, for despite the great Shadow being a two-dimensional entity that is essential negation (clearly an image of Satan since Eve notes in passing, "Even now is his head under my heel!"),[97] here Eve remarks: "When the Shadow comes here, it will be to lie down and sleep also.—His hour will come, and he knows it will."[98]

Lilith finally sleeps in Adam's cemetery, but the account raises further questions. First, she is far from submissive. On arrival, Adam offers to carry her into the house, but "she repulsed him . . . unsubmissive."[99] Eve, however, expresses universalist optimism: "Sooner or later all will be little ones, for all must sleep in my house! It is well with those that go to sleep young and willing!—Lilith . . . is neither young nor quite willing, but it is well indeed that she is come."[100] Second, although the children gladly receive bread and wine from Eve before they sleep, Lilith refuses:

> "Thy beauty slays me! It is death I would have, not food!" said Lilith, and turned from her.
> "This food will help thee to die," answered Eve.
> But Lilith would not taste of it.
> "If thou wilt nor [sic] eat nor drink, Lilith," said Adam, "come and see the place where thou shalt lie in peace."[101]

Lilith would still rather be the priestess of a counterfeit Eucharist than share in the real one. The paradox is that in refusing bread and wine she "has no life in her" (cf. John 6:53) and yet she longs for death. Third, in these scenes Lilith appears to have her own substantial being, negating the pains MacDonald has gone to to portray her as fundamentally parasitic. Who is "hosting" her now? It appears to be God.

Her final capitulation to sleep is ambiguous to the end in that she never unclenches her hand. Instead, on the basis that it has been closed for a thousand years and "the fingers have grown together and into the palm,"[102] she demands that Adam cut it off. Despite volunteering her hand for amputation, her ultimate submission to the divine will is itself "parasitic" on the will of another.

---

97. *Lilith* 299.
98. *Lilith* 302.
99. *Lilith* 296.
100. *Lilith* 295.
101. *Lilith* 297–98.
102. *Lilith* 302.

The narrative ends with Vane being instructed to travel to a desert location and bury the hand. This time he follows instructions. As a result, water flows in the desert and the land transforms into an Edenic paradise. On returning from his commission, Vane receives bread and wine from Adam and Eve and is finally laid to rest at Lona's side. (MacDonald may have had Colossians 3:3 in mind, "For you died, and your life is hidden with Christ in God.") He sleeps, dreaming that he is once more abroad in the land, a "dream" which ends with him waking once more in his own house. After four nights, he wakes once more in the house of death to find Lona standing and smiling by his side. He is now, according to Adam, "clothed-upon with Death, which is the radiant garment of Life."[103]

Thus clothed and (apparently) post-mortem, he and Lona experience "a glorious resurrection-morning. The night had been spent in preparing it!," described in MacDonald's most purple prose. An entourage of Little Ones and beasts led by Vane and Lona set out for a celestial city whose upper reaches are hidden in clouds. They traverse once more the now-fertile land flowing with the water of grace, but this Eden is not without its snakes: as they pass the "bad burrow," now a crystal lake, Vane reports:

> I gazed into its pellucid depths. A whirlpool had swept out the soil in which the abortions burrowed, and at the bottom lay visible the whole horrid brood: a dim greenish light pervaded the crystalline water, and revealed every hideous form beneath it.[104]

Are these dead forms, or might they also be resurrected if another Lilith was to arise, seduce another Vane, and make the land a desert?

On arrival at the "New Jerusalem" the group climbs towards heaven. As the children hurry forward to meet Christ,[105] at the last moment an unseen hand pushes Vane through "a little door with a golden lock":

> The door opened; the hand let mine go, and pushed me gently through. I turned quickly, and saw the board of a large book in the act of closing behind me. I stood alone in my library.[106]

---

103. *Lilith* 331.

104. *Lilith* 338–39.

105. One of the children reports (in their terrible baby language) that the "beautifullest man" said to her: "'Ou's all mine's, 'ickle ones: come along!" (*Lilith* 344; cf. Matt 19:14).

106. *Lilith* 348.

Vane has just emerged from a "book," that magic gateway to the transcendent world of imagination which is not imaginary. *We* emerge from the book pondering, with Vane, whether experienced reality is merely the product of mind—"My brain was its mother, and the fever in my blood its father." However, MacDonald locates the human mind in the divine mind, and God, like a violinist, guides the bow across the strings of experience.[107] Vane concludes: "When a man dreams his own dream, he is the sport of his dream; when Another gives it him, that Other is able to fulfil it,"[108] and thus he lives in hope. Writing in 1857 to his father, MacDonald expresses this hope in a prayer:

> May the one Father make us all clean at last by his beautiful forgiving tenderness & his well-ordered sufferings, & when the right time comes, wake us out of this sleep into the new world, which is the old one, when we shall say as one that wakes from a dream—Is it then over, & I live?[109]

---

107. *Lilith* 350.

108. *Lilith* 350.

109. Sadler, *Expression of Character*, 124. "When we lie down at last God will give a glorious waking to all our dreams; all that was lovely in them we shall find true" (Sadler, *Expression of Character*, 163).

8

Lilith—*A Summary of George MacDonald's Theology*

RONALD MACDONALD REMARKED THAT his father's

> iridescent imagination gave its colour to the religion that was his. . . . His imaginative faculty was a prism, falling through which the Great White Light was disparted into seventy times seven hues of human delight.[1]

Lilith is certainly "colorful" and this end-of-canon narrative refracts many core themes into more visible elements. This chapter attempts to identify these, clarifying specific theological ideas already discussed by considering *Lilith*'s methodology and content. Some immediate critical comments are offered; the primary aim is to shed further light on MacDonald's "theology of childhood."

A Realist Fantasy

MacDonald's reluctance to publish *Lilith* was, perhaps, that the first-person narrative implies an autobiographic dimension or at minimum an account of scenes familiar to an author. Since these describe mental states, MacDonald is necessarily making himself vulnerable to charges of, for example, sexual perversion and erotic fantasies. He is saying, in effect, that these are normal (or at least common) male fantasies, a revelation

---

1. MacDonald, "George MacDonald," 112–13.

that may not have sat too comfortably with his readership. (The genre of "Christian gothic erotic fantasy," as now, no doubt raised a few eyebrows.) But the point is that these *are* normal.[2] Furthermore, although *Lilith* appears "fantastic"—the "little world of his own" that the author has created seems, at first glance, to bear little relation to lived experience—in many respects this is "realist fantasy": this *is* how MacDonald views his world. "The world is . . . the human being turned inside out,"[3] a place where evil affects (or infects) vision and where lived reality emanates from the divine mind. That there are few "material" touchstones should not distract from the concrete nature of the proposals being made regarding issues such as identity, childhood, and evil, underscored by numerous biblical references. This is a very concrete and "realist" theological work.

I have not formally defined human imagination, but if one considers this as essentially a high-level cognitive faculty allowing us to make sense of lived reality by providing a perspective higher than the ambiguities of lived experience and convictions about the past and bridging the two,[4] then this text may be viewed as a fairy child—personified imagination, if you like—standing above the battle for religious truth, offering an alternative epistemological perspective. Plotz disparagingly suggested that the Romantic child is, in Emerson's words, "the perpetual Messiah which comes into the arms of fallen men, and pleads with them to return to paradise."[5] This text is just such a fairy child. Since "paradise" for MacDonald is the place where "the spirit of children [is the] pervading spirit throughout, from lowly subject to lowliest king,"[6] MacDonald's children plead with us to return to *childhood*. It is a protest, as noted, against adulthood with its pretensions, conventions, idolatry, and self-centeredness, forcing a reconsideration of adulthood and the world in which "adults" live.

---

2. Joyal et al., "What Exactly?"

3. *Orts* 9.

4. This is essentially the view of psychiatrist and neuroscientist Iain McGilchrist: "It is the faculty of imagination . . . which comes into being between the two hemispheres, which enables us to take things back from the left hemisphere [convictions about the past] and make them live again in the right [lived experience]. It is in this way, not by meretricious novelty, that things are made truly new once again" (McGilchrist, *Master and His Emissary*, 199).

5. Plotz, *Romanticism*, 3. See page 46.

6. *US1* 14–15.

An Alternative Epistemology—Shape-Shifting Truth

Lilith is a lesson in imaginative "fiduciary hermeneutics."[7] The shape-shifting characters and mirage-like set demand subjective interaction; the truth of such states (apparent meaning) cannot be accepted at face value, neither is "naming" them adequate. Instead, the reader (of both this narrative and God's "artwork" of life) must engage with the truth—it must be personally evaluated and internalized; faith cannot simply remain *assensus* but must become *fiducia, fidelitas,* and *visio*. The Word, one might say, must become flesh; human engagement with Christ—for Augustine, the art or "skill of the omnipotent and wise God"[8]—is also an aesthetic encounter:

> The reality of Christ's nature is not to be proved by argument. He must be beheld. The manifestation of Him must "gravitate inwards" on the soul. It is by looking that one can know.

This beatific vision is contrasted with "notions whose chief strength lay in their preconception," in other words, the conclusions of prior generations. The latter, reminiscent of J. H. Newman's "notional assent" (distilled from general principles rather than personal experience),[9] is mere theory:

> For a man to theorize theologically in any form, while he has not so apprehended Christ . . . is to bring on himself . . . such errors as the expounders of nature in old time brought on themselves, when they speculated on what a thing must be, instead of observing what it was; this *must be* having for its foundation not self-evident truth, but notions whose chief strength lay in their preconception.[10]

Lilith, especially, proposes that humans were not made to live in such a "library" of second-hand wisdom, nor that mere logic will decode the riddle of life—especially when it comes to evil. I will refer to these contrasting views of truth as "aesthetic" and "conventional."

---

7. See page 128.

8. Dods, *Works of Aurelius Augustine*, 7:177 (*De Trinitate* 6:10).

9. "Theology, as such, always is notional, as being scientific; religion, as being personal, should be real; but, except within a small range of subjects, it commonly is not real in England" (Newman, *Essay in Aid*, 53).

10. *Orts* 206–7.

There are period-specific distractions. For example, Eve is always the server who sets bread and wine on the table,[11] Adam supervises not only her but the world in general, and all the women are mothers (including Lilith, her main failure being to reject that role). Vane's infatuation with Lona, a girl half his age,[12] is also worrying to the modern reader: she represents the male fantasy of a submissive virgin who caresses the face of her "king" with childlike adoration.[13] These, however, should not distract from some very precise theological, philosophical, and moral proposals.

Learning to See Again—Imaginative Vision

The first of these positive proposals relates to aesthetic truth. Like Jesus leading the blind man out of his village (Mark 8:22–26), this fairy child leads the reader away from the bickering of contemporary religion offering a wider perspective—away from the preconceptions, presuppositions, prejudices, and the familiarity of conventional "village" life. At first we see an odd landscape, "men like trees walking," but, like Jesus, MacDonald's agenda is not just to give sight but to wake new vision—new categories, new "visual vocabulary," a new lens through which to view reality. The narrative specifically highlights the destructiveness and provisionality of conventional truth. As MacDonald remarks elsewhere: "What many men call their beliefs, are but the prejudices they happen to have picked up."[14] So, perhaps with the Congregational Leicester Conference or the Baptist "down grade" controversies in mind,[15] he has skeletal fighters slaughtering one another in a dark forest (dark religion) screaming out "*The Truth! The Truth!*" while Lilith calmly orchestrates the destruction from above.[16] "The holiest words went with the most hating blow," and, in an image that brings to mind those such as the self-appointed and pugnacious protector of Congregationalism, John Campbell, MacDonald has one frenetic fighter "who wheeled ever in a circle, and smote on all sides."

---

11. *Lilith* 38, 295, 297.

12. Biologically so, but in "reality," thousands of years old.

13. The children and Lona call Vane "king"; on Vane's reappearance after absence, Lona is full of "silent delight, expressed mainly by stroking [his] face and hands" (*Lilith* 314–15, 228).

14. *HG* 209.

15. See note pages 32–33.

16. *Lilith* 71–72.

Lilith, then—drinking the blood of children and given form and substance by the Vanes of this world—is both a product of the "pitcher of Calvinism," the "false form of true religion,"[17] and the idol at its center demanding worship and orchestrating the infighting. This narrative does not, therefore, simply champion unchecked imagination; there is a caveat: demons are reified and vivified by human imagination. Rather, it is promoting cognitive balance; that imagination is needed for, indeed the leader in, healthy cognition, *not* that rationalizing is redundant. Vane's problem is that he "saw not, felt not, and yet [was deluded into thinking that he] knew,"[18] a knowing that gives substance to Lilith. Had he truly "seen" and "felt"—that is, remained cognizant of the wider divine context beyond himself—he would have recognized that he was responsible for hosting and nourishing evil.

So although imaginative, this narrative does not propose that *anything* may be imagined. Aesthetic truth is the "topmost stone" of something, "the thing it is made for" and is, ironically, a warning against being too imaginative and attributing false meaning to something which has "obvious" meaning (after all, "To men who are not simple, simple words are the most inexplicable of riddles").[19] This may seem a bit rich coming from an author with an idealist vision who, according to Ruskin, reads whatever he likes from presenting phenomena, but it is a warning against reading badly, of accepting "unacceptable" truth—truth that fundamentally corrodes understanding of "The Truth."[20] For example, MacDonald's conviction that God is light means that he cannot accept Dante's "hell of exhausted mercy."[21] His advice—following Newman's dictum that "no religion is from God which contradicts our sense of right and wrong"[22]—is to be wary of attributing to God ungodly attributes: "If any statement is made, any word employed, that we feel unworthy of the Lord, let us refuse it":[23]

> Better to refuse even the truth for a time, than, by accepting into our intellectual creed that which our heart cannot receive, not

---

17. Pages 111 and 116.
18. *Lilith* 200.
19. *US1* 68.
20. *US1* 66–67.
21. *AF* 2:195.
22. Newman, *Essay in Aid*, 414.
23. *US3* 184.

seeing its real form, to introduce hesitation into our prayers, a jar into our praises, and a misery into our love. If it be the truth, we shall one day see it another thing than it appears now, and love it because we see it lovely; for *all* truth is lovely.[24]

Just as art is a conversation between artist and observer, aesthetic truth stresses the need for a different way of seeing; the imprecision of truth-claims does not imply inadequacy, simply that humans are dealing with "the beauty of the infinite." MacDonald's agenda, therefore, is not to help us accurately (albeit imaginatively) perceive specific truth-claims but to waken our imagination to the wider context, the depth of God's art. In *Lilith*, at every page-turn we encounter defamiliarization and paradox: fairy vision does not resolve paradox, but creates it, forcing readerly engagement. "What," one must ask, "does *this* mean?" MacDonald's thesis is that such engagement is, at least in part, responsible for *creating* reality. An individual's reality may be a construct forged by the interaction of subjective experience and objective "others," but he goes further, suggesting that human consciousness, made in the image of God, partners with God in the creation of those "others" and therefore has a moral responsibility to discern and act wisely.

Evil—Faulty Vision

A failure to accurately perceive a presenting state of affairs, allied to a preoccupation with self, results in evil—Vane resurrecting Lilith, the enemy of children. In contrast, true perception and selflessness helps to create a new heaven and the new earth. In *Lilith*, with such revitalized vision, Vane walks through the land where previously monsters had erupted from beneath his feet. He remarks:

> It was a summer-day more like itself, that is, *more ideal*, than ever man that had not died found summer-day in any world. I walked on the new earth, under the new heaven, and found them *the same as the old, save that now they opened their minds to me, and I saw into them*.[25]

On this view, the external "artwork" of the world is almost entirely shaped by the viewer; that, as Carlyle had put it, "Matter exists only spiritually,

---

24. *US1* 70.
25. *Lilith* 340 (emphasis mine).

and to represent some Idea and *body* it forth,"[26] but, rather than this being solely God's idea, human ideas play a creative, and major, part. Here, for example, Vane's experience of the "new heaven and earth" is considered entirely a matter of perception: "A wondrous change had passed upon the world—or was it not rather that a change more marvelous had taken place in us?"[27] The obverse of this is that evil results from human ideas not chiming with God's: that evil is both the creation and subjective experience of people whose God-consciousness is dimmed—that evil is located in consciousness rather than context (a prevalent nineteenth-century view).[28] These propositions are discussed more fully below.

The Child Against the Vampire

The Child

In *Lilith*, the identity of the fairy child offering us this alternative epistemology is not immediately apparent. The Little Ones, for reasons identified by Milbank and Tolkien,[29] are more parodic than metaphoric. Eve's observation that "sooner or later all will be little ones"[30] seems more of a threat than a promise. Their childlikeness represents absolute trust but little more. Their main role in the narrative is as a mirror by which other characters establish their credentials. They reveal Vane's naivety (ironically by being naive in the extreme themselves), Lilith's vampirism, and Mara's and Eve's motherliness. They also prompt reflection on the idea of a colony of children growing up in Lilith's territory, an irony not lost on Adam.[31] One might also ask why some are "elected" for salvation by Mara while others are left to become vampire prey. These issues are worthy of reflection but we do not view the world through their eyes.

The obvious candidate is Vane; however, he is hardly a child. Not only has he just come of age, he is obsessed with a girl he hardly knows (who reminds him of his mother), is erotically attracted to a vampire, prefers war to diplomacy, has delusions of becoming king and restoring

---

26. Carlyle, *Sartor Resartus*, 49.
27. *Lilith* 337.
28. Kelsey, *Eccentric Existence*, 406.
29. Note 50, page 203.
30. *Lilith* 295.
31. *Lilith* 208.

the crumbling city (with Queen Lona by his side), ignores the advice of supreme beings, and prefers reading "science" books. His "logical" military campaign to liberate the city is criticized by Adam as unimaginative.[32] While Adam, Eve, and Mara are, in a sense, perfect children, I suggest the main child protagonist of this "autobiographical" novel is MacDonald himself in the guise of Vane. As son Ronald remarked in 1911, "there has probably never been a writer whose work was a better expression of his personal character," continuing:

> The ideals of his didactic novels were the motive of his own life. . . . We have had until lately a poet . . . living among us a life of literal, and, which is more, imaginative consistency with his doctrine.[33]

In this "realist fantasy," MacDonald uses symbol and metaphor to paint as accurate a picture as he can of his vision of idealist reality and places within this ambiguous world an un-ideal child—himself. Compared to the idealized children we have met in his "realist" novels—whom he places in fantasy worlds that *look* like Aberdeen or London but where evil, it seems, is of little consequence—Vane appears normal. That he struggles to make sense of his world and often fails to make wise decisions does not make him less of a human child, simply a more real one. If childhood inheres primarily in a submissive and obedient response to divine transcendent cues, then Vane is a child in the making. The sun, waking his fairy vision by revealing the picture in his library "as if for the first time" begins the process. Realization dawns that his ancestor in the picture was once a human like himself, a predecessor who had worked out from first principles the content of many of the books now in his "library" (his consciousness). He realizes that he is not an "isolated, punctiliar, psychic monad,"[34] but is connected—not just to ancestors, but to a transcendent reality. The autobiographical dialogue reinforces this but—like that other "autobiographical" narrative of the mind, *Wilfrid Cumbermede*, that also, in many regards, offers a more faithful sketch of the human condition—it is primarily the description of mind rather than body (in the philosophical sense) that allows no other reading.

This is not to say that MacDonald sees his mind as unconnected with others. From his perspective, action and set are objective realities

---

32. *Lilith* 195–98.

33. MacDonald, "George MacDonald," 59.

34. Hart, *Beauty of the Infinite*, 170.

but are, and can only be, phenomenally perceived by that mind. It is his theological picture of the world, but not his view of total reality: transcendent reality beyond the "second death" is hinted at, but inaccessible. *Lilith* is his dramatization of the interaction between quotidian human existence and the purgatorial realm where God prepares his children for the second death (although both are purgatorial). Like Diamond, he is visiting the back of the North Wind. Apart from Lilith's proleptic experience of the fire of God, it is notable that even in this purgatorial realm God remains hidden. Christ is only hinted at in bread and wine (I believe we should read Lona, like Gibbie, as exemplary of the perfect human child). Even purgatory demands, and fosters, faith.

Considering MacDonald as a fairy-child author is revealing. Having his own particular view of Christian childhood he writes as a child, not only to foster the same in others, but by appealing to mutual childhood. His goal is to empathetically engage his "child" readers. But, as the text of *Lilith* makes clear, this child spends much of his time in fairyland: Vane's excursions to the realm of the seven dimensions in this idealist ontology are as real—more real to MacDonald, it seems—as his three-dimensional life. This appears the source of a two-fold frustration when reading his more realist novels. First, that they seem child*ish* rather than child*like* representations of the world, reflecting Lewis's comments about third-rate authorship. They are a child's sketch that tends to ignore evil and believe the best; they also have the limited perspective of a child. Nevertheless, they have a certain attraction that Lewis described as "holiness"; an aesthetic attractiveness that communicates truth if one is prepared to overlook technical ability, an attraction dependent on relationship with the child (we do not display the art of unknown children on our fridges). That MacDonald writes "for the childlike, whether of five, or fifty, or seventy-five"[35] is more than a cliché: he is assuming (and fostering) a relationship with the reader, one based on his vision of God as mutual father.

However, the optimistic claim that all humans are already part of God's family could be challenged. Christ, for example, rejected Pharisaical claims to mutual fatherhood with the blunt words, "You are of your father the devil," "you are not of God," words, moreover, spoken to "those Jews who believed Him" whom he yet described as slaves to sin (John 8:44, 47, 31, 34). This reinforces the observation that MacDonald, the childlike

---

35. *Orts* 317.

author, is drawing pictures in his nineteenth-century nursery. This is not to denigrate his work, simply to note a limited perspective reflecting the prevailing Zeitgeist and that he is drawing for the "family" around him who in some measure claim, or are familiar with the concept of, religious adherence. He is writing to those who claim childlikeness with a view to encouraging moral integrity. He would also, I believe, not be annoyed at being accused of having a limited perspective for his methodology and contribution to theology involve undermining those who claim *not* to be subject to such limitations, in other words, those who claim that their own limited "net of a presumptuous self-styled orthodoxy"[36] represents the full truth.

The second frustration, which we touched on earlier, is that the adult and the child that are MacDonald are often at odds. He insists, for example, that a picture must speak for itself:

> if I cannot draw a horse, I will not write THIS IS A HORSE under what I foolishly meant for one. Any key to a work of imagination would be nearly, if not quite, as absurd.[37]

The point being that "horse" means nothing to someone who has never encountered one and merely adding a label will not bring enlightenment. However, the adult in him often rises up to add explanatory notes or a sermon or two. Despite stubbornly refusing to explain his work on the basis that "if my dog can't bark, I'm not going to sit up and bark for him,"[38] he regularly does just that, but from within the text. For example, when Maggie, the "honest peasant" daughter of the soutar (cobbler) in *Salted With Fire* who has just prayed to see God stumbles across a crying baby on the moors, "Her first thought was, 'Can that be Himsel, come ance again as he came ance afore?'" On finding the abandoned child under a bush, she "claps[ed] it close to her panting bosom": "clearly she thought of nothing but carrying the infant home to her father."[39] The metaphor of an abandoned child being carried to a loving father is immediately obvious, but MacDonald cannot help informing us that:

36. *US3* 150.
37. *Orts* 321.
38. *Orts* 321
39. *SF* 52.

> Maggie . . . received an instantaneous insight that never left her: now she understood the heart of the Son of Man, come to find and carry back the stray children to their Father and His.[40]

As Voltaire once remarked, "*Le secret d'ennuyer est celui de tout dire.*"[41] In MacDonald's fantasy works, however, such authorial intrusions are less immediately apparent. Especially in *Lilith*, the fairy-child author explores fairyland without (on the whole) being chaperoned, censored, or explained by the ideal (possibly false) adult companion. As we look through the more honest eyes of this fairy traveler and try to understand the resulting childlike picture—"the blossom of it, the thing it is made for"[42]—without being too critical of its execution, we will understand better MacDonald's "theology of the child."

The Vampire

MacDonald, then, casts himself opposite Lilith—essential negation. If Murdoch Malison is essentially a distorted divinity (the antithesis of the child-God),[43] Lilith is a distorted creature: she is, as noted, the anti-child and, therefore, the antichrist. Whereas Christ sheds his blood on behalf of the children, she drinks it. She is also anti her true self: she refuses to accept her God-given identity. So who is she? Her essential negation has two aspects. First, she is a fallen being, that is, she was given life and a specific identity by God which was then rejected. Being Adam's first wife, she *was* human but is now "bodiless, alone"—a seemingly demonic entity (reflecting Jewish lore). She lusts after childhood (evidenced by her attraction to the cherubim) but only on her own terms, despising the corresponding need for submission. Exactly what ontological status her body has in this idealist scheme is (forgive the pun) immaterial; the issue is that by her decision to center her life on herself she is the ultimate example (with the possible exception of the great Shadow) of a *cor curvum in se* that is tending towards non-being.

---

40. *SF* 52–53.

41. "The secret of being a bore is to say everything" (Voltaire, *Discours en vers sur l'homme*, 23).

42. Note 118, page 36.

43. *US3* 69. See page 109.

The second aspect, then, is her need to find an alternative life-source. Since "blood" is needed for life,[44] her only solution is to live as a vampire. The irony is that in her parasitism she is, indirectly, dependent on the God who has given life to others. All humans, inasmuch as they reject their own God-given identity, are complicit in giving their blood to nourish this antichrist. Since this is a "religious" act, the primary arena in which the battle for true identity takes place is that of religion accounting for MacDonald's particular attention to what are, in his view, distorted religious schemes at whose center Lilith is both nourished and worshipped.

To summarize, insofar as "without shedding of blood there is no remission [of sins]" (Heb 9:22), Lilith, drinking blood, represents unforgiveness, condemnation, and judgement and is therefore guilty of the "unforgiveable sin" since God can only forgive those who want to be forgiven ("I believe that no man is ever condemned for any sin except one—that he will not leave his sins and come out of them, and be the child of him who is his father").[45] Her residence at the heart of religion makes it sacrilegious.

The Battle for the Truth

In this narrative, both fairy child and vampire are engaged in, yet in some sense above, the battle for "*The Truth!*"; they are portrayed as "principalities and powers," opposing forces behind the conflicts of earth. Each offers a perspective on the religious war raging at their feet as "skeletons and phantoms [fight] in maddest confusion." As these fight, there are—

> Wild cries and roars of rage, shock of onset, struggle prolonged, all mingled with words articulate. . . . Curses and credos, snarls and sneers, laughter and mockery, sacred names and howls of hate. . . . Phantom-throats swelled the deafening tumult with the war-cry of every opinion, bad or good, that had bred strife, cruelty in any world.[46]

This is MacDonald's jaundiced view of the nineteenth-century war for the truth, one orchestrated by Lilith who moves "at her will above the strife-tormented multitudes, now on this front, now on that, one outstretched

---

44. "Blood . . . is the life of all flesh. Its blood sustains its life" (Lev 17:13–14).
45. *US3* 154–55; cf. note 223, page 170.
46. *Lilith* 71.

arm urging the fight."[47] The scene closes with a biblical quotation: "Just before sunrise, a breeze went through the forest, and a voice cried, 'Let the dead bury their dead!'" words which MacDonald had first used in the sermon *Justice*, a withering critique of the Reformers' doctrinal efforts where he states his contrary aim to "prevent the dead from burying the living."[48] The reader must choose between a Reformed death or submissive death in Adam's cemetery. We will further consider Lilith's existential status shortly.

Key Theological Proposals that Emerge from *Lilith*

A Purgatorial, Multi-Dimensional Ontology

In *Lilith*, MacDonald's three-tier universe is evident representing a rejection of a simplistic earth/heaven duality. First, there is the "world of three dimensions" that I have referred to as quotidian reality; here I will simply call this "reality." Second, there is "the world of seven dimensions"; this I will refer to as "fairyland" (I was tempted to call it "purgatory," but, as we will shortly explore, all three tiers are purgatorial). Third, there is the transcendent realm where God is encountered, which I shall refer to as "heaven."

It will be remembered that a sonnet in *The Diary of an Old Soul* begins, "Yestereve, Death came, and knocked at my thin door" (the concept behind *North Wind*).[49] For MacDonald, a Celt raised on the borders of Faerie, there is only a thin door between reality and fairyland and much commerce between the two. Fairies are glimpsed occasionally and reality glows with a numinous presence—both fairy and divine. There are also shared phenomena: trees in fairyland grow through chimneys in the realm of reality, and "books" (humans) intersect both realms. "Ah, the two worlds! so strangely they are one," remarks Adam in *Lilith*, "And yet so measurelessly wide apart!"[50] Temporally they may be divided by human death (a doorway in a faux "bookcase") but "physically" (however that is understood) they are entwined. Both are dream-worlds prior to the final awakening. Together they make up a dualist "system of Soul-making."

---

47. *Lilith* 72.
48. *US3* 136.
49. *Rampolli* 190.
50. *Lilith* 204.

Those who might, for example, object to this model on the basis that "it is appointed for men to die once, but after this the judgment" (Heb 9:27; cf. Matt 25:31–46) must realize that MacDonald has moved the goalposts of death further "back": true death, the sleep in Adam's cemetery, is the real doorway to heaven; in the meantime, reality *and* fairyland partner together to prepare humans for that final sleep. To this end, commerce between the two realms is humanly possible: Vane's imaginative excursions to fairyland, and his "waking" back in reality illustrate this dual citizenship. Thus MacDonald, for example, has confidence that the suicidal Charley will receive a warm welcome in fairyland—that Adam will help him sleep.

The submission of sleep—choosing to relinquish consciousness—is a prerequisite for the second death symbolic of the complete renunciation of self-will. Only those so choosing will wake with joy in God's presence to be embraced as children. Thus the focus in *Lilith* is the purgatorial office of both reality and fairyland preparatory for this moment. It involves the rejection of evil couched in terms of self-will—the willful rejection of one's God-ordained identity. This, however, is beyond the power of enslaved human will. Only by accepting bread and wine prior to the second death can one overcome the power of evil and joyfully embrace the fire of God. Christ—being the only perfect *imago Dei* who has "slept" perfectly—offers others the power to sleep at peace.

Prior to the second death, then, MacDonald conceives of existence as an iterative process of purgatorial refinement involving commuting (in the mind) between reality and fairyland.[51] Although after the first death humans might not "physically" be able to return to reality, he is clear that the post-mortem influence of others folds back into reality. Lilith, for one, has continued power over the minds of "men." It is a scheme which is theodically necessary since it goes *some* way to mitigate the thorny issue of dysteleological evil in the "vale of soul making" and anticipates the work of, for example, John Hick:

---

51. According to Waite, this reflects "the Kabalistic doctrine of revolution according to Isaac de Loria" whereby Jewish souls are allowed to return to earth and enter an embryo or an adult. "Revolution occurs (1) For the cleansing of sin; (2) For the fulfilment of a neglected precept; (3) For the leading of others into the right way . . . (4) To receive a true spouse who was not deserved by the soul in the prior revolution" (Waite, *Doctrine and Literature of Kabalah*, 303). Items one and four are particularly evident in *Lilith*.

> Hick recognises this apparent failure of soul-making teleology in this world, and refers to 'further scenes of "soul making,"' and a future eschaton where one experiences 'an infinite good that would render worthwhile *any* finite suffering endured in the course of attaining it.' So he implies a future purgatorial state where soul-making activities might continue, and he proposes a future experience of such profundity that it justifies all suffering.[52]

However, for MacDonald, such purgatorial refinement does not (necessarily) end with the second death. First, the sleep in Adam's cemetery is ambiguous. Those not yet ready to wake in God's presence (that is, with residual evil that would mean a destructive encounter with God's fire) are "sent back," waking once more in either fairyland or reality, a repeated experience of Vane. So the sleep in Adam's cemetery is also purgatorial. Finally, the encounter with God is *also* purgatorial in that God's fire will purge any residual evil and finally purify the soul:

> It is not that the fire will burn us if we do not worship thus; but that the fire will burn us until we worship thus; yea, will go on burning within us after all that is foreign to it has yielded to its force, no longer with pain and consuming, but as the highest consciousness of life, the presence of God.[53]

Eve's comment that "it is well with those that go to sleep young and willing!"[54] implies that this post-(final-)mortem divine encounter can be "hell" for some. Although I remarked that Lilith "got off lightly" in her encounter with Adam, the implication is that her encounter with God—being still in some measure rebellious and having refused bread and wine—will be far from pleasant. If her proleptic experience of this at Mara's hands is indicative, the implication is that she may even be annihilated.

One might, perhaps, read too much into this model, or, indeed, into MacDonald's general tendency towards esotericism and syncretism. His willingness to explore subjects such as evolution and reincarnation should be viewed as exploratory—"aesthetic" engagement with issues to explore what they offer. The *Curdie* stories, for example, feature goblins

---

52. Stoeber, *Evil and the Mystics' God*, 75.

53. *US1* 31. This reflects Catholic doctrine; Christ himself is "purgatory." See John Paul II, "Heaven, Hell, and Purgatory."

54. *Lilith* 295.

(regressed humans)[55] who keep macabre "pets" that are either evolving or regressing. There is also the curious (and depressing) tale of the "shop in heaven" exploring "evolutionary reincarnation" where sinners are sent back to earth—

> and there must he grow up again, crawling through the channels of thousand-folded difference, from animal to animal, until at length a human brain be given to him, and after generations he become once again capable of being born of the spirit into the kingdom of liberty.[56]

The late sermon "The Hope of the Universe" (1892) likewise explores reincarnation—as well as the mid-century belief that the fetus mirrored the stages of evolutionary ascent *in utero*[57]—albeit with the caveat, "I do not care to spend thought or time, least of all argument" on such ideas. Despite the caveat, however, strong evolutionary ideas regarding creation are expressed, but, as noted, we should keep in mind that MacDonald's focus is primarily on ethics and morality rather than the "mechanics" of ontology.

The Human Demon

Further comments are needed about the existential nature of Lilith. First, that she is human. She may be "bodiless alone," but is not a non-human demon. She is Adam's ex-wife and Lona's mother. Her quintessential rebelliousness, however, has trapped her essence, her "spirit," in fairyland; only through vampirism, "possessing" and feasting on a host, can she revisit and express her lost humanity—a humanity she constantly longs for; a misguided quest for reincarnation on her terms instead of accepting her God-given identity. She, then, like Charley in *Cumbermede* (and Peter in Matt 16:23), is "demonic"; he, however, recognizes this—"*I am a devil*"—she does not. In *Lilith*, MacDonald is illustrating the connectedness of human minds; not only that ideas have power, but that through ideas ancestors haunt us. If evil, these are the "principalities," "powers," "rulers of the darkness of this age," and "spiritual hosts of wickedness in the heavenly places" in Vane's mind that he must overcome (Eph 6:12):

55. *PG* 3.
56. *TWC* 303
57. *HG* 214–15.

he is "born in sin"[58]—connected to the sin of others—and must renounce this in preparation for sleep.

It may be objected that this reading is pushing MacDonald's text too far, that the metaphor rather concerns the need for each Vane to destroy his or her Lilith. However, we face the issue that Vane does not destroy Lilith but (albeit inadvertently) saves her: his good intentions work for evil in the same way that, in MacDonald's scheme, evil intentions work for good. She is not merely *his* evil alter-ego but the nemesis of all who aspire to become children. Through the connectedness of minds, MacDonald is suggesting that he, like many others, is nourishing her, an evil entity that transcends his individual consciousness. She is an existential fallen being—"fallen" in that she has been cast from heaven (no longer free to consort with the cherubim)—and, moreover, responsible for the Fall, of causing the separation of "earth" and heaven having subsequently seduced Adam and Eve in the guise of a snake (an identity she struggles to hide).[59] The "larger hope," therefore, is synonymous with the eschaton for the precondition for "heaven and earth (fairyland and reality) to pass away"[60] is for *all* created beings to submit to God: there will be no contrary wills; all will sleep eventually in Adam's cemetery and exit the two lower realms at which point those two purgatorial realms will become redundant paving the way for the new heaven and earth where all (now true children) will live with their "elder brother," Christ.[61]

Lilith, it appears, was the first to fall and will be the last to be saved. The warning signs are, however, that her refusal of bread and wine (the last Adam) and insubmissive demeanor towards the first Adam prior to sleeping will result in a rude awakening. She will experience the full force of the wrath of God's dark fire. However, saved she will be, for in MacDonald's view:

> Annihilation itself is no death to evil. Only good where evil was, is evil dead. An evil thing must live with its evil until it chooses to be good. That alone is the slaying of evil.[62]

---

58. *RF* 1:152–53. See discussion on pages 85–86.

59. The *Zohar* concurs. See Waite, *Doctrine and Literature of Kabalah*, 259.

60. At the revelation of God's face, "the earth and the heaven fled away. And there was found no place for them" (Rev 20:11).

61. Christ is referred to as the "elder bother" eight times, for example, in MacDonald's *Unspoken Sermons*.

62. *Lilith* 212.

Furthermore, being the last creature in whom all rebellion is focused, her final repentance will be the destruction of the great Shadow. Substanceless and "hostless," the pure will of evil will be extinguished by ultimate *esse*, God's light. This is MacDonald's expression of God being "all in all." As Paul writes:

> Now when all things are made subject to Him, then the Son Himself will also be subject to Him who put all things under Him, that God may be all in all. (1 Cor 15:28)

The Polarities of Childhood and Evil

At the outset of the previous chapter I suggested *Lilith* was worthy of close reading as two of its core themes were childhood and evil. It is apparent from this discussion that this is one theme: childhood and evil are the poles of a volitional moral continuum. At one extreme we have the vampire, "perfect" disobedient rebellion; at the other, the child, perfect submissive obedience to the divine will exemplified perfectly this side of the eschaton by "the child in the midst" that "slept" in perfection and was raised from that submissive sleep. Since God is perfection, that is, as Trinity the perfect example of loving submission, God is the perfect child.

On this account, all God-created beings are located somewhere between these two extremes: none is entirely depraved just as none is perfect. (Only the great Shadow, being creature-created, is absolute negation; only God is "perfect perfection.") All, therefore, have the potential to turn towards God, and—that this might be a genuine expression of free will—creation, managed by God, conspires to that end by neither forcing obedience nor allowing slavery to sin (the moral evil in the self or others). All things *do* work together for good, for all: God ensures that the evil generated by creaturely "hosts" ultimately has no power to short-circuit free will; in addition, God uses what *seems* evil, but is really God's goodness, to bring about reformation.

George MacDonald's Universalism

Having, in chapter 5, suggested that the jury is out regarding MacDonald's universalism, *Lilith* conclusively leads us to a positive verdict. The picture presented of a purgatorial afterlife—with possibly more than one stage—prior to a purgatorial encounter with God draws on liberal theology circulating at the time. There are striking similarities, for example, to Baptist minister Samuel Cox's *Salvator Mundi* published in 1877, a work building on the views of those such as Erskine and Maurice and rejecting the anti-modernist approach of Spurgeon,[63] which may also have contributed to the ideas presented in the sermon "Justice" (in *US3*, 1889).[64] In Cox's view, "in one way or the other, in this age or in the ages to come, our sins, the sins of every one of us, must be burned out."[65] In the afterlife:

> We shall find the very discipline we need in order that we may be wholly purged from sin and imperfection. . . . We may also hope, by the very discipline and torment of our spirits, to be led to repentance, and, through repentance, unto life: we may hope that the disclosure of the spiritual world will take a spiritual effect upon us, gradually raising and renewing us till we too are prepared to enter the Paradise of God and behold the presence of the Lord and the glory of his power.[66]

Cox articulates many of the ideas found in *Lilith* as well as elsewhere in MacDonald's opus suggesting that he made a major contribution to MacDonald's thought.[67]

---

63. Instead of Spurgeon's warning against "toying with the deadly cobra of modern thought," Cox is of the opinion that the New Testament "harmonizes with, but strangely elevates, the highest conceptions of modern thought" (Cox, *Salvator Mundi*, 113).

64. "Justice" begins with Psalm 62:12, a key verse also for Cox. See *US3* 109; Cox, *Salvator Mundi*, 155, 208–9.

65. Cox, *Salvator Mundi*, 135.

66. Cox, *Salvator Mundi*, 220–21.

67. Cox was a friend of Thomas Toke Lynch, sometimes preaching at his church. See Watts, *Dissenters*, 3:63. The parallels between the work of MacDonald and Cox are numerous. In *Salvator Mundi*, for example, we find references to being "salted with fire," the Maurician view that "beneath the abyss of hell [is] a bottomless abyss of love," that suffering is always remedial, that there are at least three heavens (2 Cor 12:2–4), and that "the Jews held there were *seven* heavens" (Cox, *Salvator Mundi*, 134–35, 221, 168, 203).

9

The Implications of George MacDonald's Theology

IN THIS FINAL CHAPTER, we critically examine the theological proposals that have emerged from our focused reading of George MacDonald. It is evident that there is a strong theodical motivation to address, as Samuel Cox had phrased it, "the current libel on God";[1] it has also become clear that "the child against the vampire" is a model primarily aimed at addressing this fundamental concern. To this end, MacDonald's aim is to exorcise from religion, particularly Reformed religion, the demons of the past as well as current idols. Lilith and the great Shadow exemplify the fundamental partnership at the demonic pole of this infiltration of contemporary religion, that of human will aligned with "Satan." In contrast, the innocent child is presented to us as symbolic of an innocent God. We begin the discussion, therefore, by evaluating MacDonald's view of evil.

"Death Has Come through Our Windows"

Mara ("bitterness"), the cat-woman guardian of the children in *Lilith*, personifies MacDonald's main question. Her enigmatic fusion of tears and hope as she valiantly tries to protect the children from the vampire is modelled on the "weeping prophet," Jeremiah, who, like her, has (or at least longs for) "a lodging place for travelers in the wilderness" outside of, and in opposition to, a corrupt city (Jer 9:2). He voices God's question: "How shall I deal with the daughter of My people?" (Jer 9:7)· Lilith

---

1. Cox, *Salvator Mundi*, 132.

embodies this theological conundrum: she was created by God and, like Israel, is God's daughter, but is evil. Jeremiah summarizes the problem succinctly in words that, perhaps, inspired *Lilith*:

> Death has come through our windows,
> Has entered our palaces,
> To kill off the children. (Jer 9:21)

The great Shadow haunting the streets "seeking those he may devour," and Lilith's subsequent nocturnal feasting, is at the heart of the drama. Death *has* come through our windows to kill off the children: how did death come to have such brazen access to humanity, and who is responsible?

Since "windows," for MacDonald, are access points to the human mind, his answer is clear: humans are responsible. They have genuine free will and, therefore, the right—indeed the tendency—to open their "windows" to evil. Second, all evil is used by God for good purposes. God is sovereign. This familiar theological tension permeates his work. For him, evil is uniquely a question of sin, that is, *all* negative circumstances and experiences result from human rebellion against God and God's response is an entirely appropriate solution to that rebellion. But what is that response? How does MacDonald answer God's question: "How shall I deal with the daughter of my people?" In short, it is to remind God that Lilith *is* God's daughter. If this is the case, and since she is also the most depraved, "the vilest of God's creatures,"[2] all "lesser" created beings must also be God's children meaning that God has a moral obligation to ensure that "all things work together for good"—for *all*. God therefore has a responsibility to expose all creation to "necessary evil" in order to refine and redeem all souls. Since God is good, what we call evil is, in reality, "the best good" in disguise for a person at a particular time; the "aching" we call evil is "the unpleasant cure of evil"; and if you sin, "then some evil that is good for you will follow," and so on. Ultimately, as Vane realizes, "evil was only through good!"[3]

This divine project to purge creation of willful evil is expressed as a universe with a divine child of light at its center set against a kingdom of darkness ruled by the "anti-child." It is a moral metaphor focusing on the nature of God and those made in God's image; however, it is, therefore, also an ontological model: one cannot speak of the moral nature of

---

2. *Lilith* 205.
3. See note 9, page 240; note 55, page 204; *Lilith* 113.

things "made" without making ontological claims, however secondary. Put differently, his focus on the "vale of soul-making" as a moment in an *exitus–reditus* trajectory necessarily demands an account of the nature of that "vale" and its relationship to the being of God. We therefore need to consider the moral and ontological import of MacDonald's thought, beginning with the stage of his drama before looking more closely at the actors.

"A Problematic Attitude to the World"

While materiality, the spatio-temporal "world of three dimensions," is not completely negated, it appears marginalized; we have repeatedly noted the felt unreality of MacDonald's fictive settings—a disconnect between his fictional "stage" and normal human experience. J. P. Stern identifies this as a fundamental issue related to idealism:

> In realism the relation that obtains between a work of literature and the world outside is positive, expressive of a fundamental assent, whereas in idealism it is negative, expressive of a problematic attitude to the world.[4]

Such a problematic attitude is evident. For example, in *Lilith* there is almost no "3D" action. Although Vane expresses regret that he has neglected to foster relationships with others in the "real" world ("I had not cared for my live brothers and sisters"),[5] all that has meaning takes place in his other-worldly mental reality and the relationships formed *there* uniquely focus on the goal of him finding his true identity conceived as God's timeless and unchanging idea of who he should be.

It will be objected that MacDonald's narratives, through their use of fantasy and "making strange," *are* truly concerned with the human quotidian context and force a fresh consideration of that context; this is no doubt the case, however, the problem one faces is that narratives such as *Lilith* tend not to look back on the quotidian world from the other side of fairyland's hedge but *away* from it towards the eschaton, and when they do look towards it, it is considered illusory—just a dream. This devaluing of materiality is theologically problematic as the biblical narrative takes the opposite view. Three issues are of concern.

---

4. Stern, *On Realism*, 44.
5. *Lilith* 113.

Creation and Materiality

The first concerns the stage of the drama. That the mind (both divine and human) plays a key role in the construction of that stage is admitted; we also noted the need to evaluate the human context "aesthetically," a process involving the subject's engagement with the "art" of life. But this should not distract from the biblical emphasis on the objective nature of that art, a focus which speaks less of its ontic status as its radical otherness from God. The biblical phrase "before the foundation of the world," for example, implies that God's being, and certain actions, "pre-date" creation (e.g., John 17:24; 1 Pet 1:20). Creation also has intrinsic value, so much so that God will create a new heaven and a new earth, an event, according to Paul, anticipated by a personified creation that "eagerly waits for the revealing of the sons of God" (Rom 8:19). In contrast, MacDonald, with this verse in mind, remarks:

> I am inclined to believe the apostle regarded the whole visible creation as, in far differing degrees of consciousness, a live outcome from the heart of the living one, who is all and in all.[6]

The "degrees of consciousness" referred to here are the various levels of sentience in creatures, but "live outcome" nevertheless implies a lack of otherness that may be a problem. It would appear to be a Neoplatonic, highly monistic version of Platonism, "one that posits a superexistent Source of all being that extends itself into various lower levels of being" where "non-materiality is the highest form of reality"; and this allied to "a belief in some form of immortality" and "that the universe is essentially good."[7] Rowan Williams summarizes the problem of such a world view:

> There is a growing trend, of course, towards the view finally expressed in the great Plotinus's work . . . that the entire complex world of things that can be known and talked about depends on or flows out of a simple, wholly unified primary reality, the One; but it would be odd to describe this as an *action* in the way "creating" seems to be an action.[8]

Rather than a "fallen" creation in some sense other than God, where genuine human free will can have negative consequences (the biblical context of discussions relating to evil), MacDonald focuses on corruption

---

6. HG 204.
7. Honderich, *Oxford Companion to Philosophy*, 612–13.
8. Williams, *On Christian Theology*, 67.

as a good individual's rejection of God's "idea." Corruption, in other words, is not "out there" but a personal problem. All being is essentially good. Only what is good, argues MacDonald, can suffer, for suffering is felt, can only be felt, by that part of a being that longs for deliverance from corruption:

> Corruption brings in vanity, causes empty aching gaps in vitality. This aching is what most people regard as evil: it is the unpleasant cure of evil. It takes all shapes of suffering—of the body, of the mind, of the heart, of the spirit. It is altogether beneficent.[9]

It is this insistence that all suffering—including that orchestrated by the "bad fairies" and "all demons"[10]—is "the unpleasant cure of evil" and "altogether beneficent" that raises questions. MacDonald's fusion of Neoplatonic monism and Christianity necessarily implies that Christ is *already* "all, and in all,"[11] the implication being that those who suffer do so because they are impenitently encountering the omnipresent Christ. This is a misapplication of Colossians 3:1–11, which refers to those who "were [proleptically] raised with Christ" not the whole population or cosmos, an error which necessarily makes God complicit in evil. In Paul, however, the present "all in all" applies only to those already citizens of the in-breaking new kingdom.[12] That Christ will be "all in all" is an eschatological hope rather than a present reality (1 Cor 15:28) leaving the question open as to whether the future "all" is a residue or the totality of created being. MacDonald believes it is the latter for reasons we will explore.

For MacDonald, then, materiality is the lower expression of something greater: nature displays God's being; the human body is the visible expression of a human soul on a trajectory towards its perfect, God-thought expression. This foundational duality is exemplified in his discussion of Christ's temptation: "the whole Temptation may be regarded as the contest of the seen and the unseen, of the outer and inner, of the likely and the true, of the *show and the reality.*"[13] Such dualism contrasts with the New Testament emphasis that, rather than humans needing to escape from, or overcome, materiality, God's solution to the human

---

9. *HG* 219–20.
10. Pages 160–62.
11. Note 6, page 239. In MacDonald's KJV, the phrase "all, and in all" only appears in Colossians. Elsewhere it is "all in all."
12. The "brethren" (1 Cor 12:6); "the church" (Eph 1:23).
13. *US1* 154 (emphasis mine).

condition—that of genuinely destructive evil in the created sphere—was to share, fully identify with, and therefore in some sense redeem, materiality: Christ not only died, but "was buried" (1 Cor 15:4). That the risen Christ embodied a new kind of materiality is not the issue; the point is that the incarnation was just that—God putting on flesh and blood, a Eucharistic physicality necessary to resolve the estrangement of physical creatures: "as the children have partaken of flesh and blood, He Himself likewise shared in the same, that through death He might destroy him who had the power of death, that is, the devil" (Heb 2:14)—not that he should destroy physicality.

It is not that MacDonald ignores materiality, rather that in his thought "flesh and blood" are not intrinsic to what it means to be human. Ontologically speaking, materiality is inferior to the spiritual world of divine ideals and not "good" *in se* as declared by God. Thus salvation—that is, becoming a "true" child, morally and existentially—involves escaping from a materiality that is primarily a delusional dream-state (so Novalis).[14] After Plotinus, MacDonald views the descent of the soul into materiality as a "necessary evil," a preparatory and transient state prior to reunion with God, which, if experienced as evil, is the fault of the individual soul, not of God. However (unlike Plotinus), evil will be overcome if that soul opens itself to Christ's devil-defeating power, that is, the power to overcome *its own* recalcitrance. On this basis—and in contradistinction to the Neoplatonic emphasis on the impersonal return of the many to the One—salvation is a *personal* reunion with God prior to which the soul must be purged of all sin through a cyclical process of self-atonement by which the "cunning and deceitful Self—ever cunning and deceitful until it is informed of God . . . is thoroughly and utterly denied, and God is to it also All-in-all—till we have left it quite empty of our will and our regard."[15] It is "self atonement" in that the self is responsible for "denying itself" by turning to Christ and engaging in "repentance, restitution, confession, prayer for forgiveness, righteous dealing thereafter, [which] is the sole possible, the only true make-up for sin. For nothing less than this did Christ die."[16] The eschaton, therefore, is conceived as the time when all have repented. Put differently, the consummation of the present age

---

14. Note 13, page 194.
15. *US2* 220.
16. *US3* 128.

will happen when the "All-in-all" becomes a personal reality *in all* since at that point Satan, bereft of "hosts," will be destroyed.

How, then, does MacDonald view physical resurrection? He suggests animals will be resurrected[17] and speaks of human resurrection as being the final step when God "clothes" God's newly-embraced children as the "prodigal son" received a new cloak. The body is a "cloak" that is, in some sense, external, the expression of a higher order of being. Speaking of the present human body he writes, for example, that:

> There is glory and might in this vital evanescence, this slow glacier-like flow of clothing and revealing matter, this ever uptossed rainbow of tangible humanity. It is no less of God's making than the spirit that is clothed therein.[18]

As for the resurrection body, "since all matter is radiant of spiritual meaning," it will be—

> the same body, glorified as we are glorified, with all that was distinctive of each from his fellows more visible than ever before. The accidental, the non-essential, the unrevealing, the incomplete will have vanished. That which made the body what it was in the eyes of those who loved us will be tenfold there.[19]

On this basis, MacDonald clearly *does* have a positive view of materiality since he is affirming that the body, especially the resurrection body, is the "clothing" of "the idea of each . . . carried out in the perfection of beauty."[20] The issue is, however, that despite being perfect and "no less of God's making" it is nevertheless subordinate to the spirit it expresses. Thus, set against such bodily perfection is the notion that bodily imperfection and distortion (such as disease) is evidence of distorted (sinful) personhood, Lilith being the ultimate example of this in her "anti-theophany" incarnation as a snake.

Undergirding these views of incarnation and resurrection is the view that the soul is immortal. This tacit acceptance of an unbiblical Greek doctrine[21] necessarily leads to universalism since God, being love, cannot sustain immortal creatures in a state of reprobation, neither (he

---

17. *HG* 210–13.
18. *US1* 238–39.
19. *US1* 240.
20. *US1* 244.
21. Brown, *Dictionary of NT Theology*, 2:208; Wenham, *Facing Hell*, 241–42.

submits) can they, without reflecting badly on God, be destroyed.[22] The doctrine reinforces the view that *physical* resurrection, if not redundant, is at least a lower state of being. Despite MacDonald's praise of the resurrection body, he espouses an incipient dualism which does equate to a devaluation of materiality. In themselves, these ontological observations may seem peripheral in that MacDonald's primary concern is to make moral claims; however, the issue is that they reveal flaws in his world view which have moral implications. We consider first the implications for human identity.

Human Identity

The devaluing of the quotidian human context leads to a corresponding devaluing of social interaction as a mechanism that forges human identity (as we noted in the context of Gibbie's muteness, Diamond's communication difficulties, and Vane's solipsism, for example). In contrast, Paul's assertions that "so we, being many, are one body in Christ, and individually members of one another" (Rom 12:5) and that God is creating a "new man [people]" (Eph 2:15) highlight the positive and mutually-constructive nature of quotidian social interaction as a forger of human identity. This "vale of soul-making" forges communities (Israel and the church being prime examples) as well as individuals, and—as recent scholarship insists—the latter are not only a product of social interaction but inherently socially constructed.[23] Michael Banner goes as far as saying, "It is not that we have relationships, but that we are relationships."[24] Human personhood is not simply a fixed divine idea (discussed further below).

It will be objected that there *is* social interaction in MacDonald's fiction. Gibbie, for example, is mentored by his adoptive parents, the old shepherd and his wife; the curate, Thomas Wingfold, is similarly coached by the disabled social outcast Polwarth, and so on. However, these relationships generally follow the pattern of the mentor providing a confirmatory rather than a formatory role. God is the true coach, present at the poles of being, that is, internally as the "candle of consciousness" and externally in nature, and mentors are "honest peasants" qualified to fulfil

---

22. Note 212, page 167.
23. Explored further below, pages 266–68.
24. Banner, *Ethics of Everyday Life*, 190.

their office by being themselves close to God and nature having remained untainted by the affectations of culture.

For MacDonald the Romantic, society, with its cultural mores, is a barrier to faith built on pretense.[25] He writes: "It is better to be a child in a green field than a knight of many orders in a state ceremonial."[26] Thus *Sir* Gibbie's ascent to the mountain—the "grand nursery" of nature[27]—is contrasted with his persecutor's (Fergus Duff's) downward trajectory into the city to become a minister. Farmer's son Fergus "would have been much more of a man if he had thought less of being a gentleman," and, in a quest to impress what he hopes will be his future congregation, for example, has no qualms about memorizing a printed sermon and passing it off as his own.[28]

Regarding evil, this devaluing of social interaction as a positive force results in a corresponding denial of socially embedded evil as a destructive force—of the genuine destructiveness of dysfunctional, damaged societies. More broadly, it reflects the view that the Holy Spirit and "the devil" work primarily through personal, rather than social, means. Again, it equates to a focus on (individual) sin rather than (social) evil. David Kelsey, however, calls for cognitive "realism" in order to articulate "with precise, accurate, and full truth just what the condition of the quotidian presently is," a realism that admits that human relationships are forged "in the midst of evil's deformations."[29] He notes that, "It is important for theological reasons . . . to distinguish between sin and evil"; a failure in this regard results in "confusions in theological anthropology." Whereas humans are morally accountable for the former, the latter acts *on* them through living in a distorted world. So rather than, as MacDonald implies, evil being simply the result of a God-dimmed consciousness, Kelsey writes:

> By contrast, I want to stress that we neither ascribe nor bestow reality and power to evil conditions or situations as evil; rather we acknowledge their reality and power as we suffer from their energetic reality.[30]

---

25. This is especially evident in the destructive, brittle relationships in *WC*.
26. *Orts* 226.
27. *SG* 188.
28. *SG* 319–23.
29. Kelsey, *Eccentric Existence*, 353–54.
30. Kelsey, *Eccentric Existence*, 406.

While individuals may or may not contribute to aspects of quotidian distortion, such distortion is evil and acts against creaturely good: creatures are recipients of the "energetic reality" of evil, not—at least directly or necessarily—responsible for it. In MacDonald's work it does result in "anthropological confusion": whereas Christ, who was "without sin," experienced the full force of destructive evil, characters such as Gibbie or Clare Skymer—also perfect children—do not. The biblical emphasis, in contrast, is that humans are given strength to bear the negativity of evil, not that it will have no purchase (Rom 5:5; 8:35–39).

With regard to epistemology, MacDonald's individualism leads to a corresponding unshakeable belief that an imaginative individual has the ability to discern truth rightly on the basis that God primarily speaks to individuals. This reflects a nineteenth-century climate. Reardon notes, for example, that the erudite Unitarian, James Martineau, later in his career moved away from viewing an infallible Bible as the primary source of revelation:

> Rather, if personality is the highest value known to man it is to be expected that revelation will be made through personal media and that the real criterion of divine truth is provided by the heart and conscience. In short, if a man would know the will and purpose of God let him first search the depths of his own nature. The primal authority in religion is experience itself, the inner witness of moral feeling and perception.[31]

F. D. Maurice, however, although expressing similar views that all humans have an innate sense of right and wrong, puts his finger on the problem: a person "may be very much deceived about his own preference for truth over falsehood in any particular case; he may be bribed to like a lie better than the truth."[32] Or, as in the case of Charley Osbourne's domineering religious father in *Wilfrid Cumbermede*, a person may be, perhaps unaware, guilty of "branding the truth of religion with the private mark of opinion," the outcome being inevitably "persecution and cruelty."[33] The problem, though, is that such as Osbourne senior are merely following MacDonald's advice. Lilith's success in seducing Vane is also a salutary example of the danger of relying on individual discernment. The issue is that the judgement that such discernment is misguided must necessarily

---

31. Reardon, *Victorian Age*, 315.
32. Maurice, "What is Revelation?," 260; cf. Jer 17:9.
33. *WC* 456.

come from others, others who, if MacDonald's scheme is pushed to its limits, are *de facto* denied an opinion. MacDonald would respond to this by arguing that when the true heart *acts* on perceived truth, God will, if necessary, correct error. He thus locates the problem in volition rather than perception on the basis that humans have the genuine ability to choose the good should they so desire. However, if, as we sense, Charley Osbourne is truer to life than Sir Gibbie, this argument is refuted: Charley wants to perceive the truth but is prevented by quotidian circumstances. Furthermore, we are faced with the issue that many individuals act, with integrity, on their perception of the truth that results in evil consequences that God does not address.

This discussion reveals a general principle when evaluating MacDonald's work. His emphasis on the need to personally discern truth is not so much a foundational epistemological principle as a pastoral call to obedience underlining two key issues: that faith cannot be second-hand, nor can it remain merely theoretical. His sweeping assertions do not necessarily have universal applicability since he writes pastorally for a specific audience. One might observe, for example, that he himself is socially embedded and part of a wide conversation. We have identified numerous voices that have contributed to his understanding of the truth, not least that of childhood Calvinism. It could be argued, for example, that his criticism of faithful Calvinists as possessing faith despite, not because of, their religion might be aimed at himself: he has a vibrant faith despite the shortcomings in his own scheme—a scheme which owes a significant debt to its Calvinist heritage and the input of others. Put differently, he rightly underscores the need to personally evaluate and appropriate truth but in the process has championed a methodology that potentially leads to error. The Apostle Paul asserted that even he only "knew in part" and stressed the limited nature of personal prophecy (1 Cor 13:12; Rom 12:6); since we live in a distorted world and each is subject to a very limited perspective, the truth about God must primarily be discerned communally, not individually.

Satan's Identity and the Existential Nature of Evil

While there are numerous divine representatives, even theophanies, in the form of great-great-grandmothers (*The Princess and Curdie*) or old men (*The Golden Key*) in MacDonald's narratives, it is striking that

MacDonald's cosmology omits beings such as demons or angels; such, after all, are staples of fantasy. Where these are mentioned, they appear to be the literary expressions of evil or good *ideas* rather than references to created beings. Their origin is inevitably traced back to either human or divine creative thought; in other words, like Lilith, their existence is contingent. If we are to believe the narrator of *The Shadows*, for example, angels are "white shadows cast in heaven from the Light of Light," in contrast to earthly shadows which, in a strongly Platonic image, are either frightening "body ghosts" or good "soul ghosts."[34] It may be objected that the cast of the fairy stories, which includes giants, witches and fairies, refers to such beings, but I would argue that these are either the creations of fantasy (often moral metaphors), or, more often, images symbolic of divine or human being—even children. As MacDonald notes:

> all the powers that vivify nature must be children. The popular imagination seems to have caught this truth, for all the fairies and gnomes and goblins, yes, the great giants too, are only different sizes, shapes, and characters of children.[35]

The strongest demonic image is the great Shadow in *Lilith*, the immaterial personification of aggregate human rebellious will; a kind of negative Hegelian *Geist* that will cease to exist when the last human child has repented. This reading is confirmed by Charley Osbourne's words on recognizing his own willful selfishness: his comment "*I am a* devil" is set within an understanding of cosmic evil that conceives of God as the antithesis of such selfishness:

> I am the most selfish creature in the world—always taken up with myself. I do believe there is a devil, after all, *I* am *a* devil. And the universal self is *the* devil. If there were such a thing as a self always giving itself away—that self would be God.[36]

To which his friend Cumbermede replies: "Something very like the God of Christianity, I think"; that is, the divine Child.

However, with regard to evil, it is that last *human* child—who was also the original serpent, Lilith—who is Satan. Satan/Lilith is human.[37] All

---

34. *Fairy Tales* 79, 73.

35. *AF* 1:162.

36. *WC* 330.

37. In the *Zohar*, Samael and Lilith are inseparable, an unholy, hermaphroditic fusion representing a counterfeit Trinity—an ultimately distorted, uncircumcised (that is, rebellious) humanity: "Samael is said to be the uncircumcised and his bride

evil, in MacDonald's view—from first sin to last sin—is down to human rebellion. It is a perennial refrain. Self-worship is devil-worship, a good churchman or a good dissenter can be a devil, "*self* is our demon-foe": only rarely is the urge to rebel attributed to "some roar of a wandering bodiless devil"[38] which, if Lilith's pedigree is to be believed, might simply be a bodiless human rather than a demon (see below). Aware, no doubt, that "God cannot be tempted by evil, nor does He Himself tempt anyone," MacDonald, biblically, locates the source of evil in the human heart but does not put this down, as Jesus did, to the work of the "father of lies," the father of lying Pharisees (Mark 7:21; Matt 15:19; John 8:24). For him, Satan is a (human) person who has "resisted the truth with some amount of perception that it was the truth" (echoing Jesus's verdict on Peter); "Is not this to be Satan? to be in hell? to be corruption? to be that which is damned?"[39]

In the Bible, however, Satan is spoken of as a created non-human being. In the Old Testament he has access to heaven and accuses the righteous (Job 1:6–2:7; cf. Zech 3:1); in the New, he has angels at his command, is referred to by Jesus as the "ruler of this world" whom he saw "fall like lightning from heaven" and, according to John, "was cast to the earth, and his angels were cast out with him" (Matt 25:41).[40] But is this merely an anthropomorphism of evil? After all, a personified Death will be thrown into the lake of fire as well as the devil (Rev 20:10, 14); the former can only be metaphoric—why not the latter? It is also unclear whether Jesus's followers are to pray "deliver us from evil," or "deliver us from the evil one," and some have argued that since the Bible never

---

[Lilith] is the prepuce [foreskin], which, [the *Zohar*] adds significantly, is the serpent" (Waite, *Doctrine and Literature of Kabalah*, 82). The fusion of Lilith and the Shadow therefore represents the "flesh" and "spirit" of ultimate human depravity. This reading is confirmed by Mathers; regarding demons, he writes: "Their prince is *Samael*... the angel of poison and of death. His wife is the harlot, or woman of whoredom... and united they are called the beast.... Thus the infernal trinity is completed, which is, so to speak, the inverse and caricature of the supernal Creative One" (Waite, *Doctrine and Literature of Kabalah*, 30; cf. Rahner's Trinitarian *mysterium iniquitatis* [discussed on page 250]).

38. *US1* 145; *US3* 242; *US2* 155; *WC* 92.

39. *US1* 89, 90.

40. Cf. Paul's "messenger of Satan," 2 Cor 12:7; John 12:31; 14:30; Luke 10:18; Rev 7:9.

speaks of the salvation of Satan, he cannot be personal.[41] What issues are relevant here?

One key issue is MacDonald's attribution of "evil" to God, permissible only if evil *is* a good: in this sanitized (apparently) monist cosmos without demons, this is logically possible (indeed necessary) and, on the surface, biblical. There are numerous biblical allusions to God both creating and controlling evil: did not God place a tree of good *and* evil in the garden?; "if there is calamity in a city, will not the Lord have done it?" (Amos 3:6); and did not "the Spirit of the Lord depart from Saul" to be replaced by "a distressing spirit from the Lord" (1 Sam 16:14)? The theme continues into the New Testament. According to John, for example, writing concerning ten kings who "make war with the Lamb": "God has put it into their hearts to fulfill His purpose, to be of one mind, and to give their kingdom to the beast, until the words of God are fulfilled." In the apocalyptic setting of Revelation Satan does appear to be God's evil sheepdog, sometimes on a short leash (Rev 17:17; cf. 20:1–3).

MacDonald's understanding of evil is limited since a monist cosmos, understood as the expression of God's good thoughts, cannot admit evil creatures or destructive distortion without indicting God. Instead, and worryingly, God sometimes masquerades, or is perceived, as the devil. For example, commenting on John's observation, quoting Isaiah, that unbelief is because "He has blinded their eyes and hardened their hearts, Lest . . . I should heal them" (John 12:40), MacDonald suggests that "in St. John's reference, the blinding of the heart seems attributed directly to the devil." In other words, "he," in this verse, is the devil who has blinded people to prevent them turning to God. The Isaiah passage quoted (Isa 6:10), though, implies "he" is Isaiah, God's agent, bearing—and in some sense enacting—the message of God's judgement to his peers, and the following verse (in John) suggests that "he" is Christ: "These things Isaiah said when he saw His glory and spoke of Him." Perhaps MacDonald is thinking of "the god of this age" blinding people to the truth (2 Cor 4:4), but the point is that for him the distinction is trivial:

> Whether this [blindness] follows as a psychical or metaphysical necessity, or be regarded as a special punishment, it is equally the will of God, and comes from him who is the live Truth. They shall not see what is not for such as they.[42]

---

41. Brown, *Dictionary of NT Theology*, 1:566.
42. *US2* 99–100.

In other words, if it is the devil, he is simply doing God's will; if God, it is God perceived badly, for, as he notes: "God must be terrible to those that are far from him"—so much so that such "must prefer a devil."[43] On this view, the French Revolution must be labelled "the righteous plague of God," at least by permission: when there is contempt for the truth, "the wild beast in man breaks from its den."[44]

This blurring of the boundaries between good, evil, and sin weakens MacDonald's theology simply because in his quest to rehabilitate God he has made God complicit in evil. This is not because he views God as other than pure (moral) light; on the contrary, a core theme is "in Him there is no darkness."[45] Rather, it is his reluctance to concede that genuine depravity exists that cannot be co-opted for good and must be destroyed, or to allow that events such as the Lisbon earthquake (we might think of Hiroshima or Auschwitz) serve no good purpose. As one contemporary put it:

> His optimism scarcely allows him to reckon with the terrors that sometimes run riot in the world. . . . He ignores the scientific interpretation of Nature, and never attempts to adjust it to his rosy Wordsworthian aestheticism.[46]

This theological problem becomes sharper when one compares the "marriage" of Lilith and the great Shadow to that of the antichrist and the beast in Revelation. As Hans Urs von Balthasar notes, "The whole abyss of the *mysterium iniquitatis* yawns in the way it opposes the *mysterium Trinitatis*."[47] We have already noted how Lilith, with her counterfeit stigmata and Eucharist, represents that opposition. Von Balthasar notes that at every level, "the blasphemous structure of the trinity of hell [Antichrist, beast, and dragon] contradicts the divine Trinity in every last detail."[48] The beast has a fake wound; it, like Lilith, stages a fake resurrection. It also represents a fake incarnation: the dragon does not "beget"

---

43. US2 159. In *The Princess and Curdie*, the great-great-grandmother, the "Mother of Light," says that a thief would perceive her as a demon: "his evil eyes would see me as I was not." Note 127, page 39.

44. EA 303–4.

45. US3 163–81.

46. Selby, *Theology of Modern Fiction*, 137, 40.

47. Von Balthasar, *Theo-Drama*, 4:450.

48. Von Balthasar, *Theo-Drama*, 4:451.

the beast from itself, it arises out of the sea, a product of creation. Von Balthasar remarks:

> there is nothing here of divine self-emptying and so nothing of the Trinity's self-disclosure and truth. The Dragon, absolute evil, remains hidden behind its hideous offspring and utterance, the beast [it has "blasphemy" written all over it], but in such a way that the latter continues to put forth its monstrous seductive power [over all tribes and nations].[49]

Lilith, one might say, assuming a counterfeit, bodily eroticism (her true nature is snake-like)—the "monstrous seductive power" made visible—represents the Whore of Babylon, one who feeds on the "merchants of the earth" who eventually mourn the destruction of her city.[50] The issue is simply this: inasmuch as both the Whore and Lilith are personifications of seductive evil, they must be destroyed ("her smoke rises up for ever and ever" [Rev 19:3]). Neither are they in any sense human: the beast is a product of creation. As a metaphor for the last deposit of aggregate evil will in humanity, Lilith serves an illustrative role, but to suggest that somehow she will be reconciled with "Adam" and live in eternal bliss makes a mockery of Revelation's claim that in the Whore—as in Lilith—"was found the blood of prophets and saints, and of all who were slain on the earth" (Rev 18:24)—blood that cries for vengeance, that is, for genuine justice: "And she will be utterly burned with fire, for strong is the Lord God who judges her" (Rev 18:8). Put simply, if God's eschatological embrace of Lilith did not result in her annihilation, "blasphemy" would be found in God.

"If We Are Not Little Ones of a Perfect Love, I Can See No Sense in Things"

These observations regarding shortcomings in MacDonald's view of evil must be borne in mind but do not nullify his work; they simply alert us to the dangers of pushing his scheme beyond its pastoral remit. This caveat does not detract from some significant and incisive theological proposals that we have a duty to explore. As Thomas Toke Lynch remarked (as quoted by MacDonald):

---

49. Von Balthasar, *Theo-Drama*, 4:451.

50. According to *Zohar* 1.86a: "The female of Samäel, which is the serpent, is called the harlot" (Waite, *Doctrine and Literature of Kabalah*, 260).

> the critic is more than the censurer; and in his higher and happier aspect appears before us and serves us, as the discoverer, the vindicator, and the eulogist of excellence.[51]

What "excellence" is revealed by MacDonald's child?

First, the child offers a new way of seeing the world; it challenges the conventional approach to cognition and epistemology. We may be unconvinced that such as Diamond and Gibbie are seeing the world truly, but this does not detract from the message that we should look at it differently. The child, for example, challenges conventional anthropological assumptions by forcing a fresh look at the child itself. In a world that believed (albeit briefly) in female genital mutilation as a cure for insanity or that children were born deaf and were sexually deviant, and so on, the child pleads with us to take a more honest and holistic look at reality. Similarly, it offers a fresh perspective on religion, warning us not to accept beliefs at face value, however sanctified by church or time, that do not "ring true." The child, in effect, calls us to become childlike: apart from the moral and religious implications discussed, it represents a call for a more balanced cognitive approach emphasizing the need to contextualize knowledge within a wider field and to be suspicious of truth-claims that appear to offend wider moral or logical sensibilities. Those wider "sensibilities" include openness to scientific and philosophical advances. The child represents an attitude of wonder to an evolving world not constrained or intimidated by revelation, from whatever quarter, on the basis that God not only indwells the world, but that faith is beyond the vicissitudes of evolving world-views. The year that MacDonald died, Einstein produced his theory of relativity. We now have advanced quantum mechanics, we understand more the processes of evolution, and the term "big bang"—anticipated in Boehme's "ethereal blaze"[52]—is no longer a term of derision. MacDonald's legacy is a child who is at peace in such a changing world.

Second, the childlike, imaginative disposition towards the "artwork" of the world reminds us of the connectedness of God's creation and the role of humanity as stewards. It will be remembered that one of Plotz's criticisms of the Romantics was, citing Piaget, that their emphasis on the child's connectedness with nature was unhealthy; that, instead, disassociation—the awareness of individuality—was necessary for healthy

---

51. *Orts* 220.
52. Page 148.

development.⁵³ However, it could be argued that we have become "over dissociated." Recent work has claimed, for example, that humans have, to their detriment, completely lost a sense of connectedness to the cosmos or to divinity and in the process become disassociated from the human family, with catastrophic environmental consequences.⁵⁴ In contrast, "when we receive the child in the name of Christ . . . we receive all humanity."⁵⁵ The child reminds us of the need to connect imaginatively with "nature," to discern its catholicity, that is, a sense of the wholeness and connectedness of the cosmos,⁵⁶ to sense the abductive drawing of the Spirit, to sense the numinous in the mundane. MacDonald's child is perhaps intuitively anticipating the post-Einstein equation of energy with matter. Although I have been somewhat critical of MacDonald's idealist negation of materiality, it reflects the view that God, as the loving and sustaining "mind-energy" of the universe *is* intimately invested and present in the cosmos; a recognition that "heaven unfolds when we see the world for what it truly is, 'pregnant with God'"⁵⁷; a reminder, as Rowan Williams remarked, that "the overcoming of 'nature' as a proper goal for spirituality is highly problematic."⁵⁸

Finally, the child challenges conventional Christian power narratives relating to the misguided quest for Christendom. This is a by-product of MacDonald's focus on the other-worldly nature of the kingdom of God, but more specifically—as a counter-Enlightenment position—challenges the tendency towards religious fundamentalism that results in violence: the view that those privy to the truth of the universe have the right, and duty, to suppress those not so enlightened. The contrasting vision of MacDonald is that "the spirit of children"—mutual dependence and humility—is the hallmark of the kingdom of God.⁵⁹ Emphasizing the need for loving, mutual submission instead of power, MacDonald writes:

> Not all the sovereignty of God, as the theologians call it, delegated to the Son, and administered by the wisdom of the Spirit

---

53. Page 48.
54. Delio, *Making All Things New*, 30.
55. *US1* 16.
56. Delio, *Making All Things New*.
57. Delio, *Making All Things New*, 96. The phrase Delio quotes comes from Angela of Foligno.
58. Williams, *On Christian Theology*, 69.
59. *US1* 15.

> that was given to him without measure, could have wrought the kingdom of heaven in one corner of our earth. Nothing but the obedience of the Son, the obedience unto the death, the absolute *doing* of the will of God because it was the truth, could redeem the prisoner, the widow, the orphan. But it would redeem them by redeeming the conquest-ridden conqueror too, the stripe-giving jailer, the unjust judge, the devouring Pharisee himself with the insatiable moth-eaten heart.[60]

Even divine sovereignty, supported by all the resources of heaven, cannot alone inaugurate the kingdom of God. The "idea of the universe" is the father–son relationship,[61] and only loving obedience, not coercion, can be the foundation of a kingdom of love. Rather than the god of popular religion that demands obeisance, the Son, the perfect child, is our model, and the appropriate human response is also to live as a child, that is, to renounce coercive, repressive behavior. The above quotation underlines that salvation inheres in Christ being "all in all," including oppressors; that sin is defeated when sinners repent, not when they are condemned.

I close this section with comments that offer another perspective on "the idea of the universe" reinforcing MacDonald's view that divine power is the servant of love and grace. Williams's comment above regarding "highly problematic" adversarial attitudes to nature follows the observation:

> creation is not an exercise in divine power, odd though that certainly sounds. Power is exercised *by* x *over* y; but creation is not power, because [being *ex nihilo*] it is not exercised on anything.[62]

Creation is fundamentally an act of powerless grace; it is "unnecessary," a gift expressing the graciousness of God but not needed by God to complete God's identity.[63] One might say that creation represents God's playfulness, the perfect, joyful expression of the divine child; in the words of Robin Stockitt, something "fundamentally concerned with aesthetics . . .

---

60. *US1* 158–59.

61. Kelsey notes that this "idea" dates back to the Nicene-Constantinopolitan Creed. See Kelsey, *Eccentric Existence*, 63.

62. Williams, *On Christian Theology*, 68.

63. Von Balthasar, *Theo-Drama*, 4:323. Delio makes this error by suggesting that "divinity and humanity have, from the birth of consciousness, been opposites united in an ongoing process of mutual redemption. Both divinity and humanity are related to each other from the outset and attain the completion of their respective consciousness in the reciprocity of their relationship" (Delio, *Making All Things New*, 88).

THE IMPLICATIONS OF GEORGE MACDONALD'S THEOLOGY

enjoyment, beauty, joy and delight" and, in a utilitarian sense, pointless.[64] The implication being that "the very heart of the coming kingdom of God announced by Christ is portrayed in terms that insist that we become like children."[65] As MacDonald put it: "If we are not little ones of a perfect love, I can see no sense in things."[66]

"His Quarrel Is with All Churches at Home and Abroad"

"Evangelical Christianity," writes David Hempton of the nineteenth-century situation, "under the pressure of new and threatening questions, was particularly prone to fundamentalist answers, thereby further undermining its appeal to thoughtful adherents."[67] F. D. Maurice, for example, alert to this danger, called for action:

> it is a duty and a necessity to strike continually at a cancer which is eating out the heart of Christendom, the poisonous quality and deadly effects of which our most vehement Protestant declaimers do not exaggerate but underrate.[68]

The "cancer" concerned false convictions that "outrage the conscience... misrepresent the character of God, [and] generate a fearful amount of insincere belief, positive infidelity, also, I think, of immorality."[69] To be clear, it is not simply that Maurice objects to firmly held beliefs being worshipped above Christ, bad as that might be; he is objecting to a fundamentalism that, under these conditions, has begun to worship false concepts—Liliths, as it were. In the words of Pope Francis, "Fundamentalism

---

64. This understanding of the "pointlessness" of creation does not necessarily imply purposelessness; play may have "profoundly purposeful" outcomes. See Stockitt, *Imagination and the Playfulness of God*, 102.

65. Stockitt, *Imagination and the Playfulness of God*, 101. In my view, though, Stockitt is wrong to suggest that: "It is to George MacDonald's credit that he was sufficiently prescient to realize that the playfulness of God would one day need to be explored in much greater detail": MacDonald, as we have noted, views reality as a "school time" rather than a playground. He does, though, suggest that we are imaginative children loved by a "playful" (though somewhat Victorian and moralizing) God.

66. Sadler, *Expression of Character*, 357.

67. Hempton, *Evangelical Disenchantment*, 197.

68. Maurice, *Theological Essays*, 136.

69. Maurice, *Theological Essays*, 133.

is a disease that is found in all religions . . . religious fundamentalism isn't religion, it's idolatry."[70]

Misguided certainty is the issue. As Nicholas Lash remarks regarding such fundamentalism: "In many respects, the withdrawal of the fideist into his world of private certainties is a greater betrayal of Christian faith than the open-minded uncertainty of the agnostic."[71] Iain McGilchrist remarks that such private certainties are "the greatest of all illusions":

> whatever kind of fundamentalism it may underwrite, that of religion or science, it is what the ancients meant by *hubris*. The only certainty, it seems to me, is that those who believe they are certainly right are certainly wrong.[72]

As is clear from our reading of MacDonald, he considered much of the religion of his day to be "the greatest of all illusions," not simply because it was enamored with false propositions, but because its epistemological foundations were entirely false. The familiar tension between "Enlightenment" ("logical") and "Romantic" ("imaginative") epistemology is the root issue; the former, for reasons discussed, necessarily breeds idolatry since it is incapable of engaging with the person of Christ. That said, it is important to remember that MacDonald is not simply replacing "logical falsehood" with "imaginative falsehood," rather the fairy child is arguing for cognitive balance. This is essentially Iain McGilchrist's plea in *The Master and His Emissary*: Western society, he argues—particularly during and since the Reformation—has swung too far towards a ruthlessly logical, "left hemisphere" approach to cognition and, as a result, is increasingly delusory; "right hemisphere" balance is urgently needed.[73] MacDonald is championing this.

Noting MacDonald's views on hell, one contemporary critic observed, "his quarrel is therefore with all the Evangelical Churches at home and abroad."[74] However, I believe one might go further: since "hell" is symbolic of the false epistemology discussed above, MacDonald's

---

70. Wooden, "Pope Says He Was Surprised." The Vatican has recently expressed the opinion that American fundamentalist Evangelicalism is based on "a logic that is no different from the one that inspires Islamic fundamentalism" (Spadaro and Figueroa, "Evangelical Fundamentalism").

71. Lash, *Theology on Dover Beach*, 59.

72. McGilchrist, *Master and His Emissary*, 460.

73. See especially McGilchrist, *Master and His Emissary*, 314–29.

74. McCrie, *Religion of Our Literature*, 305.

critique goes far beyond the walls of Evangelicalism; it is a fundamental challenge to much of Western theology. In this penultimate section, therefore, we explore this claim by considering further the moral nature of MacDonald's cosmos for, despite the flaws noted, it represents a challenge to the morally suspect "watchmaker" model of Newton, an Enlightenment model creating the conditions for propositional fundamentalism to flourish.

An Alternative Ontology

From an ontological perspective, the central issue is that if creation is entirely other than God—a basic claim of Western theology—God is within God's rights (as it were) to act as Pilate did: to wash his hands, turn his back, and say "this is nothing to do with me." According to John Milbank, such handwashing equates to a "purely rational relation to the world" symptomatic of the Enlightenment turning its back on transcendent truth.[75] The nub of the issue is that while Western soteriology stresses that God in Christ has *not* "washed his hands," naive views of creation as entirely independent of God have precipitated doctrines of damnation that imply that God is unable to intervene salvifically for a subset of God's creatures and implies a realm where God is not sovereign, not present, and unable to act. At root are certain articulations of the doctrines of original sin and *creatio ex nihilo*, the doctrine of hell being the outworking of these.

As is clearly evident, vindictive and libelous (with respect to God) doctrines regarding the fate of the wicked exercised MacDonald and were symptomatic of a cataphatic, literalist fundamentalism that had prized God away from God's creation and installed an idol. Focusing on Newton as exemplary of this move, John Milbank summarizes the issue:

> Newton no longer conceived of God as Being as such, and as the source of finite being produced from nothing but sharing by various degrees in his infinite simple *esse*. His God was rather a supremely powerful entity who had shaped alongside himself other entities with whom he communicated.[76]

This sums up the main objection of Milbank and his "radical orthodox" colleagues to schemes that collapse the ontological difference between

---

75. Milbank et al., *Radical Orthodoxy*, 25.
76. Milbank, "Life, or Gift and Glissando," 121.

God and creation: that univocal speech about God—that is, speaking of the being of God in the same terms as created being—necessarily reduces God to a subordinate deity. MacDonald counters such views by insisting that we are not forged by God in, and from, some universal ground of being—but from God's created "*nihil.*" The spatio-temporal stage of the drama, MacDonald insists, emerges from the heart of God rather than existing "alongside" it. "If God were not, there would not even be nothing. Not even nothingness preceded life. Nothingness owes its very idea to existence."[77] Creation exists in some sense "in" God and is not independent of God: "This world is not merely a thing which God hath made, subjecting it to laws; but it is [not was] an expression of the thought, the feeling, the heart of God himself."[78] Since the essential being of God is love, "Love is the one bond of the universe, the heart of God, the life of his children."[79] This focus on the loving immanence of God and the graciousness of nature leads MacDonald to insist that God cannot "wash his hands" in regard to certain of his creatures, for all are God's children:

> [God] is bound in himself to make up for wrong done by his children, and he can do nothing to make up for wrong done but by bringing about the repentance of the wrong-doer.[80]

For this reason, MacDonald must conclude that the *mysterium iniquitatis* is "in" God, and that God will eventually act such that God will be "all in all." It leads to the universalist perspective recently articulated, for example, in Rob Bell's short popular apologetic, *Love Wins* (resulting also in significant backlash from the Evangelical community).[81] MacDonald is clear on this issue:

> For nothing less than this did Christ die. . . . He brings and is bringing God and man, and man and man, into perfect unity: "I in them and thou in me, that they may be perfect in one."[82]

We need, however, to reiterate that MacDonald's emanationist model is metaphorical (as is all language about God) rather than ontological.

---

77. *US2* 144.
78. *Orts* 246.
79. *HG* 212.
80. *US3* 128.
81. Bell, *Love Wins*. For Kevin DeYoung, "It is the last rung for evangelicals falling off the ladder into liberalism or unbelief" (DeYoung, "God Is Still Holy").
82. *US3* 128–29.

It may have ontological, that is "scientific" in MacDonald's language, implications, but is primarily a metaphor for God's moral relationship with humanity. As noted, MacDonald refuses to speculate on the ontic nature of the human proximate context; that said, he is nevertheless making claims that, for example, resonate with the current quest of the radical orthodox "movement" to overturn erroneous embedded ideas related to ontology that have structurally warped Western theology. At the heart of the radical orthodox perspective are claims that MacDonald shared: that there is no "territory independent of God," that it represents an alternative to the standard Christian polarities of conservatism and liberalism, and that radical truth may be found in medieval theology.[83] Furthermore, it is fundamentally suspicious of a "Barthianism [that] can tend to the ploddingly exegetical" (MacDonald's "plodding brother" of imagination, reason, perhaps).[84] I briefly outline a recent debate between Catherine Pickstock (John Milbank's colleague) and David Kelsey in order to provide some context for the following discussion and to draw attention to some key issues. This brief excursus also illustrates that MacDonald's ideas speak to contemporary theology.

David Kelsey has produced an extensive theological anthropology that appears to espouse many of the principles that MacDonald rejected.[85] It is based on a thought-experiment: What can we learn about God's relating to creation if we consider, hypothetically, how each "person" of the Trinity might act towards creation if acting unilaterally? Kelsey, for example, posits that God's presence in creation by the "circumambient" Spirit or the incarnate Son is truly "gracious" whereas the gift of creation itself—the "thoroughly other-than-God" gift of the Father—should not be considered intrinsically "graceful."[86] On this basis, he suggests that

---

83. Milbank et al., *Radical Orthodoxy*, 3–4.

84. Milbank et al., *Radical Orthodoxy*, 2.

85. Kelsey, for example, stresses that creation has value "simply in its being just what God creates in all its everydayness." God's creation does not have a noumenal quality which is more desirable or important than the quotidian "surface," moreover, it is "deeply informed by evil." With regard to materiality, Kelsey suggests, contra MacDonald, that: "The real human person is God's good creature precisely in his or her quotidian everydayness and finitude, and not because they satisfy some one, universally applicable, ideal of a human person completely—that is, 'perfectly,' actualized in all respects. The status of 'real' human person is not constituted by transcending the quotidian, any more than it is a degraded (i.e., 'fallen') version of a historically once or future human perfection" (Kelsey, *Eccentric Existence*, 191–92, 207).

86. Kelsey, *Eccentric Existence*, 214.

creation considered as the Father's stand-alone project would still have meaning even if shorn of its eschatological *telos*.[87] This troubles Catherine Pickstock who feels that this amounts to "an espousal of univocity,"[88] and that Kelsey has misrepresented God by seeming "to endorse a (mis)reading of the Cappadocians in terms of a relational play between hypostatic centers somewhat independent in their own right."[89] Despite Kelsey's protestations of innocence,[90] Pickstock feels strongly that a theological crime has been committed; that Kelsey has lost sight of the traditional view that creation *does* have a *telos*—"that creation was for the sake of human deification and cosmic transfiguration, in such a way that God would finally be 'all in all.'"[91]

The heated nature of this discussion underlines that issues relating to ontology, far from being peripheral to faith, strike at the very core of belief with far-reaching implications for how one views God's relationship with "all that is not God." That MacDonald was chastised for his "heretical" views, therefore, should come as no surprise as his model of reality was fundamentally challenging received wisdom; his quarrel *was* "with all Evangelical churches at home and abroad," and his critique of Calvinism cannot simply be dismissed as a reaction to contemporary excesses, as David Bentley Hart realizes. To explore this and the moral implications of MacDonald's emanationist model, we read Hart's paper, "God, Creation, and Evil: The Moral Meaning of *creatio ex nihilho*."

"The Moral Meaning of *Creatio Ex Nihilo*"

The key issue we have identified is MacDonald's seeming inability to articulate a convincing account of evil. Hart summarizes the dilemma:

---

87. Kelsey, *Eccentric Existence*, 191.

88. Kelsey insists "*Eccentric Existence* emphatically does *not* espouse the 'univocity of being'" (Kelsey, "Response," 78).

89. Pickstock, "One Story," 27.

90. Kelsey affirms "the Creator-creature ontological difference between God . . . and all that is not God," that "the triune God is not one more causal factor in the complex of energy systems that make up the creaturely cosmos," and that "God and creatures are by definition not on a common spatio-temporal framework, God and creatures are by definition not on a common ontological level" (Kelsey, *Eccentric Existence*, 714, 718, 844).

91. Pickstock, "One Story," 29.

> God *in se* is not determined by creation and . . . consequently, evil does not enter into our understanding of the divine essence. All of this is true, of course, but left to itself it inexorably devolves toward half-truth, and then toward triviality—a wave of the prestidigitator's hand and Auschwitz magically vanishes.[92]

MacDonald does tend to wave such a "prestidigitator's hand." The other side of the coin, Hart notes, is that since the relationship between God and creation is one of contingency, one cannot simply assume that God's "morality" is alien to the human. MacDonald agrees:

> To say on the authority of the Bible that God does a thing no honourable man would do, is to lie against God; to say that it is therefore right, is to lie against the very spirit of God.[93]

For Hart, the issue is: "precisely because God and creation are ontologically distinct in the manner of the absolute and the contingent, they are morally indiscerptible."[94] In other words, existential, but dependent, otherness does not imply moral otherness; on the contrary, it implies moral congruence.

In Hart's view, following Gregory of Nyssa, since *nihil* is itself *ex* the "heart of God" (to use MacDonald's phrase), *creatio ex nihilo* necessarily implies an eschatological *telos*—a return to that heart. (One might say that the funereal phrase should be "heart to heart" rather than "dust to dust.") And, agreeing with MacDonald's view that the whole purpose of creation is that, having been flung into existence by God's creative "sun" we are destined to return such "that his life might be our life, that in us, too, might dwell that same consuming fire which is essential love,"[95] Hart writes:

> In the end of all things is their beginning, and only from the perspective of the end can one know what they are, why they have been made, and who the God is who has called them forth from nothingness.[96]

Such a concept only has meaning if God's creatures are genuinely such, that is, created beings with independent existence without which a return

---

92. Hart, "God, Creation, and Evil," 2.
93. *US3* 116–17.
94. Hart, "God, Creation, and Evil," 2.
95. *US1* 30.
96. Hart, "God, Creation, and Evil," 2.

to their source would simply be absorption rather than relationship. For Gregory, therefore, unlike David Kelsey's tripartite scheme which can countenance (but does not necessarily imply) a creation without such a *telos*, true creation is only the *result* of consummation (not absorption); anything prior to that is necessarily contingent and, in a sense, provisional.[97]

Hart notes that as long as an emanationist theology is not reduced to "a kind of gross *material* efflux of the divine substance into lesser substances" (Milton's misconception), there is no tension here with the doctrine of *creatio ex nihilo*. It still means that "all that exists comes from one divine source" and, perhaps contra Kelsey, "*subsists* [rather than exists] by the grace of impartation."[98] MacDonald expresses this by suggesting we are distinguished from God, but not divided from God: "that between creator and poet lies the one unpassable gulf which distinguishes—far be it from us to say *divides*—all that is God's from all that is man's."[99] This is not to say that God and creation are ontologically on the same plane, but it is to say that God is intimately involved in "all that is not God." One might say that the "distinguishing" gulf separates ontologically but not experientially.

This involvement by God in creation, a creation which is not in any sense "needed" by God but a gift for which God takes full responsibility, means that in its graciousness and radical dependence on God as its final cause, "there can be," in Hart's words, "no residue of the pardonably tragic, no irrecuperable or irreconcilable remainder left at the end of the tale; for, if there were, this too God would have done, as a price freely assumed in creating."[100] This is why MacDonald insists that "annihilation itself is no death to evil. Only good where evil was, is evil dead. An evil thing must live with its evil until it chooses to be good. That alone is the slaying of evil."[101] The conclusion, then, is not that God is responsible for the genesis of, or condones, evil—with the implication that "every evil that time comprises . . . is an arraignment of God's goodness"—but God is responsible for its resolution, a solution that will only be fully visible in the eschaton. Hart again: "until the end of all things, no answer

---

97. Hart, "God, Creation, and Evil," 3.
98. Hart, "God, Creation, and Evil," 4 (emphasis mine).
99. *Orts* 2. See page 68.
100. Hart, "God, Creation, and Evil," 5.
101. *Lilith* 212.

has been given."¹⁰² Thus Hart rejects the morality of an Augustinian hell, MacDonald's "hell of exhausted mercy":

> When Augustine lamented the soft-heartedness that made Origen believe that demons, heathens, and (most preposterously of all) unbaptized babies might ultimately be spared the torments of eternal fire, he made clear how the moral imagination must bend and twist in order to absorb such beliefs.¹⁰³

Instead, he too insists that "the greater hope" is the only reasonable position to take:

> Even Paul asks, in the tortured, conditional voice of Romans 9, whether there might be vessels of wrath stored up solely for destruction only because he trusts that there are not, that instead all are bound in disobedience only so that God might prove himself just by showing mercy on all.¹⁰⁴

The key issue, to which both Hart and MacDonald object, is that Western Christianity in particular has evolved an erroneous theology of which the doctrine of hell is the prime *reductio ad absurdum* leading to evangelical zeal effectively motivated by the need to save people *from* God. Singling out Calvin for particular criticism, Hart observes that:

> Calvin had the courage to acknowledge that his account of divine sovereignty necessitates belief in the predestination not only of the saved and the damned, but of the fall itself; and he recognized that the biblical claim that "God is love" must, on his principles, be accounted a definition not of God in himself, but only of God as experienced by the elect (toward the damned, God is in fact hate).¹⁰⁵

Hart seems to summarize MacDonald's inability to accept such a schizophrenic characterization of God when he describes Calvinism as "an immensely influential but deeply defective theological tradition"¹⁰⁶ whose infernal toxicity has infected "just about the whole Christian tradition."¹⁰⁷

---

102. Hart, "God, Creation, and Evil," 5.
103. Hart, "God, Creation, and Evil," 7–8.
104. Hart, "God, Creation, and Evil," 5–6.
105. Hart, "God, Creation, and Evil," 8. MacDonald makes a similar claim, see note 177, page 160.
106. Hart, "God, Creation, and Evil," 8.
107. Hart, "God, Creation, and Evil," 11.

The issue of univocity underlies this toxicity in that it is assumed that the mystery of faith may be logically investigated on the same terms as the created realm. This is not to say that rationality is suspect, simply that when grace and nature are divorced, human logic is inexorably drawn towards absurdity. It results in "thin" and insubstantial schemes that hide the true nature of God's gracious creation and God's relationship to it. For Hart, the many individual texts that speak of universal salvation, along with the wider panoply of the biblical story as a whole, point to a consummation inhering in Christ being "all in all."[108] Anything less than this, he argues, morally compromises God. "It is odd," he remarks concerning passages that imply universal salvation, "that for at least fifteen centuries such passages have been all but lost behind so thin a veil as can be woven from those three deeply ambiguous verses that seem (and only seem) to threaten eternal torments for the wicked."[109] Hart's "thin veil" is reminiscent of the "robe of imputed righteousness" made by the Reformers from "legal cobwebs spun by spiritual spiders."[110] MacDonald's work represents an attempt to draw back this curtain and rediscover ancient Christian orthodoxy.

Perennially suspicious of such "logical" schemes that hide the truth of Christ, MacDonald focuses on the eschaton as providing resolution to the enigma of life at the expense of a robust theological account of *social* evil. Instead he focuses on *religious* evil. This is simply because he sees religious evil as the fundamental cause of all social evil. This is well articulated by David Kelsey who suggests that for every worshipful response to the three fundamental ways that God relates to God's creation—as creator, redeemer, and consummator—there are distorted responses; that the distortion of the appropriate doxological responses of faith, love, and hope is the essence of sin, and that such responses inevitably further distort the context in which humans live. This is the root of social evil. So while there is a tendency in MacDonald to wave his "prestidigitator's hand so that Auschwitz magically vanishes," this is because he firmly believes that God will ultimately resolve the issue of evil and be "all in all." He can only see resolution in an eschatological future. In a world where social evil was seen as almost inevitable, and where there was still a lingering view that God had ordained the social

---

108. For a wide biblical perspective, see O'Collins, *Salvation for All*.

109. Hart, "God, Creation, and Evil," 15. The texts referred to (at the head of the paper) are Rom 5:18–19; 11:32; 1 Cor 3:15; 15:22, 28; 1 Tim 2:3–4; 4:10.

110. *US2* 103.

order, he prefers not to dwell on evil but instead address what he sees as its root cause. It is not an erroneous doctrine of evil *per se*, rather it is the consequence of a limited perspective of the "now" and the "not yet" of the kingdom of God—a failure to appreciate that present reality is not simply a "school time" to prepare humanity for the eschaton, but that the kingdom of God is already proleptically present in the present age. This latter (more Maurician) perspective might have given MacDonald a more pragmatic view of the need to actively engage in the fight against social ills, a perspective that is clearly only in the background in his work. Instead, he brings before us idealized saints and critical fairy children to stir those who claim faith towards living more faithfully.

Hart closes his paper by contrasting the vision of Gregory—of all souls being drawn towards the joyous source of their being—with that of Augustine's eschatological vision of two cities in the most populous of which are quarantined those who are under God's judgement and destined for perpetual sorrow. He concludes:

> There is no question to my mind which of them saw the story more clearly. Or which theologians are the best guides to scripture as a whole: Gregory, Origen, Evagrius, Diodore, Theodore, Isaac of Ninevah [sic] ... George MacDonald.[111]

"The Idea of the Universe"

The child, while primarily expressive of humanity's "vertical" relationship with God, also underlines the connectedness of humanity under the headship of Christ—that, in carrying the *imago Dei*, the child is related to siblings. Although there are numerous historical and scholarly views of what it means to be a child and carry the *imago Dei*,[112] it is certainly contrary to Calvin's view that "he who perverted the whole order of nature in heaven and earth [Adam] deteriorated his race by his revolt" with the result that "the heavenly image in man was effaced,"[113] and that "the impurity of parents is transmitted to their children, so that all, without exception, are originally depraved."[114] For Calvin, humanity is connected

---

111. Hart, "God, Creation, and Evil," 15–16.
112. Grenz, *Social God*, 186–200.
113. Calvin, *Institutes* 2.1.5.
114. Calvin, *Institutes* 2.1.6.

by depravity; for MacDonald, the connection is divinity. The child thus instinctively question the morality of eternal judgement. Although MacDonald concurs with the many nineteenth-century voices rejecting a Dantean hell, his Job-like criticism of God is more subtle for, as noted above, he is rather questioning the nature of a God who is content to be "defeated" by evil such that good creatures that God has given life to are eternally punished, or perhaps summarily destroyed, despite the fact Christ submitted to evil in order to emasculate it on their behalf (Col 2:15).[115]

However, there is another aspect of the theology of final judgment to which the child speaks. Recent scholarship concerning human personhood highlights that while individuality is a meaningful concept, it cannot be divorced from community; that an "individual" is not just forged in the crucible of social interaction but is in some measure constituted by it, echoing Maurice's assertion that God sees people as connected through participation in the kingdom of God, rather than "partially, or each in reference to a separate centre."[116] Grenz, for example, quoting John Zizioulas, writes:

> "Communion does not threaten personal particularity; it is constitutive of it." Such communion establishes the uniqueness of each person, in that the person is an indispensable and irreplaceable part of a relational existence.[117]

Grenz suggests that the monadic, independent self typical of both medieval and Enlightenment thinking is untenable; rather, "communion," he argues, implies that the "*self* does not amount to much, no self is an island; each exists in a fabric of relations,"[118] and that "the postmodern self is constituted by social relationships."[119] David Kelsey concurs, reminding us not to forget that the "vertical" relationship with God is also a dimension of human social embeddedness: "the proximate contexts into

---

115. MacDonald does not seem to discuss conditional immortality (that is, the final annihilation of the wicked) as articulated, for example, by Wenham (Wenham, *Facing Hell*, 229–57). His views chime more with such as Moltmann who regards both hell and annihilation as equally morally suspect. See Moltmann, "Logic of Hell."

116. Morris, *Maurice and the Crisis*, 154. See page 26.

117. Grenz, *Social God*, 52.

118. Jean-François Lyotard quoted in Grenz, *Social God*, 135.

119. Grenz, *Social God*, 136, 331.

which we are born make us social beings all the way down, and all the way up to our responding to God as well."[120]

So not only are there moral questions concerning eternal retribution for finite sin, there is the issue that if some of God's creatures are to be destroyed this necessarily implies that some of the relational-structural content of the personhood of the eschatologically blessed will be lost. To put it crudely: can John Piper truly enjoy heaven as "himself" knowing that his sons are eternally suffering?[121] David Bentley Hart puts it like this:

> After all, what is a person other than a whole history of associations, loves, memories, attachments, and affinities? Who are we, other than all the others who have made us who we are, and to whom we belong as much as they to us? We are those others. To say that the sufferings of the damned will either be clouded from the eyes of the blessed or, worse, increase the pitiless bliss of heaven[122] is also to say that no persons can possibly be saved: for, if the memories of others are removed, or lost, or one's knowledge of their misery is converted into indifference or, God forbid, into greater beatitude, what then remains of one in one's last bliss? Some other being altogether, surely: a spiritual anonymity, a vapid spark of pure intellection, the residue of a soul reduced to no one. But not a person—not the person who was. But the deepest problem is not the logic of such claims; it is their sheer moral hideousness.[123]

In response, it could be argued that "moral hideousness" would equally result if God allowed, say, an abusive individual responsible for damaging others during earthly life to continue to abuse eternally, or if the distortions resulting from that influence were not beatified.[124] Evil, as MacDonald argues, must be destroyed and sin atoned for—hence his purgatorial emphasis. Hart's words, though, do reveal the bankruptcy of simplistic and voluntarist notions of election such as Piper's.

---

120. Kelsey, *Eccentric Existence*, 274.

121. Page 139.

122. Hart notes that this was the view of Tertullian, Peter Lombard, Thomas Aquinas, and Luther.

123. Hart, "God, Creation, and Evil," 9.

124. I am thinking here of the "Lamb as though it had been slain" (Rev 5:6) or the post-resurrection stigmata of Christ, the eternal evidence of evil defeated.

In contrast, MacDonald's universalism allows him to look forward to a resurrection body not only perfectly expressive of the individual, but cognizant of the many others to whom it owes its existence.[125] He views eschatological resolution as more than simply blessing for the elect surrounded by ambiguity; with Paul, he looks for the redemption of the whole of creation (Rom 8:22). Anything less than this, he maintains, amounts to defeat for God. These anthropological implications directly inform MacDonald's doctrine of God. The divine image carried by the human child relates to childlikeness as a category. God, too, is "a child":

> It is *like king like subject* in the kingdom of heaven. No rule of force, as of one kind over another kind. It is the rule of *kind*, of *nature*, of deepest nature—of *God*.[126]

Judith Plotz, with, I believe, some justification, locates the Romantic child as stranded between earth and heaven; neither connected with transcendence nor with the (sometimes grim) realities of earth. Wordsworth's child may attempt to connect with God—and MacDonald may laud Wordsworth as the "high priest of nature" who "in all things felt the presence of the Divine Spirit"[127]—but, in many respects, Wordsworth's Nature, with whom "The Child" communes, is a surrogate deity somewhat divorced from Christ. As MacDonald himself notes, the "inclined plane from . . . nature to . . . the Son of Man" is "what we miss in Wordsworth."[128] Plotz, although perhaps overstating the case, notes that in this godless Romantic mid-realm the child itself assumes the role of God.[129]

The Christian child, however—especially the Calvinist child—was, ironically, moved earthwards: the image of God having been effaced, it, like its secular counterparts burdened with evolutionary baggage, was in some sense less than human; a human in the making, perhaps, but deeply flawed. Notably, and again ironically (noting the lack of childhood sexual awareness), it was considered to over-indulge in "passion," which was

---

125. *US1* 242–44.

126. *US1* 14.

127. *Orts* 247.

128. *EA* 307. Elsewhere MacDonald notes: "[Wordsworth] saw God present everywhere; not always immediately, in his own form, it is true" (*Orts* 247).

129. Page 46.

deeply feared as, since Augustine, sexual awareness had been equated with the Fall.[130]

Against this backdrop, MacDonald places a child whose perfect model is Christ who, despite shortcomings in its dramatization, connects both earth and heaven. Despite Plotz's protestations, the Romantic child was, perhaps, the most positive incarnation of childhood of the period. MacDonald certainly thought so, and his child bears the marks of Romanticism; however, one must not lose sight of how MacDonald's child—rather than floating in the mid-realm—genuinely bridges, or attempts to bridge, earth and heaven. The hesitancy is on the earthward side: wanting to reconnect the child with transcendence, in his idealist enthusiasm he has perhaps over-disconnected it, even uprooted it, from the earth; his fictional children *do* tend to float implausibly above nineteenth-century grime; the social dimension of human life *is* lacking.

However, our close reading of MacDonald has revealed a nuanced challenge to contemporary theology, many aspects of which have continuing application, especially addressing the issue of Christian (or other religious or secular) fundamentalism. In an era broadly suspicious, or fearful, of childhood, MacDonald's choice to make God a child—meaning that humans carrying the *imago* are thus also, in some sense, children—was a radical challenge to the orthodoxy of the day. That MacDonald's child has Romantic flaws must be admitted, the most notable being its aversion to facing the true horror of evil, however, this should not distract from the radical nature of the claims being made. MacDonald's theological embrace of the child has redeemed the child, that is, the child, instead of being viewed as less than human, has been reinstated as *essentially* human: the tables are turned. The child questions whether "adulthood," with its self-centeredness, affectations, power-hunger, and conventional beliefs, is a valid expression of humanity. The child claims that it is the pretentious adult that is the sinner. It claims to see truly, imaginatively; it is the logical, Pharisaical adult who is blind.

Looking heavenwards, the false Romantic deity, "The Child," as well as the Calvinist headmaster, are exposed as idols. However much one might want to soften this and argue that MacDonald is simply attacking what in his view is a distortion of Calvinism—simply misguided "popular religion"—will not wash. As I have argued above, I believe there is

---

130. Augustine, *City of God* 15; 18–20. Calvin insists that no human "has not felt the power of concupiscence" and generally blames this on Adam (Calvin, *Institutes* 2.7.5).

a strong case that MacDonald's child fundamentally quarrels with "all the churches," that is, not simply Calvinism or Evangelicalism and their offshoots; his theology is corrosive to ideas considered foundational, especially in Western Christianity. At the heart of this is a rejection of the power narratives embedded in faith which suggest that God, instead of being the world's advocate, has become its "infinite contrary"[131] and that, in consequence, the world has to be "overcome" in God's name. MacDonald's ontology and cosmology may, in many respects, be flawed or naive, but one cannot deny that his valuing of "nature"—the quotidian world in which humans live, however idealized—has reinstated creation as a place wholly "in" God and infused by God. Neither can one deny that, despite flaws in his account of evil, his emphasis that Christ will be all in all represents a challenge to the tacit assumption in Western theology that Christ will *not* be all in all; that there will be a residue of God's creation impervious to God's inexorable love.

These priorities are summed up in MacDonald's claim that "the child-relation is the one eternal, ever enduring, never changing relation" that is "the idea of the universe."[132] An "idea" which, since rooted in the "abyss of love," means that the pursuit of aesthetic truth—that is, God—is an open-ended, eternal vocation. In Hart's words, it is "perpetually to transcend any fixed identity: a transcendence which is always more transcendent, an infinite scope within the self that no self can comprise, and to which the self belongs. The *imago Dei*." Being a child, in other words, "is not simply a possession of the soul as much as a future, a hope."[133] MacDonald phrases it thus:

> Nobody knows to what the relation of father and son may yet come. Those who accept the Christian revelation are bound to recognize in it depths infinite. For is it not a reproduction in small of the loftiest mystery in the human ken—that of the infinite Father and the infinite Son?[134]

---

131. Hart, *Beauty of the Infinite*, 134.
132. *HG* 161.
133. Hart, *Beauty of the Infinite*, 114.
134. *CW* 170.

Works Referenced

Alabaster, Henry. *The Wheel of Law: Buddhism*. London: Trübner, 1871.
Amell, Barbara. "'A Man of Beatitudes': George MacDonald and John Hunter." *Wingfold* 89 (2015) 13–22.
———. "On MacDonald and Maurice." *Wingfold* 91 (2015) 25–33.
Auden, W. H. *Forewords and Afterwords*. Edited by Edward Mendelson. London: Faber and Faber, 1979.
Augustine. *The City of God against the Pagans*. Edited by Philip Levine. 7 vols. London: William Heinemann, 1966.
Baldwin, Nicholas. "The History of The Hospital for Sick Children at Great Ormond Street (1852–1914)." *Historic Hospital Admission Records Project*, 2009. http://www.hharp.org/library/gosh/general/history.html.
Banner, Michael. *The Ethics of Everyday Life*. Oxford: Oxford University Press, 2014.
Barringer, Tim. *The Pre-Raphaelites*. London: Orion, 1998.
Barth, Karl. *The Doctrine of Creation*. Vol. 3/2 of *Church Dogmatics*. Edited by G. W. Bromiley and Thomas F. Torrance. 14 vols. Edinburgh: T&T Clark, 1960.
Bebbington, David W. *The Dominance of Evangelicalism: The Age of Spurgeon and Moody*. Leicester: InterVarsity, 2005.
Beilby, James K., and Paul R. Eddy, eds. *Justification: Five Views*. London: SPCK, 2012.
Bell, Rob. *Love Wins: At the Heart of Life's Big Questions*. London: Collins, 2011.
Black Koltuv, Barbara. *The Book of Lilith*. Berwick, ME: Nicolas-Hays, 1986.
Boehme, Jakob. *The Signature of All Things*. Edited by Clifford Bax. Cambridge: J. Clarke, 1969.
Bonhoeffer, Dietrich. *Act and Being*. London: Collins, 1962.
Borg, Marcus. *The Heart of Christianity: Rediscovering a Life of Faith*. New York: HarperOne, 1989.
British Library. "Silly." *Oxford English Dictionary 1879–1928*. Online. https://www.bl.uk/learning/langlit/dic/oed/silly/silly.html.
Brown, Colin, ed. *Dictionary of New Testament Theology*. 4 vols. Grand Rapids, MI: Zondervan, 1986.
Buckland, Adelene. *Novel Science: Fiction and the Invention of Nineteenth-Century Geology*. Chicago: University of Chicago Press, 2013.
Bunge, Marcia J., ed. *The Child in Christian Thought*. Grand Rapids: Eerdmans, 2001.
Calvin, John. *Institutes of the Christian Religion*. Grand Rapids: Christian Classics Ethereal Library, 2012. Online. http://www.ccel.org/ccel/calvin/institutes.
Campbell, John McLeod. *The Nature of the Atonement*. London: Macmillan, 1848.
Carlyle, Thomas. *Past and Present*. London: Chapman and Hall, 1843.

———. *Sartor Resartus*. London: Chapman and Hall, 1872.
Chesterton, G. K. *Heretics*. London: Bodley Head, 1905.
———. *Orthodoxy*. Edited by Philip Yancey. New York: Doubleday, 2001.
Cohen, Morton N., ed. *The Letters of Lewis Carroll*. 2 vols. London: Macmillan, 1979.
Coleridge, S. T. *The Collected Works of Samuel Taylor Coleridge*. Edited by James Engels and W. Jackson Bate. London: Routledge and Kegan Paul, 1983.
Colvin, Sidney, ed. *Letters of John Keats*. London: Macmillan, 1891.
Cox, Samuel. *Salvator Mundi: or, Is Christ the Saviour of All Men?* London: Kegan Paul, 1878.
Cummings, Brian. *The Literary Culture of the Reformation: Grammar and Grace*. Oxford: Oxford University Press, 2011.
Cusick, Edmund. "MacDonald and Jung." In *The Gold Thread*, edited by William Raeper, 56–86. Edinburgh: Edinburgh University Press, 1990.
Dale, A. W. W. *The Life of R. W. Dale of Birmingham*. London: Hodder and Stoughton, 1898.
Danielson, Dennis Richard. *Milton's Good God: A Study in Literary Theodicy*. Cambridge: Cambridge University Press, 1982.
Dart, Ron. "'Would We Have Been Friends?': Piper/Keller Contra Lewis/MacDonald." *Clarion: Journal of Spirituality and Justice*, April 23, 2015. http://www.clarion-journal.com/clarion_journal_of_spirit/2015/04/would-we-have-been-friends-piperkeller-contra-lewismacdonald-by-ron-dart.html.
de Jong, John R. "The Innocence of George MacDonald." In *Innocence Uncovered*, edited by Elizabeth S. Dodd and Carl E. Findley, 41–57. Abingdon: Routledge, 2017.
Dearborn, Kerry. *Baptized Imagination: The Theology of George MacDonald*. Aldershot: Ashgate, 2006.
Delio, Ilia. *Making All Things New: Catholicity, Cosmology, Consciousness*. New York: Orbis, 2015.
DeYoung, Kevin. "God Is Still Holy and What You Learned in Sunday School is Still True: A Review of *Love Wins*." *The Gospel Coalition*, March 14, 2011. http://www.scribd.com/doc/50772118/Love-Wins-Review-by-Kevin-DeYoung.
Dickens, Charles. *Dealings with the Firm of Dombey and Son*. London: Oldhams, n.d.
Dods, Marcus, ed. *The Works of Aurelius Augustine, Bishop of Hippo*. 15 vols. Edinburgh: T&T Clark, 1872–1876.
Dostoyevsky, Fyodor Mikhail. *The Brothers Karamazov*. Translated by David Magarshack. 2 vols. Harmondsworth: Penguin, 1973.
Douven, Igor. "Abduction." *Stanford Encyclopedia of Philosophy*, March 9, 2011. http://plato.stanford.edu/archives/spr2011/entries/abduction.
Dunne, John S. "The Friends of God 'Guided and Guarded' J. R. R. Tolkien." *Journal of Law and Religion* 11.1 (1994) 323–42.
"Education on Church Principles." *Christian Remembrancer* 21.5 (1839) 299–300.
"Education with Respect to Religion." *Scots Magazine* 43 (1781) 149–52.
Eliot, George. *The Mill on the Floss*. Oxford World's Classics. Edited by Gordon S. Haight. Oxford: Oxford University Press, 2008.
———. "Worldliness and Other Worldliness; the Poet Young." *Westminster Review* 67 (1857) 1–42.
Eliot, T. S. *The Sacred Wood*. London: Methuen, 1920.
"Essays on Practical Education." *Christian Remembrancer* 51.131 (1866) 21–49.
Forsyth, P. T. *Positive Preaching and the Modern Mind*. London: Independent, 1964.

Frei, Hans W. *The Eclipse of Biblical Narrative: A Study in Nineteenth-Century Hermeneutics*. New Haven and London: Yale University Press, 1974.
Gabelman, Daniel. *George MacDonald: Divine Carelessness and Fairytale Levity*. Waco, TX: Baylor University Press, 2013.
"George Macdonald on Dante: Reprinted from the *Glasgow Evening News*, Sept. 18, 1889." *Wingfold* 89 (2015) 31–38.
Gillies, Mary Ann. *The Professional Literary Agent in Britain, 1880–1920*. Toronto: University of Toronto Press, 2007.
Goodloe, James C., IV. *John Mcleod Campbell: The Extent and Nature of the Atonement*. Studies in Reformed Theology and History, New Series 3. Princeton: Foundation for Reformed Theology, Princeton Theological Seminary, 1997.
Grenz, Stanley J. *The Social God and the Relational Self: A Trinitarian Theology of the Imago Dei*. Louisville: Westminster John Knox, 2001.
"*Guild Court*. By George Macdonald, M.A. Author of 'Alec Forbes of Howglen,' 'David Elginbrod,' &c. In Three Volumes. London: Hurst and Blackett." *Examiner* 3121 (1867) 741.
Hale White, William. *The Autobiography of Mark Rutherford*. London: Trübner, 1889.
Hanna, William, ed. *Letters of Thomas Erskine of Linlathen*. Edinburgh: David Douglas, 1878.
Hardy, Daniel W., et al. *Wording a Radiance: Parting Conversations on God and the Church*. London: SCM, 2010.
Hardy, Thomas. *Jude the Obscure*. London: Everyman, 1995.
Hart, David Bentley. *The Beauty of the Infinite: The Aesthetics of Christian Truth*. Grand Rapids: Eerdmans, 2004.
———. "God, Creation, and Evil: The Moral Meaning of *Creatio Ex Nihilho*." *Radical Orthodoxy* 3.1 (2015) 1–17.
Hein, Rolland. *George MacDonald: Victorian Mythmaker*. Nashville: Star Song, 1993.
———. *The Harmony Within: The Spiritual Vision of George MacDonald*. 1982. Reprint, Eureka, CA: Sunrise, 1989.
Hempton, David. *Evangelical Disenchantment: Nine Portraits of Faith and Doubt*. New Haven: Yale University Press, 2008.
Hill, Christopher. *The World Turned Upside Down: Radical Ideas During the English Revolution*. London: Temple Smith, 1972.
Hilton, Boyd. *The Age of Atonement*. Oxford: Oxford University Press, 1986.
———. *A Mad, Bad, Dangerous People?: England 1783–1846*. Oxford: Oxford University Press, 2006.
Holmes, Andrew R. "Biblical Authority and the Impact of Higher Criticism in Irish Presbyterianism, ca. 1850–1930." *Church History: Studies in Christianity and Culture* 75.2 (2006) 343–73.
Honderich, Ted, ed. *The Oxford Companion to Philosophy*. Oxford: Oxford University Press, 1995.
Hopkins, Mark. *Nonconformity's Romantic Generation: Evangelical and Liberal Theologies in Victorian England*. Carlisle: Paternoster, 2004.
Humm, Alan. "Lilith." *Jewish and Christian Literature*. 2013. http://jewishchristianlit.com/Topics/Lilith/lilith.html.
I. P. "Thoughts on the Education of the Poor." *Monthly Magazine, or, British Register* 31.211 (1811) 217–21.

Ingelow, Jean, et al. *Home Thoughts and Home Scenes*. London: Routledge, Warne, and Routledge, 1865.

"Interesting Discourse at St. Paul's by Dr. Hunter on George MacDonald (Reprinted from the *Meridian Morning Record*, [CT] June 7, 1910)." *Wingfold* 89 (2015) 23–25.

International Theological Commission. "The Consciousness of Christ Concerning Himself and His Mission." Congregation for the Doctrine of the Faith. 1985. http://www.vatican.va/roman_curia/congregations/cfaith/cti_documents/rc_cti_1985_coscienza-gesu_en.html.

John Paul II. "Heaven, Hell, and Purgatory." *L'Osservatore Romano*, July 28–August 18, 1999. English: Cathedral Foundation. Online. https://www.ewtn.com/catholicism/library/heaven-hell-and-purgatory-8222.

Johnson, Dale A. *The Changing Shape of English Nonconformity, 1825–1925*. Oxford: Oxford University Press, 1998.

Johnson, Joseph. *George MacDonald: A Biographical and Critical Appreciation*. London: Pitman, 1906.

Johnson, Mark D. *The Dissolution of Dissent, 1850–1918*. New York: Garland, 1987.

Joyal, Christian C., et al. "What Exactly Is an Unusual Sexual Fantasy?" *The Journal of Sexual Medicine* 12.2 (2015) 328–40.

Kelsey, David H. *Eccentric Existence: A Theological Anthropology*. Louisville: Westminster John Knox, 2009.

———. "Response to the Symposium on *Eccentric Existence*." *Modern Theology* 27.1 (2011) 72–86.

Knoepflmacher, U. C. *Ventures into Childland: Victorians, Fairy Tales, and Femininity*. Chicago: University of Chicago Press, 1998.

Kussmaul, Adolf. *Untersuchungen Über Das Seelenleben Des Neugeborenen Menschen*. Leipzig: C. F. Winter'sche Verlagshandlung, 1859.

Lash, Nicholas. *Theology on Dover Beach*. London: Darton, Longman, and Todd, 1979.

Leavis, F. R. *The Great Tradition*. New York: George W. Stewart, 1950.

Leibniz, Gottfried Wilhelm (von). *Theodicy: Essays on the Goodness of God, the Freedom of Man, and the Origin of Evil*. Edited by Austin Farrer. 1710. Reprint, London: Routledge & Kegan Paul, 1952.

Lewis, C. S. *George MacDonald: An Anthology*. London: Geoffrey Bles, 1946.

———. *Surprised by Joy*. New York: Harcourt, Brace, 1956.

"Literature and Imagination." *Cambridge University Magazine* 2.7 (1841) 58–67.

Lynch, Thomas T. *The Rivulet*. London: Longmans, Green, Reader, and Dyer, 1868.

MacDonald, George. *Alec Forbes of Howglen*. 3 vols. London: Hurst and Blackett, 1865.

———. *Annals of a Quiet Neighbourhood*. 1867. Reprint, London: Kegan Paul, Trench, Trübner, n.d.

———. *At the Back of the North Wind*. 1871. Reprint, London and Glasgow: Blackie, n.d.

———. *Castle Warlock*. Previously published as *Warlock o' Glen Warlock*. 1881. Reprint, London: Kegan Paul, Trench, Trübner, n.d.

———. *Complete Fairy Tales*. Edited by U. C. Knoepflmacher. Penguin, 2000.

———. *David Elginbrod*. 3 vols. London: Hurst and Blackett, 1863.

———. *The Disciple and Other Poems*. 1867. Reprint, Eureka, CA: Sunrise, 1989.

———. *A Dish of Orts*. London: Sampson Low Marston, 1895.

———. *Donal Grant*. 1883. Reprint, Eureka, CA: Sunrise, 1990.

———. *England's Antiphon*. London: Macmillan, 1868.
———. *God's Words to His Children: Sermons Spoken and Unspoken*. New York: Funk & Wagnalls, 1887.
———. *A Hidden Life and Other Poems*. 1864. Reprint, Eureka, CA: Sunrise, 1988.
———. *The Hope of the Gospel*. 1892. Reprint, Eureka, CA: Sunrise, 1989.
———. *Lilith*. London: Chatto & Windus, 1896.
———. *Malcolm*. 3 vols. London: Henry S. King, 1875.
———. *Mary Marston*. London: Samson Low Marston, 1894.
———. *The Miracles of Our Lord*. London: Strahan, 1870.
———. *Phantastes*. London: Smith, Elder, 1858.
———. *The Poetical Works of George MacDonald*. 2 vols. London: Chatto & Windus, 1893.
———. *The Portent, and Other Stories*. London: T. Fisher Unwin, n.d.
———. *The Princess and Curdie*. 1883. Reprint, London: Blackie, 1888.
———. *The Princess and the Goblin*. London: Strahan, 1872.
———. *Rampolli: Growths from a Long-Planted Root*. London: Longman, Green, 1897.
———. *Robert Falconer*. 3 vols. London: Hurst and Blackett, 1868.
———. *A Rough Shaking*. London: Blackie, [1897?].
———. *Salted with Fire*. 1897. Reprint, Eureka, CA: Sunrise, 1989.
———. *Sir Gibbie*. London: Hurst and Blackett, 1880.
———. *Thomas Wingfold, Curate*. 1876. Reprint, Eureka, CA: Sunrise, 1988.
———. *Unspoken Sermons: First Series*. 1867. Reprint, Eureka, CA: Sunrise, 1988.
———. *Unspoken Sermons: Second Series*. 1886. Reprint, Eureka, CA: Sunrise, 1989.
———. *Unspoken Sermons: Third Series*. 1889. Reprint, Eureka, CA: Sunrise, 1996.
———. *What's Mine's Mine*. 3 vols. London: Kegan Paul, Trench, 1886.
———. *Wilfrid Cumbermede*. 1872. Reprint, London: Kegan Paul, Trench, Trübner, n.d.
MacDonald, Greville Matheson. *George MacDonald and His Wife*. Introduction by G. K. Chesteron. London: G. Allen & Unwin, 1924.
MacDonald, Ronald. "George MacDonald." In *From a Northern Window*, edited by F. Watson, 55–113. London: James Nisbet, 1911.
MacLachlan, Christopher, et al., eds. *Rethinking George MacDonald*. Glasgow: Scottish Literature International, 2013.
Macritchie, Iain A. M. "Celtic Culture, Calvinism, Social and Mental Health on the Island of Lewis." *Journal of Religion and Health* 33.3 (1994) 269–78.
Makman, Lisa Hermine. "Child's Work is Child's Play: The Value of George MacDonald's *Diamond*." In *Behind the Back of the North Wind*, edited by John Pennington and Roderick McGillis, 109–27. Hamden, CT: Winged Lion, 2011.
Manning, Henry Edward. *Sermons*. Vol. 3. 3rd ed. London: William Pickering, 1848.
Manlove, Colin N. "A Reading of *At the Back of the North Wind*." In *Behind the Back of the North Wind*, edited by John Pennington and Roderick McGillis, 148–74. Hamden, CT: Winged Lion, 2011.
Manlove, Colin N. "MacDonald and Kingsley: A Victorian Contrast." In *The Gold Thread*, edited by William Raeper, 140–62. Edinburgh: Edinburgh University Press, 1990.
Mathers, S. L. MacGregor. *The Kabbalah Unveiled*. London: Kegan Paul, Trench, Trubner, 1887.
Maudsley, Henry. *The Physiology and Pathology of Mind*. London: Macmillan, 1868.

Maurice, F. D. *The Kingdom of Christ*. 2nd ed. New York: D. Appleton, 1843.

———. *Theological Essays*. Cambridge: Macmillan, 1853.

———. "What is Revelation?" In *Religious Thought in the Nineteenth Century*, edited by Bernard M. G. Reardon, 257–62. Cambridge: Cambridge University Press, 1966.

McCrie, George. *The Religion of Our Literature*. London: Hodder and Stougton, 1875.

McGilchrist, Iain. *The Master and His Emissary: The Divided Brain and the Making of the Western World*. New Haven: Yale University Press, 2009.

McGrath, Alister E. *Heresy*. London: SPCK, 2009.

McIntyre, John. *Faith, Theology, and Imagination*. Edinburgh: Handsel, 1987.

Milbank, Alison. *Chesterton and Tolkien as Theologians*. London: T&T Clark, 2009.

Milbank, John. *Being Reconciled: Ontology and Pardon*. London: Routledge, 2003.

———. "Life, or Gift and Glissando." *Radical Orthodoxy* 1.1–2 (2012) 121–51.

Milbank, John, et al., eds. *Radical Orthodoxy: A New Theology*. London: Routledge, 1999.

Moltmann, Jürgen. "The Logic of Hell." In *God Will Be All in All*, edited by Richard Bauckham, 43–47. Edinburgh: T&T Clark, 1999.

Montemaggi, Vittorio. *Reading Dante's Commedia as Theology: Divinity Realized in Human Encounter*. Oxford: Oxford University Press, 2016.

Moore, A. L. "The Influence of Calvinism on Modern Unbelief." In *Sources*, edited by James R. Moore, 333–39. Vol. 3 of *Religion in Victorian Britain*. Manchester: Open University Press, 1988.

Morency, Kenneth. "Religion and Education." *The Critic* 9.217 (1850) 183–84.

Morris, Jeremy N. *F. D. Maurice and the Crisis of Christian Authority*. Oxford: Oxford University Press, 2005.

Morrow, John. *Thomas Carlyle*. London: Hambledon Continuum, 2006.

Newell, J. Philip. "Unworthy of the Dignity of the Assembly: The Deposition of Alexander John Scott in 1831." *Records of the Scottish Church History Society* 21 (1983) 249–62.

Newman, John Henry. *Apologia Pro Vita Sua*. London: Longmans, Green, 1908.

———. *Essay in Aid of a Grammar of Assent*. London: Burns, Oats, 1870.

Nishitani, Keiji. *On Buddhism*. New York: State University of New York Press, 2006.

Novalis (Friedrich von Hardenberg). *Henry of Ofterdingen*. Cambridge: John Owen, 1842.

O'Collins, Gerald. *Salvation for All: God's Other Peoples*. Oxford: Oxford University Press, 2008.

Okely, Francis. *Memoirs of the Life, Death, Burial, and Wonderful Writings, of Jacob Behmen*. London: J. Lackington, 1780.

Paslick, Robert H. "From Nothingness to Nothingness: The Nature and Destiny of the Self in Boehme and Nishitani." *Eastern Buddhist* 30.1 (1997) 13–31.

Pennington, John. "Alice at the Back of the North Wind, or the Metafictions of Lewis Carroll and George MacDonald." In *Behind the Back of the North Wind*, edited by John Pennington and Roderick McGillis, 52–62. Hamden, CT: Winged Lion, 2011.

Pennington, John, and Roderick McGillis, eds. *Behind the Back of the North Wind*. Hamden, CT: Winged Lion, 2011.

Pickstock, Catherine. "The One Story: A Critique of David Kelsey's Theological Robotics." *Modern Theology* 27.1 (2011) 26–40.

Piper, John. "How Does a Sovereign God Love? A Reply to Thomas Talbott." *Desiring God Foundation*, February 1, 1983. http://www.desiringgod.org/resource-library/articles/how-does-a-sovereign-god-love.

Plotz, Judith. *Romanticism and the Vocation of Childhood*. New York: Palgrave, 2001.

Poole, William. *Milton and the Idea of the Fall*. Cambridge: Cambridge University Press, 2005.

Prickett, Stephen. *Romanticism and Religion: The Tradition of Coleridge and Wordsworth in the Victorian Church*. Cambridge: Cambridge University Press, 1976.

———. *Victorian Fantasy*. Waco, TX: Baylor University Press, 2005.

Pridmore, John. "George MacDonald and the Languages of Liberal Spirituality." *Modern Believing* 39.1 (1998) 28–36.

———. "George MacDonald's Estimate of Childhood." *International Journal of Children's Spirituality* 12.1 (2007) 61–74.

Raeper, William. *George MacDonald*. Tring: Lion, 1987.

———, ed. *The Gold Thread: Essays on George MacDonald*. Edinburgh: Edinburgh University Press, 1990.

Rahner, Karl. "Ideas for a Theology of Childhood." Translated by David Bourke. In *Theological Investigations*, 33–50. Vol. 8/3. London: Darton, Longman & Todd, 1971.

Ramsay, Edward Bannerman. *A Manual of Catechetical Instruction: Compiled and Arranged for the Use of Young Persons*. 6th ed. Edinburgh: R. Grant, 1851.

Reardon, Bernard M. G. *Religious Thought in the Victorian Age: A Survey from Coleridge to Gore*. London: Longman, 1980.

"Recent Novels." *The Times*, November 5, 1895.

Reis, Richard H. *George MacDonald's Fiction: A Twentieth-Century View*. Eureka, CA: Sunrise, 1989.

"The Religious Education of Children (Art. IV)." *Westminster Review* 48.2 (1875) 374–90.

Reynolds, David S. *Faith in Fiction: The Emergence of Religious Literature in America*. Cambridge: Harvard University Press, 1981.

Robb, David S. "Fiction for the Child." In *Behind the Back of the North Wind*, edited by John Pennington and Roderick McGillis, 26–32. Hamden, CT: Winged Lion Press, 2011.

Rowell, Geoffrey. *Hell and the Victorians: A Study of the Nineteenth-Century Theological Controversies concerning Eternal Punishment and the Future Life*. Oxford: Oxford University Press, 1974.

Rowland, Ann Wierda. *Romanticism and Childhood: The Infantilization of British Literary Culture*. Cambridge Studies in Romanticism. Cambridge: Cambridge University Press, 2012.

Ruskin, John. "April 13, 1864." Letter to George MacDonald. King's College London archives, GB0100 KCLCA K/PP82, 1/1/28.

———. "July 22, 1863." Letter to George MacDonald. King's College London archives, GB0100 KCLCA K/PP82, 1/1/27.

———. *Modern Painters*. Vols. 2–4. London: Smith, Elder, Routledge, 1848–1856.

———. *The Stones of Venice*. 4th ed. Vol. 2. Orpington, Kent: George Allen, 1886.

Russell, W. M. S., and Katherine M. Briggs. "The Legends of Lilith and of the Wandering Jew in Nineteenth-Century Literature." *Folklore* 92.2 (1981) 131–40.

Sacks, Jonathan. *The Great Partnership: God, Science, and the Search for Meaning.* London: Hodder & Stoughton, 2011.
Sadler, Glenn Edward, ed. *An Expression of Character: The Letters of George MacDonald.* Grand Rapids: Eerdmans, 1994.
Schwartz, Howard. *Lilith's Cave: Jewish Tales of the Supernatural.* Oxford: Oxford University Press, 1991.
Selby, Thomas G. *The Theology of Modern Fiction: Being the Twenty-sixth Fernley Lecture delivered in Liverpool, July, 1896.* London: C. H. Kelley, 1896.
"Sermon by Dr. George Macdonald (Reprinted Courtesy of the *Huntly Express* from Their September 21, 1889, Issue)." *Wingfold* 89 (2015) 29–30.
"Shall Religion Be Separated from Secular Education?" *Wesleyan-Methodist Magazine* 10 (1854) 343–49.
Sherwood, Mary Martha. *The History of the Fairchild Family: Or, The Child's Manual; Being a Collection of Stories Calculated to Shew the Importance and Effects of a Religious Education.* London: J. Hatchard, 1822.
Shuttleworth, Sally. *The Mind of the Child: Child Development in Literature, Science, and Medicine, 1840–1900.* Oxford: Oxford University Press, 2011.
Spadaro, Antonio. "Evangelical Fundamentalism and Catholic Integralism in the USA: A Surprising Ecumenism." *La Civiltà Cattolica*, July 13, 2017. https://laciviltacattolica.com/june-2017/evangelical-fundamentalism-and-catholic-integralism-in-the-usa-a-surprising-ecumenism.
Spencer, Herbert. "Religious Retrospect and Prospect." *Popular Science Monthly* 24 (1884) 340–51.
Stern, J. P. *On Realism.* London: Routledge and Kegan Paul, 1973.
Stockitt, Robin. *Imagination and the Playfulness of God: The Theological Implications of Samuel Taylor Coleridge's Definition of Human Imagination.* Eugene OR: Pickwick, 2011.
Stoeber, Michael. *Evil and the Mystics' God: Towards a Mystical Theodicy.* Basingstoke: Macmillan, 1992.
"Sunday-Schools." *Theological Review* 2.6 (1865) 74–92.
Sutherland, Helen. "George MacDonald and the Visual Arts." In *Rethinking George MacDonald*, edited by Christopher MacLachlan, et al., 216–34. Glasgow: Scottish Literature International, 2013.
Sutphin, Christine. "Victorian Childhood: Reading Beyond the 'Innocent Title': *Home Thoughts and Home Scenes*." In *Children's Literature: New Approaches*, edited by Karín Lesnik-Oberstein, 51–77. Basingstoke: Palgrave Macmillan, 2004.
Tennyson, Alfred Lord. *In Memoriam.* London: Edward Moxon, 1850.
Thisted, Valdemar Adolph. *Letters from Hell.* Introduction by George MacDonald. London: Richard Bentley, 1885.
Tolkien, J. R. R. "Tree and Leaf." In *Tree and Leaf, Smith of Wootton Major, the Homecoming of Beorhtnoth.* London: Unwin, 1975.
Torrance, Thomas F. *Scottish Theology: From John Knox to John McLeod Campbell.* Edinburgh: T&T Clark, 1996.
Travers, Martin P. A., ed. *European Literature from Romanticism to Postmodernism: A Reader in Aesthetic Practice.* London: Continuum, 2001.
Voltaire. *Discours en vers sur l'homme.* 1734. École Alsacienne. https://www.ecole-alsacienne.org/CDI/pdf/1400/14110_VOLT.pdf.

Von Balthasar, Hans Urs. *The Realm of Metaphysics in the Modern Age.* Vol. 5 of *The Glory of the Lord: A Theological Aesthetics.* Edinburgh: T&T Clark, 1991.
———. *Theo-Drama.* 5 vols. San Francisco: Ignatius, 1994.
Waite, Arthur Edward. *The Doctrine and Literature of the Kabalah.* London: Theosophical Publishing Society, 1902.
Watts, Michael R. *The Dissenters.* 3 vols. Oxford: Clarendon, 2015.
Wenham, John William. *Facing Hell: An Autobiography 1913–1996.* Carlisle: Paternoster, 1998.
West, Charles. *On Some of the Disorders of the Nervous System in Childhood: Being the Lumleian Lectures delivered at the Royal College of Physicians of London in March 1871.* London: Longman, Green, 1871.
"What is the Zohar?" Bnei Baruch Kabbalah Education and Research Institute. http://www.kabbalah.info/engkab/mystzohar.htm.
White, Christopher G. "Minds Intensely Unsettled: Phrenology, Experience, and the American Pursuit of Spiritual Assurance, 1830–1880." *Religion and American Culture* 16.2 (2006) 227–61.
"Wilfrid Cumbermede." *Spectator,* March 9, 1872.
Williams, Rowan. *Dostoevsky: Language, Faith, and Fiction.* London: Bloomsbury, 2008.
———. *Lost Icons: Reflections on Cultural Bereavement.* London: Morehouse, 2000.
———. *On Christian Theology.* Oxford: Blackwell, 2000.
Wilson, Samuel Law. *The Theology of Modern Literature.* Edinburgh: T&T Clark, 1899.
Wilton, Andrew, and Robert Upstone, eds. *The Age of Rossetti, Burne-Jones, and Watts.* London: Tate Gallery, 1997.
Wingrove, David Melville. "La Belle Dame: *Lilith* and the Romantic Vampire Tradition." In *Rethinking George MacDonald,* edited by Christopher MacLachlan, et al., 175–97. Glasgow: Scottish Literature International, 2013.
Wooden, Cindy. "Pope Says He Was Surprised by Crowds, Joy in Africa." *Catholic News Service,* November 30, 2015. http://www.catholicnews.com/services/englishnews/2015/pope-says-he-was-surprised-by-crowds-joy-in-africa.cfm.
Wordsworth, William. *Selected Poems.* Edited by John O. Hayden. London: Penguin, 1994.
Wright, N. T. *Justification: God's Plan and Paul's Vision.* Downers Grove, IL: InterVarsity Academic, 2009.

www.ingramcontent.com/pod-product-compliance
Lightning Source LLC
Chambersburg PA
CBHW071240230426
43668CB00011B/1526